ENTRYWAYS TO CRIMINAL JUSTICE

ENTRYWAYS TO CRIMINAL JUSTICE

GEORGE PAVLICH & MATTHEW P. UNGER, Editors

UNIVERSITY of ALBERTA PRESS

ACCUSATION AND CRIMINALIZATION IN CANADA

Published by

University of Alberta Press
Ring House 2
Edmonton, Alberta, Canada T6G 2E1
www.uap.ualberta.ca

Copyright © 2019 University of Alberta Press

LIBRARY AND ARCHIVES CANADA
CATALOGUING IN PUBLICATION

Entryways to criminal justice : accusation
and criminalization in Canada / George
Pavlich and Matthew P. Unger, editors.

Includes bibliographical references and index.
Issued in print and electronic formats.
ISBN 978–1–77212–336–4 (softcover).—
ISBN 978–1–77212–436–1 (EPUB).—
ISBN 978–1–77212–437–8 (Kindle).—
ISBN 978–1–77212–438–5 (PDF)

1. Criminal justice, Administration of—
Canada. 2. Criminal procedure—Canada.
3. Crime—Canada—Sociological aspects.
I. Pavlich, George, 1960–, Editor II. Unger,
Matthew P., editor

HV9960.C2E58 2019   364.971
C2018–906382–3
C2018–906383–1

First edition, first printing, 2019.
First printed and bound in Canada by
Houghton Boston Printers, Saskatoon,
Saskatchewan.
Copyediting and proofreading by
Angela Pietrobon.
Indexing by Stephen Ullstrom.

University of Alberta Press is committed to
protecting our natural environment. As part
of our efforts, this book is printed on Enviro
Paper: it contains 100% post-consumer
recycled fibres and is acid- and chlorine-free.

University of Alberta Press gratefully
acknowledges the support received for its
publishing program from the Government
of Canada, the Canada Council for the Arts,
and the Government of Alberta through the
Alberta Media Fund.

CONTENTS

ACKNOWLEDGEMENTS

THIS COLLECTION was born out of a Canada Research Chair in Social Theory, Culture and Law symposium held at the University of Alberta in January 2016. Sincere thanks are due to all the participants. They generously shared, and engaged carefully with, work-in-progress ideas to help trace the contours of new directions in the study of criminal entryways. It is through these challenging and rigorous conversations and discussions that this collection was eventually made possible. The editors also thank the Department of Sociology and Faculty of Arts at the University of Alberta for supporting the initiative. The research assistance of Jean-Philippe Crete is appreciated, as is the support and careful attention of Linda Cameron and Peter Midgley from University of Alberta Press.

INTRODUCTION

GEORGE PAVLICH & MATTHEW P. UNGER

Gatekeepers to Law

In a well-known passage of *The Trial*, Franz Kafka offers a puzzling account of a man from the country seeking entry to the law. The main character of the book, K., asks a priest to help him understand why he has been arrested, and what he might expect from the law. The priest answers through a parable:

> *In front of the law there is a doorkeeper. A man from the countryside comes up to the door and asks for entry. But the doorkeeper says he can't let him in to the law right now. The man thinks about this, and then he asks if he'll be able to go in later on. "That's possible," says the doorkeeper, "but not now." The gateway to the law is open as it always is, and the doorkeeper has stepped to one side, so the man bends over to try and see in. When the doorkeeper notices this he laughs and says, "If you're tempted give it a try, try and go in even though I say you can't. Careful though: I'm powerful. And I'm only the lowliest of all the doormen. But there's a doorkeeper for each of the rooms and each of them is more powerful than the last. It's more than I can stand just to look at the third one." The man from the country had not expected difficulties like this, the law was supposed to be accessible for anyone at*

any time, he thinks, but now he looks more closely at the doorkeeper in
his fur coat...The doorkeeper gives him a stool and lets him sit down to
one side of the gate. (Kafka 2009, 154)

The man spends his life waiting to be granted entry, but is ultimately
refused. Seemingly haunted by a potential to grasp the law, the man
confronts its inscrutability through an encounter with its doorway, its
threshold. The law seems to compel his presence, but simultaneously
distances him by a relentlessly deferred justice. Frail and at the end of
his life, the man pleads with the doorkeeper to be admitted:

"Everyone wants access to the law," says the man, "how come, over all
these years, no-one but me has asked to be let in?" The doorkeeper can
see the man's come to his end, his hearing has faded, and so, so that
he can be heard, he shouts to him: "Nobody else could have got in this
way, as this entrance was meant only for you. Now I'll go and close it."
(2009, 155)

This enigmatic parable may be read in many ways. One might, for
example, focus on the labyrinthine and opaque proceedings that befall
those arrested and called upon to journey through interwoven justice
institutions. Symbolized by K.'s baffling arrest and trial, the encounter
with such bureaucracy often feels alienating, mysterious, and even inac-
cessible to those subject to its force. Or, it is possible to read into this work,
as does Agamben (2008), a different idea; namely, that Kafka's character
K. is a self-accuser, and a false one at that, who confronts law precisely
through the act of self-accusation. Agamben's point here is that accusation (and self-accusation) brings subjects into contact with a sense of law
that is predicated on judgmental recrimination of one sort or another.
This is what allows us to glimpse why law's justice remains inscrutable
and at a vague distance—it is an unendingly deferred promise of justice
aroused by accusation.

As important as these readings undoubtedly are, the following collection fixes its gaze in another direction; namely, on the oft-neglected

doorkeepers authorized to institute entryways into fluid criminal justice arenas. While one might valuably concentrate on the allegorical symbols of K. or the countryman standing before the law, the following collection, in other words, emphasizes the doorkeepers who figuratively open or close doors to criminalizing processes—their history, authority, cultural ambiguities, connections to changing images of crime, reliance upon situated suspicions and subtle interactions, and shifting identifications of which subjects to detain as criminals, or potential criminals. These historically shaped accusers and authorities occupy liminal thresholds that serve to mark out the law-abiding subjects from "criminals," and to channel selected persons from everyday life to criminal regulation. The political rationales and rituals of these thresholds significantly shape the lives of participants, who in the end serve as vehicles for historically formed boundaries to criminal justice.

Such boundary-creating activities happen and are deployed in multiple ways, using diverse and context-specific ideas and rituals for granting entry to criminal justice to selected subjects. Resulting criminal justice entryways reflect situated cultural, social, and political tendencies; their modern incarnations often drew authority from—and indeed claimed to operate in the name of—specific sovereigns. Inasmuch as such gatekeeping mechanisms decide on who to enter and who to evict from facing criminal courtrooms, they recursively help to shape the sovereignty politics from when they derived authoritative legitimacy. From this point of view, historically sanctioned criminal procedures that select who to criminalize do more than usher people in or out of criminal justice institutions: they help to define, police, and exclusively regulate the borders of normal social orders (see Foucault 2015).

Working with these and allied issues, the following chapters explore how criminalizing processes have shaped different entryways to Canadian criminal justice across time and place. This is a relatively unique focus. Furthermore, it is one that has—with few exceptions (Ericson and Baranek 1982)—escaped detailed analysis. As noted below, much critical criminological and sociological-legal thinking valuably focuses on the real costs (economic and otherwise) of governing through crime via policing, alienating courtroom trials, mass incarnation and so on. Yet few have paid much attention to the complex apparatuses that populate criminal justice arenas in the first place. Such omissions allow processes that select specific subjects for criminalization to remain obscured, and eclipse the local ways that expanding criminal justice arenas are populated, replenished, and indeed expanded. Bluntly stated, diverse entryways have surfaced in Canada via shifting procedures and gatekeeper identities, both of which have a constitutive impact on the size, profile, and continued existence of unequal and exclusionary criminal justice systems.

In broad terms, the chapters of this collection examine various historical (colonial) and contemporary entryways to criminal justice in Canada, but tap two more specific themes (*albeit* in different ways). First, they investigate different dimensions of *criminal accusation* as a key way by which criminalizing processes have been, are, or may be instigated at criminal justice entryways. Secondly, the chapters explore different elements of what might be called a politics of truth-telling that reflects a vital moment for criminal accusations stationed at thresholds to colonial and contemporary juridical forms. This allows for discussion on how criminality is initiated in context, how the identities of subjects (the accused, accusers, authorities) are thereby negotiated, and how these initiate specific criminalizations, as well as images of crime. Nonetheless, we suggest that these points of focus are not to be read as attempts to obscure the richness and diversity of what is engaged throughout—merely to provide integrating points of departure for readers.

Criminal Accusation and Entryways

On the first theme, one might say that despite differences, authors in this book describe and name ideas, rituals, and the socio-legal implications of criminal accusation in unfolding legal forms. Whether focused on colonial or current juridical examples, the chapters highlight ways by which subjects come to be accused of crimes at gateways to criminal justice. They explore, for instance, how criminal accusations are implicitly launched through complex and oft unequal relations of power, culturally structured notions of suspicion and habit, Goffmanesque obligations and expectations, written legal lexicons, local battles of spite and malice, victim and offender demeanours, political fluctuations in what is defined as criminal (e.g., self-murder, genocide, prize fighting, HIV non-disclosure, beggars, insurrectionists), and regulatory technologies that identify specific traits as revealing persistent offenders. Through these discussions, this collection highlights and reassesses key dimensions of what it is to accuse someone of criminality.

One of the persistent questions here involves the difficult issue of if, when, or how, criminal accusation might legitimately be evoked. In some cases (genocide, domestic violence, murder, etc.), authors are led to reflect on how devastating wrongs may be contained through democratic accusations that enable effective governance that do not replicate self-lauding settler colonialism, or exclude the voices of domestic violence victims. They challenge existing ways by which entrances to criminal justice accuse subjects. This allows us to think through the possibility of alternative—perhaps less exclusionary—genres of accusation. In turn, such thinking raises the difficult, and yet critically important, matter of whether or not accusation could ever accomplish such feats—perhaps a topic for further work. Others come at this issue by questioning the imperial auspices of colonial accusations of crime, or problematizing definitions of criminality (self-murder, prize fighting, horse-eaters, insurrectionists, HIV non-disclosure, etc.) and hypostatized regulatory categories (break and enter, habit, persistent offenders, etc.). They meet in offering critiques of the starting, accusatory moments of criminalizing processes, pondering how inclusive governmental patterns could change the very auspices of current entryways to criminal justice. As such, the analyses offered throughout the volume allow us to recognize how multiple forms of criminal accusation occupy diverse entryways to criminal justice, holding out the promise of changing or refining accusatory logics to enable the promise of greater justice for those who now are accused of falling foul of criminal law.

By their focus on accusation at criminal justice entryways, the chapters highlight a largely overlooked facet of crime control cultures that analysts like Simon (2007), Brown (2009) and Garland (2002) have perceptively recounted. In a socio-political ethos that so pervasively—using Simon's (2007) terminology—"governs through crime," unequal and exclusionary forms of criminal control have ballooned. This has produced Christie's (1994) famously described "crime control industry" that claims a monopoly over the regulation of crime. Like other industries, its overall influence is tied to a vested interest in continuously expanding, and hence a seemingly limitless stream of people is directed into criminal justice institutions. Many have noted the tenaciously unequal race and class profiles of such criminal justice expansion (Alexander 2010; Wacquant 2009), while others point to the significant socio-economic costs and failures (Simon and Sparks 2013), and even the very constitutionality of mass incarceration (Simon 2014). But then, one might ask, how could such costly expansions be checked?

In pointing to accusation's mechanisms and procedures at entrances to criminal justice, the chapters refuse to hypostatize images of crime and criminals, and open discussion to the wider effects of specific accu-satory forms. If one is to restrain bloated and expanding criminal justice systems, it is essential at least to understand the initiating processes that populate or sustain them. Attending to the transformation of accusa-tory entryways, then, promises to allow for an alternative focus on how to limit population flows into criminal justice by scrutinizing why, how, and with what effects particular criminalizations are historically deployed. In all cases, that is, a consequential politics of accusation that shapes figurative entrances to criminal justice ought to be engaged directly rather than furtively assumed.

Accusation, Truth-telling, and Crime

On a second theme, the chapters draw attention to the role of "truth" in the overarching politics of criminal accusation, and so indicate how this issue shapes the kind of criminality initiated in particular Canadian contexts. This broad focus on the crime as a socio-political creation of context runs up against a prevalent cultural assumption about crime as an absolute phenomenon and as necessarily requiring punitive responses. In turn, crime and criminals appear as having a fixed, and so discoverable, essence. By contrast, focusing on initiating moments of criminalization allows the authors of this collection to approach crime and criminality as the outcome of historical processes. To highlight the stakes of this move, Nietzsche (2011) points us, for example, to the "lowly beginnings" that allow such issues as "crime" to appear as absolute beings—with causes, nature, and effects (see Chapter 1). He urges us instead to focus on the political "becoming" that yields the appearance of such being, and on the sheer historical amnesia required to sustain myths about the absolute being of crime and criminals. In addition, he draws our attention to a "will" to power and truth generally, but which also play out through the truths required by criminal law and its accusatory procedures. Exemplifying his repudiation of dominant conceptions of truth, Nietzsche famously writes:

> What is truth? A mobile army of metaphors, metonyms, anthropomor-
> phisms, in short, a sum of human relations which were poetically and
> rhetorically heightened, transferred, and adorned, and after long use
> seem solid, canonical, and binding to a nation. Truths are illusions
> about which it has been forgotten that they are illusions, worn-out
> metaphors without sensory impact, coins which have lost their image
> and now can be used only as metal, and no longer as coins. (as quoted
> in Gilman et al. 1989, 250)

Whatever one makes of this aphorism, it could be used to alert us to a kind of historical amnesia that shrouds criminal justice entryways— namely, one that has forgotten the changing rituals of truth-telling that have variously shaped what it is to accuse another person of wrongdoing (and indeed to accuse someone of a crime that needs to be punished). Here, one might refer to a complex genealogy of the "apparatuses of accusation" detectable in ancient Athenian rituals of accusation (e.g., Socrates' trial), tests and oaths, the Roman republic's rhetoric for proper accusations, medieval blood accusations or ordeals, modern discipline's confessions, the turn to a science of criminal identification, and so on (Pavlich 2006, 2007). In each case, different images of crime (e.g., as immoral, socially dangerous, etc.) and rituals of truth-telling were demanded in order for a criminal accusation to count as a credible one in juridical contexts (Nietzsche 2011).

Foucault (2015) develops such ideas by alerting us to the rationales and "political technologies" that help to create historical visions of crime. At the same time, his Leuven lectures highlight shifting forms of avowal—the truth-telling rituals and practices—required by accusations of crime in different contexts (Foucault 2014). These lectures offer nicely honed interpretations of Sophocles' *Oedipus Rex* and Homer's account of a conflict in games held by Achilles. In each case, we are shown how truth-telling was variously countenanced by juridical attempts to resolve disputes. The lectures also draw attention to a subsequent ethos in which early medieval juridical forms underwent significant change from an earlier process of accusation. Specifically, he tells us that,

> the accusatory procedure through which someone—whether it was the victim or someone representing the victim—…accused another of having wronged him, this procedure…centred the entire penal mechanism on the confrontation between two adversaries or two partners. And these two, the accuser and the accused, then had to settle their litigation according to the rules and sometimes through arbitration, or eventually they had to pursue their vengeance in a private war. (2014, 202–03)

However, when sovereigns usurped the task of settling disputes, new rituals of accusation emerged around avowal, of telling specific truths in particular ways. As forms of law developed through monarchical and early state forms of sovereignty, a key juridical problem came to reside around "establishing the truth and...determining a sanction based on the established facts" (2014, 203).

Now conflicts were to be resolved not by struggles between accusers and the accused, but by a knowledgeable decision of a "sovereign court" or "the sovereign himself" that was based on truths avowed in juridically specified ways (2014, 203). This made a particular kind of truth-telling an essential aspect of criminal procedure, and in turn,

> the affirmation of the truth by the accused himself would become an important element. Avowal became—or rather, became again, because in fact, throughout Roman law, proof by avowal was recognized and admitted, but this type of procedure had almost disappeared, or in any case had declined in a massive way from the 17th or 18th centuries on—the establishment of the truth through the avowal of the culprit became once again an important piece of the procedure [sic]. (2014, 203)

Here, Foucault points out that the renewed role of avowal was possible precisely as medieval accusatory procedures based on tests and ordeals gave way to "new procedures of inquisition" that determined truth by inquiry (2014, 203). That role was further developed in the truth-telling of disciplinary powers and its subtle attempts to contain social enemies (Foucault 2015, 34, 441–49; Foucault 2016, 221–27).

These brief allusions to a complex body of work suffice to underscore the contingency of accusatory entryways, and to highlight the historically specific rituals used to open subjects to criminalizing processes. That is, such legal rituals became a requirement for enunciations to count as legal truths, and as valid evidence from which to make decisions of entry to criminal justice. Subjects now had to avow, to "tell the truth, the whole truth..." in ways considered appropriate to the juridical forms at hand. Whether oath swearing, regulated confession, legally transcribed testimony, court rulings, or expert, scientific knowledge, one glimpses historical demands for particular kinds of truth-telling to conform to accusatorial procedures within different juridical forms. That types of accusation at entryways to criminal justice are dependent upon how one tells the truth may also be referenced by his neologism "veridiction" (*veri* = truth; *diction* = speaking), which suggests how subjects are required to avow truths within changing juridical forms. In other words, the term highlights how different forms of avowal are employed by given accusatory procedures. Rather than viewing accusation as an abstracted being, then, one might use Foucault's approach to understand that in criminal justice contexts, accusation takes form through specific kinds of avowal, truth-telling practices about purportedly criminal circumstances. Understood thus, avowal enables law's subjects to speak the truth in ways that are meaningful and understood as juridical truths to an audience or judge at hand. His approach nicely highlights the close relation between rituals of truth-telling testimony, mechanisms of legal speech or writing, and how people enter into criminal justice systems. It also alerts us to how truth-telling practices that shape criminal accusation at entryways to criminal justice recursively form the identities of accuser, accused, and even sovereign-authorized legal agents.

The chapters implicitly or explicitly tackle such matters in various ways. Criminal law's lexicons allow only limited kinds of subject formations by contextually restricting: what it is to accuse someone legally of a crime; what one may be accused of doing; the grammars of accusation to be used by accusers when laying information before officials; who can say what, who can hear what, and who is authorized to decide on whether there is enough truthful, and so legally validated, evidence to indict the accused for committing a crime. On this note, several chapters refer to how particular subject identities are generated by the very performances of avowal required by legal procedures in context. At one level, genres of avowal may be associated with identities of criminal subjects that appear as guilty or innocent of crime, of habitually good character or bad, and so on. Equally, the accepted voices of accusers have an impact on the limited kinds of accusing identities that are possible in context. Various accuser identities (victims, police, prosecutors, justices of the peace) are both shaped and negotiated through power relations that accuse through legally sanctioned truth-telling practices. Different authorized officials surface as meaningful beings (e.g., judges, prosecutors, grand juries, magistrates) via their participation. In all instances, subjects (the accused, accusers, legal agents) are recursively shaped, in part, by the avowals that are enabled by local accusatorial processes and lexicons—how and what they enunciate as truth through processes of accusation shape the kinds of legal personhood that can be ascribed to them (Pavlich 2018).

The chapters, then, interrogate the different kinds of entry into the criminal justice system, whether those accused of criminal activity or those seeking to accuse (in the case of the chapter from Sibley et al.), and how these different entry points are predicated upon contingent social flows of political currents, privileged forms of knowledge and technology, as well as aesthetic and rhetorical claims. As such, the truth elicited from within the different contexts is also performative, as Hogeveen rightly asserts, in the fashioning of criminal fields and subjects. The performance of regulations and procedures associated with particular forms of truth-telling produces the subjects that are required by, and so able to engage with, the law. In other words, through rituals that render persons subject to criminal law, particular identities surface. Hence, we see, for instance, the complicated relational dynamics that victims of domestic violence face when they encounter the police and legal system. In this case, the experience of the engagement with law reposes upon conceptions of deference, demeanour, and the "proper victim." Another consequence with which the chapters contend is the avowal of truth-telling in judicial contexts and the risk that people face in their attempt to come forward with complaints, witness statements, or accusations of domestic violence. Several of the chapters also reflect on performances that effect accusation and entryways, who has access to the system, who is able to speak, and the subjectivities ascribed to individuals who appear before those deciding on the sufficiency of evidence to proceed to trial.

Chapter Overview

The first chapter in the collection, by George Pavlich, explores the changing politics of gatekeeping at thresholds designed to criminalize selected colonial subjects through two late nineteenth-century cases—one in Edmonton, and the other in Nanaimo. From surviving records deposited in archives, Pavlich interprets key political ideas and practices of accusation that were—with the expansion of Dominion law's jurisdiction over "criminal" matters—mobilized to identify wrongdoers as "criminal." By giving a reading of selected documents, the chapter highlights how the Dominion consolidated its criminal law in the first instance by deploying legally regulated criminal accusation rituals in local contexts. A complex politics enabled such accusatory processes to arrest everyday relations in particular cases, forging Dominion law over local relations in bids to forge an amorphously conceived "west." Drawing on both Nietzsche and Foucault, the chapter shows how the growth of criminal accusation at entryways plays a formative role in creating particular images of crime, and enables the possibility of regulating certain acts and subjects as criminal. Pavlich also points to initiating fractures of everyday meaning that spark accusations of crime, and shows how this possibility is only available in cultural and socio-political contexts where criminal justice controls have started to take root. He also shows how legally required lexicons unleashed highly constrained and regulated ways for subjects to avow the truth about putative crimes. Their transcription in written legal documents further truncated the scope of narratives of criminal events, and had significant effects on what sort of colonial subjects—the criminally accused, accusers, or authorized agents of Dominion law—were possible. The accusatory processes exacted from the cases indicate the early legacy of expanding colonial criminal jurisdiction—a legacy that tenaciously endures in the shadows of today's vast criminal justice networks.

Developing the theme of how accusation arrests everyday processes and meaning frameworks, Matthew Unger examines the deployment of colonial law in British Columbia through a single tragic case dating back to 1879. This chapter offers a close reading of how accusation remained unsettled in the murder of Thomas Poole and his two children, the proprietor at Halfway House, a popular roadhouse that travellers and gold diggers used as a waypoint in Lillooet, BC. The ensuing grand juries and criminal trials were quick to accuse people based on recommendations by validated members of the settler society of the time. Between the years 1879 and 1891, multiple accusations and counter accusations surfaced in what were by all accounts deeply divided and dividing attempts to make sense of the tragic loss of life. Unger argues that precisely who was able to accuse another effectively depended on the relations between the hegemonies of settler society (and hence hierarchies of the day), the accuser, and the accused. Not only this, but the manner in which accusations were levelled in context reflected how rhetoric, speech practices, and truth-telling could be mobilized to shape normative contours of entry to the then legal processes. As such, by examining who had "the right to speech" during the course of these trials, one might expect to find privileged forms of knowledge, political and legal boundaries, and what constituted proper legal subject identities. The trials, witness depositions, and grand jury inquests exemplified accusatory processes embedded within the colonial dynamics of dispossession in British Columbia's early legal history. Unger argues, however, that the trials, accusatory processes, and criminal entryways were indelibly shaped through a series of complicated misrecognitions in the encounters between different forms of justice.

Interrogations into beginnings of colonial law over the Canadian west now go back decades with Aaron Henry's analysis of how Hudson's Bay Company (HBC) officials targeted, accused, and punished individuals in the Red River colony during a famine in the winter of 1825–1826. By carefully examining the entries in the journal of Francis Heron, an HBC clerk in charge of Fort Garry, Henry's chapter shows how unique accusations of crime were born out of a famine. This devastating event prompted not only starvation, but fears of an imminent insurrection by racially defined groups who were seen not to be self-sufficient and as lacking a capacity for self-control. In context, a version of criminal accusation appeared that was directed not to individuals as such, but to the potential threat of an "immoral mob." Heron's post log reveals to Henry a cast of suspicious characters—"beggars," "horse-eaters," and "insurrections"—who Heron considers worthy of criminalization and control. These forms of accusation had profound effects on those accused of being indolent as they were denied aid and shut outside the fort to learn the "lessons of the season." The chapter then explores how Heron's text may fruitfully be read against Foucault's image of habit as a stabilizing political technology amendable to emerging forms of capitalism, and Heron's nascent use of disciplinary accusations to render accused criminals observable and controllable as social enemies in a politically retooled conception of the "fort." Henry's analysis of Heron's post log further traces how entryways into the criminal justice system were conditioned by normative structuring principles disproportionately directed at governing those that presented threats to a sovereign imaginary.

Amy Swiffen and Martin French also tackle the matter of how mechanisms of accusation govern observable subjects, and thereby create particular kinds of entryways. Their chapter examines the criminalization of people with HIV/AIDS in Canada, and specifically those who are alleged not to have disclosed that status to a sexual partner. By focusing on three precedent-setting HIV non-disclosure criminal cases in Canada, Swiffen and French analyze how Canadian courts interpret epidemiological knowledge through interpretations of criminal law centred on moral blameworthiness and individual responsibility. Having described how courts in Canada use epidemiological information in the context of HIV non-disclosure cases, the authors extract a legal principle that is usually taken to justify criminal prosecution in such cases. They then examine how this legal principle was actually evoked in three cases between 2008 and 2015. On the strength of the preceding analysis, the chapter coins a neologism, "seropolitics," to describe how juridical interpretations evoke a biopolitics that relies on epidemiological ideas about blood. In such contexts, the entryways to potential criminalization revolve around judgments of liability determined by an accused individual's biological status. Such medico-legal forms of governmentality create and link two kinds of subjects, individuals and populations, through epidemiologically determined blood levels that create new versions of criminality.

That accusatorial pathways are productive of criminal categories, social relationships, and identities is something that Bryan Hogeveen examines through an analysis of how early twentieth-century Canadian law criminalized prize fighting. Hogeveen argues that even though the establishment of a law is often understood as an attempt to reduce or repress a specific behaviour or action, the creation of a legal category shows a rather more productive side to law—one that forms new kinds of legal subjects as criminal, and places them in sight of the criminal justice system. In attempting to criminalize prize fighting in Canada, the judicial system inadvertently privileged a particular kind of fighting that exhibited forms of behaviour and rationalities, and thus fighting went from "science to slugging." Through somewhat dramatic performances of accusation, we see how local enunciations of the truth can frame a legal subject as criminal, thus creating conditions for possible entry into the criminal justice system. Prize fighting, for Hogeveen, may be analyzed as an element within a truth regime established through the bordering mechanisms of a legal system that creates specific images of what is criminal.

Dale Ballucci's analysis of a prolific offender category within contemporary Canadian policing practices explores just how criminal justice entryways are reconfigured. If, as Swiffen and French argue, blood can create the basis for criminal accusation, Ballucci's chapter shows how emerging criminal justice entrances are no longer dependent on the commission of a crime. Now, by framing a nebulously conceived predilection for criminal activity, Canadian policing institutions have developed a unique kind of governance based on controlling the very possibility of criminal activity—in advance. Such governance constructs altered entryways that target accused subjects less as those shown truthfully to have committed an offence, and more as an amorphous probabilistic grouping of prolific offenders who are regulated because of past rather than present criminal acts. Through an analysis of the technologies, processes, and kinds of surveillance that come out of the establishment of a prolific offender list, Ballucci suggests that a "perpetual state of accusation" surfaces in efforts to curb recidivism. This form of governance has several unintended consequences, including reformulating past images of criminal accusation to enable further extensions of the criminal justice system into people's lives. Ballucci's reference to prolific offender programs shows how their initiatives may offer new dimensions to crime control, with the possible negative effect of justifying the perpetual intervention of police, surveillance, and prefigured accusations. This perpetual accusation may be viewed as an exceptional trope, but it is one that indicates how newly emerging entryways may enable a form of governance that extends the scope of criminal justice controls.

Andrew Woolford's contribution to this collection pursues a different jurisdiction, showing how entryways might be reconfigured by launching alternative kinds of accusations and criminalizations. Specifically, Woolford explores what Pavlich (2007) calls a "lore of accusation" as it pertains to the criminalization of genocide and Canada's role in the promotion of the United Nations *Convention on the Prevention and Punishment of the Crime of Genocide* (1948). By drawing on Raphael Lemkin's writings (the originator of the legal definition of genocide), Woolford argues that Canada's engagement with the development of genocide law was compromised by not fully entertaining this possibility: "cultural" genocide might constitute an appropriate legal category in context. Though some might view the reasons for this response as political expediency, allowing the state to absolve itself of committing genocide. However, it also had the effect of allowing Canada to avoid contending with the genocidal dimensions of its own settler-colonial history. Woolford suggests that a secure Canadian sovereignty need not shun such a past, but should try to come to grips with it, and partially predicate itself upon its response to accusations of cultural genocide. In this way, Woolford's chapter points to an aspect of Canada's colonial past marked by a complex history of dispossession and genocidal activities against Indigenous cultures; it also suggests a poignant avoidance of working through that past. By examining Canada's role in the negotiations and its rejection of the "cultural genocide" accusation, Woolford argues that one can see a way to a kind of absolution of Canadian national identity; but, coming to grips with accusations of cultural genocide may be necessary to develop more inclusive political forms in the future.

Marcus Sibley, Elise Wohlbold, Dawn Moore, and Rashmee Singh discuss entryways and criminalization through the vantage of someone attempting to influence entrances to criminal justice by examining the complexities of accusation in cases of domestic violence. The experience of being effectively able to level and shape accusations in domestic violence (and sexual assault) cases reveals, according to the authors, complex relational dynamics that often silence women, who are overwhelmingly the victims here. Drawing on Goffman's notion of "demeanour" to expand on current literature that looks predominantly at the victim's presentation of self, Sibley et al. broaden this concept to ensure that all participants— including the demeanour of the police—are taken into account. Expected rituals of deference and demeanour reflect how police will likely respond to victims, but also how victims respond to police. In the accusatory contexts under review, victims often experience what Berlant (2011) calls "cruel optimism" in a stark disjuncture between expectations of help and support, and their disheartening experience of shaping accusations when confronted by authorized agents of criminal justice entryways. They argue that a sense of who the victim is, characterized by a sense of her demeanour, may be crucial to the shape of accusations and eventual prosecutions. How victims are perceived as subjects is often a deciding factor in whether police lay charges, and whether judges find them to be credible witnesses. Such perceptions may even in some cases determine whether or not she will be charged with a crime. Avowal is important here, for telling the truth always entails risk, and victims of sexual assault face this harsh reality when they relay their experiences. Drawing on case law as well as interviews with domestic violence survivors, Sibley et al. suggest that a complex image of victim personhood in law is contingent on the kinds of performance that establish whether she is perceived as a legally recognized victim able to level a convincing accusation.

Conclusion

Overall, this collection seeks to ameliorate a relative lacuna in Canadian scholarship directed at critically examining the discourses, mechanisms, apparatuses, and rituals that inaugurate entry into criminal justice arenas. We see the impact of accusation in several different registers and social spheres: from the beginnings of crime control and the codification of English Law to the technologically driven management and interrogation of blood; from the criminalization of prize fighting to the criminalization of genocide; and from the perpetual accusation of prolific offenders to the difficulty of levelling accusation for domestic violence victims. In all, these seemingly disparate subjects reveal a continuity in forms of governance that rely on foundational rituals, patterns, and mechanisms of accusation. Through the course of this collection what stands in stark relief against the background of differences is the contextualization of a criminal law that calls for the subject to stand before its fluid, yet tenacious, patterns of criminal judgment. Embedded within these enduring patterns is a politics of recognition that begins with the truths of certain accusations of crime and ends up reinforcing wider patterns of domination, dispossession, disenfranchisement, and power. The law's ability to frame social potential is disclosed by examining the contingent and politically salient sanctioning of criminal identities and actions through the validation of particular criminal accusations. In the end we ask as a whole: what implicit social discourses and long-standing structures undergird the putative rationality of law; in short, what "lore of accusation" governs entryways into Canada's changing criminal justice systems?

References

Agamben, Giorgio. 2008. "K." In *The Work of Giorgio Agamben: Law, Literature, Life*, edited by Justin Clemens, Nicholas Heron, and Alex Murray, 13–27. New York: Oxford University Press.

Alexander, Michelle. 2010. *The New Jim Crow: Mass Incarceration in the Age of Colorblindness*. New York: New Press.

Berlant, Lauren Gail. 2011. *Cruel Optimism*. Durham, NC: Duke University Press.

Brown, Michelle. 2009. *The Culture of Punishment: Prison, Society, and Spectacle.* Alternative Criminology Series. New York: New York University Press.

Christie, Nils. 1994. *Crime Control as Industry: Towards Gulags, Western Style.* London: Routledge.

Ericson, Richard V., and Patricia M. Baranek. 1982. *The Ordering of Justice: A Study of Accused Persons as Dependants in the Criminal Process.* Toronto: University of Toronto Press.

Foucault, Michel. 2014. *Wrong-Doing, Truth-Telling: The Function of Avowal in Justice.* Translated by Fabienne Brion, Bernard E. Harcourt, and Stephen W. Sawyer. Chicago: University of Chicago Press.

―――. 2015. *On the Punitive Society: Lectures at the Collège de France, 1972–1973.* Edited by Bernard Harcourt. Translated by Graham Burchell. London, New York: Palgrave Macmillan.

Garland, David. 2002. *The Culture of Control: Crime and Social Order in Contemporary Society.* Chicago: University of Chicago Press.

Kafka, Franz. 2009. *The Trial.* New York: Dover Publications.

Nietzsche, Friedrich. 1989 [1873]. "On Truth and Lying in an Extra-Moral Sense." In *Friedrich Nietzsche on Rhetoric and Language,* edited by Sander L. Gilman, Carole Blair, and David J. Parent, 246–57. Translated by D.J. Parent. New York: Oxford University Press.

―――. 2011. *The Will to Power.* Knopf Doubleday Publishing Group.

Pavlich, George. 2018. *Criminal Accusation: Political Rationales and Socio-legal Practices,* London: Routledge.

―――. 2006. "Accusation: Landscapes of Exclusion." In *The Geography of Law: Landscape, Identity and Regulation,* edited by William Taylor, 85–100. Oxford: Hart Publishing.

―――. 2007. "The Lore of Criminal Accusation." *Criminal Law & Philosophy* 1 (1): 79–97.

Simon, Jonathan. 2007. *Governing Through Crime: How the War on Crime Transformed American Democracy and Created a Culture of Fear.* New York: Oxford University Press.

―――. 2014. *Mass Incarceration on Trial: A Remarkable Court Decision and the Future of Prisons in America.* New York: The New Press.

Simon, Jonathan, and Richard Sparks, eds. 2013. *The SAGE Handbook of Punishment and Society.* London: Sage Publications.

Wacquant, Loic. 2009. *Punishing the Poor: The Neoliberal Government of Social Insecurity.* Durham NC: Duke University Press.

1

ACCUSATORY ENTRYWAYS TO CRIMINAL JUSTICE

GEORGE PAVLICH

Introduction

Through an analysis of oft-overlooked accusatory entryways to colonial justice in Canada, this chapter attends to practices that selectively define people to face law as potential criminals. These contests heralded suspensions of everyday life and enabled sanctioned authorities—police officers, prosecutors, magistrates, coroners, justices of the peace, juries, and judges—to serve as legal gatekeepers to law's criminalizing trials. What rites condensed complex social events into legal narratives of criminality? What contextual procedures claimed a monopoly on "legally" valid methods to receive and process information that a crime has taken place? How did local legal practices establish the identities of accuser, accused, and authorized agent at entrances to criminal justice? And which truth-telling practices served to decide who should face criminal trials?

Such questions no doubt support critical sociological and criminological analyses that emphasize crime's contingent socio-political, cultural, and economic foundations (e.g., Christie 1994; Foucault 2014; Reiman 1990; Taylor, Walton, and Young 1973). Yet my accent here is specific: I focus on two cases that reflect newly forming crime control rituals in late nineteenth-century western Canadian contexts—one in 1888 at Edmonton (North-West Territories—NWT—now Alberta) and the other in 1890 at Nanaimo, British Columbia. These cases indicate how those in charge of colonial governance established legal entryways as they expanded the jurisdiction of an emerging criminal justice system, and secured a monopoly over rituals to define and regulate criminally accused subjects. Clearly, with two arbitrarily selected examples, the aim can be neither to capture a colonial past where, following an 1867 confederation, Canada looked westwards, nor to detail comprehensively the imposition of Dominion law over a vast territory occupied by Indigenous peoples, Métis, and growing numbers of settlers, many associated with the fur trade (Innis 2015; Komar 2015; Loo 1994b). Readers seeking histories of this general background might refer to well-established enunciations (Foster 1994; Harring 1998; Loo 1990, 1994a; Strange and Loo 1997). They might also turn to analyses of how Dominion law was enforced by the quasi-military North West Mounted Police's (NWMP) march west (Beahen 1998; Macleod 1976, 2004; Wilkins 2012), alongside the deployment of the British Columbia Provincial Police over the Vancouver Island Colony (Foster 1994; Foster, Buck, and Berger 2008; Loo 1994b; Marquis 2015; Parker 2015; Stonier-Newman 2006, 1991), or the Province of British Columbia (Barman 2007, 2008; Ferguson 2009) and the expansion of court configurations over the prairies (Farr 1967, 1944; Gavigan 2012).

By contrast, critically interpreting the selected cases, I tap into surviving texts that offer a glimpse of officially preserved narratives, the likes of which enabled the western expansion of Dominion criminal law. They spawned practices at opening moments of criminalization, recursively laying the foundations for what would become a vast criminal justice edifice (Foster 1992, 1990). Such foundational developments also imposed Dominion criminal law over an amorphously conceived west, and in so doing created versions of crime and its control in local contexts. Indeed, the acts and subjects (persons) that the emerging legal force criminalized played an important role in expanding the jurisdiction of criminal law (Dorsett and McVeigh 2012). This expansion was premised upon erected entryways by which definitions of crime could be enforced over a vast terrain. The following is then a tale of a largely unspoken jurisdictional legacy—one that tenaciously endures in the shadows of today's expansive criminal justice networks.

Entryway Narrative I
Information and Accusations of a Break and Enter

Consider these reported events. On March 9, 1888, Thomas Rees, a miner and resident in the east side of Edmonton (then part of the NWT), presented an "information and complaint" to a police inspector Casey, who also served in the capacity of a justice of the peace (Chiste 2005). Rees informed him that a crime had taken place; he accused John Sunday of breaking and entering into his house near Fraser's Mill, intending to steal his watch. One day later, on March 10, Casey transcribed the accuser's sworn information and complaint using the appropriate legalese of the day:

> *That John Sunday did on the ninth day of March in the year above mentioned feloniously break and enter my dwelling contrary to the statutes in such cases made and provided.*[1]

One might imagine these events playing out in a dwelling described by a newspaper report of the day as a "shanty."[2] Its simple fireplace offered, at that time of the year, life-preserving warmth and shelter from a disabling winter cold that was also familiar to those who, some fourteen years prior, at the command of Macdonald's government, were to "bring law" to an imperially defined west (Macleod 1976, Chap. 3).

Once a fort in the Hudson's Bay Company's fur trading network (Hesketh and Swyripa 1995; Palmer and Palmer 1990), the now larger settlement of Edmonton offered no witnesses to confirm or deny Rees's account. Doubling up as a justice of the peace, Casey had to decide, on the strength of the information provided, whether the first of several figurative gates should be opened so that the accused, John Sunday, might stand before the

Dominion's colonial criminal justice. Casey apparently thought so and signed a Warrant to Apprehend him, addressed to all constables and peace officers of the NWT. Two days later, on February 12, a rudimentary magistrate's court (with Casey and J.A. Macdougal presiding) was convened,

> upon a charge laid upon the information of William Thompson Rees of Edmonton—miner who saith that John Sunday an Indian did feloniously break and enter his dwelling house with the intent to committ a felony therein contrary to the statutes in such cases made and provided.

Whatever else might have been said in the earlier confrontation between the neighbours, they now faced each other as accuser and accused in a legally organized magistrate's court.[3] This court was to decide whether to open figurative gates to the "due courses of law," beginning with a criminal trial. In "evidence" sworn before this court, Rees is said to have stated these words before the magistrates and the accused:

> I was away from my house working, on my return I found the door ajar and some strange keys in the locks which was opened on entering I saw the prisoner John Sunday standing opposite the wall directly in front and close to where my vest hung with my watch in the pocket— the chain had been detached from the Button hole and was hanging down the watch remaining in the pocket—I asked the prisoner what he was doing there he said to see what time it was. I recognized the keys produced in court as the ones that were in the lock when I found Sunday in the house. My dwelling is in the east end of Edmonton the prisoner lives in the next house to me about 2000 yards away...The door was locked in the morning by me before I went to work.

In Casey's handwritten "Statement of the Accused," Sunday was legally cautioned by these words:

Having heard the evidence do you wish to say anything in answer to
the charge. You are not obliged to say anything unless you desire to
do so but whatever you say will be taken down in writing and may be
given in evidence against you at your trial.

In response, the accused reportedly said:

I tried my key in the lock of course I opened it I did not think it would
open it I was hungry I saw a pot on the stove. I took off the lid I took
not quite half a plate full of beans after I had eaten the beans I took the
watch in my hand and took the chain out of the button hole I opened
the watch to see what time it was I shut the watch and put it back in
the pocket and I was just going to leave when the prosecutor came and
caught me in the house.

Even with the imposition of the justice of the peace's attempt at legalese,
and the lack of routine punctuation, one senses differently arranged horizons behind such phrases as "of course I opened it" and "I was hungry...
I took not quite half a plate full of beans." Sunday seemed by such phrases
to regard his actions as perfectly ordinary, even mundane. The records refer
to Sunday as an Indigenous man, and a neighbour of the accuser, who by
virtue of his differently arranged cultural horizons did not consider the
phrase "break and enter" as an appropriate way of describing the events,
or that eating some beans, or holding a watch, were actions that warranted
much further comment.

Regardless, the magistrates sided with Rees's account and a "Warrant
of Commitment" propelled Sunday's journey further into criminal justice
networks. He was taken into custody in anticipation of being "delivered by Due courses of law" at the next Supreme Court. Reflecting the
contact between local social context and imposed law (Gavigan 2012), his
sense of the world was subjugated to the advancing Dominion's "law and
order" as he found himself in legal custody answering charges against

him (see Harring 1998). That journey was temporarily interrupted by a "Recognizance of Bail" for $200 dollars—$100 from Sunday, and $50 each from Charles Stewart (a "merchant" at Edmonton) and Bella Croaknose (a "widow"). Sunday's bail condition required him to plead to,

> *such indictment as may be prepared against him for and in respect to the charge aforesaid and takes his trial upon the same and does not defeat the said court without leave then the said recognizance to be void otherwise to stand in full force and virtue.*

On Saturday May 12, *The Edmonton Bulletin* reported that this case was to be heard the following Monday before Judge Rouleau of the NWT Supreme Court, who had travelled up from Calgary to Edmonton to hold court.[4] The following week, it followed up with a report that in the case "Queen vs John Sunday, housebreaking, with felonious intent," a certain R. Strachan had appeared on behalf of the Crown, with Shaw and Prince for the defence, to be heard before a jury of six men—who, as it turned out, "rendered a verdict of acquittal."[5] If nothing else, this indicates the social complexity of legal decisions; but it also reaffirms how—regardless of outcome—entryways helped to ensconce Dominion criminal justice.

Entryway Narrative 2
Accusations of Attempted Self-Murder

A second case may be recovered from scattered texts deposited in a state-funded archive that tell a tragic tale of an attempted suicide as a "crime." The narratives take us to William Boyle's house in Nanaimo on Vancouver Island at approximately 7:10 A.M. on October 28, 1890. In witness depositions,[6] recorded on December 2, we are told that a Joseph Macdonald, the local milkman, did as he usually did at Boyle's house—he called out "milk."[7] But something struck him as odd that morning:

the door was open for about an inch and a half. The can for his milk was usually set on the railing of the Veranda, but this morning it was not there.

His curiosity raised, he again called "milk" and this time, "Boyle came to the door his face, neck and hands up to his elbow were covered with blood." Macdonald also noticed a pool of blood on the floor and immediately enquired as to what was happening. Boyle apparently responded by saying, "I cut my throat yesterday," pointing to the blood and saying that a hog had been killed there. Strangely, Macdonald continued with his milk delivery and "served four or five" customers before thinking that he had "better inform" the city constable, O'Connell, whose house was not far away. At about half past seven, on finding the constable asleep following the previous night's duty, he left his "information with Mrs. O'Connell." A note in the archived documents indicates that the "prisoner" had no questions to ask, suggesting that the accused was present when this witness testified.

Constable Thomas O'Connell's sworn deposition claims that he received the information at roughly 7:40 A.M. and saw a man walking to the nearby hospital en route to Boyle's house. He found the door "wide open," and

I went into the house and saw blood all about the floor and a large dish pan of water was coloured with blood—and clothes such as pants, socks and a coat, were lying on the floor soaked with blood—I found a razor upon the floor...the razor was covered with blood.

He then proceeded to the hospital and encountered Boyle, who had "an ugly gash in his throat"; when asked how that happened, Boyle confessed to doing it. O'Connell escorted Boyle to the police station. His testimony also indicates that Boyle had been drinking to excess "for some weeks previously—he had neglected his work and given himself to drink"; seemingly, this all happened after his wife and two children had left him.

Peter Joseph Rice, a registered medical practitioner, examined Boyle in the Nanaimo gaol at about 9:00 A.M. on October 28 with a Dr. Davis attending. Rice noted the blood and "some cloths around his neck, also saturated with blood." When he removed these cloths, he found an "incised wound at the throat" with a cut,

> extending from 3 inches to the right of the middle line of the body to 2 inches to the left of the middle line...It was 4 inches in depth—the windpipe and gullet were not injured but only a severed membrane was left between the back part of the wound and the base of the tongue... A number of the muscles of the throat were severed...But bleeding had arrested before I saw him.

He dressed the slash with a temporary antiseptic dressing and sent Boyle back to the hospital, where later that afternoon "Dr. Davis and myself stitched up the wound," which had since "progressed most favourably."

These complex relations were reduced to a standard form stating, "The information and complaint of Thomas O'Connell of Nanaimo, Constable... before the undersigned...Her Majesty's Justices of the Peace in and for the said district or county of Nanaimo." That information was recorded thus:

> On the 28th day of October in the year 1890 aforesaid one William Boyle of Nanaimo in the said district, at the city of Nanaimo in the said district, did unlawfully cut and worked himself in the throat with a certain razor with intent, thereby then and there feloniously wilfully and of his malice aforethought to kill and murder himself against the peace of Our Lady, the Queen, Her Crown and Dignity.

A form for indictable offences entitled "Statement of the Accused" stated the law's formal indictment. It was read by a sanctioned authority (police officer, justice of the peace), seemingly in the presence of "prosecution witnesses" and the accused. When asked whether he had any response, Boyle simply replied, "I make no statement."

He was then indicted, but granted bail on the condition that he appear before,

> *the next court of competent Criminal Jurisdiction to answer any indict-*
> *ments that may be found against him by the Grand Jury in respect of*
> *the charges aforesaid.*

A subsequently convened grand jury concluded with this presentment:

> *And the jurors aforesaid upon their oath aforesaid do further present*
> *that the said William Boyle afterwards to wit on the day and your*
> *aforesaid did unlawfully attempt feloniously wilfully and of his malice*
> *aforethought himself to kill and murder against the peace of Our Lady*
> *the Queen Her Crown and dignity.*

To hedge their bets, since it was two years before the introduction of the Criminal Code in Canada (see Brown 1989), this jury decided too that Boyle,

> *did unlawfully cut and wound himself in the throat with a razor with*
> *intent thereby to commit suicide against the peace of our Lady the*
> *Queen.*

Such a decision set the course of Boyle's life down the road of a criminal trial, the outcome of which is unknown.

Interpretative Orientations
Understanding the "Lowly Beginnings" of Crime

How might one interpret these cases? The Introduction to this collection suggests that crime emerges from contextual legal negotiations that decide on whether to criminalize specific acts or subjects. Echoing the point in his analysis of the "long march" of the NWMP westwards, expressly to enforce Dominion law, Macleod astutely observes that,

Every society in every age works out its own definition of antisocial
and therefore proscribed behaviour...In theory the police are merely the
agents of society in identifying and apprehending offenders to whom
the courts then apply the appropriate punishment. In fact the police
play a mediating role in determining which offences will be taken most
seriously...This kind of selective perception and enforcement of the law
is apparent in the history of the North-West Mounted Police. (1976, 114)

That "selective perception and enforcement of the law" followed from dominant perceptions of crime,[8] and how to enforce Dominion law and order in local contexts. The attempt to forge a monopoly over the use of legal violence, and to define materially what its order required, is nicely framed by Nietzsche's scattered—if iconoclastic—references to crime (see Pavlich 2009).

Whatever its liabilities, the value of Nietzsche's thinking on criminal law lies in a call to understand the "lowly beginnings" of western (imperial) morality, politics, and law (Sedgwick 2013). His approach helps us to grapple with a far-flung "will to power" behind the imposition of Dominion law and its creation of crime. Nietzsche insists that,

More strictly: one must admit nothing that has being—because then
Becoming would lose its value and actually appear meaningless and
superfluous. Consequently one must ask how the illusion of being could
have arisen (was bound to arise)... (2011, 708)

In this sense, we should not consider crime and criminal subjects as ontologically distinct beings, but as elements of historical formations (the "becoming") whose powers shape subjects and social forms. Furthermore, Nietzsche indicates that the "most decisive act" performed by a "supreme power" as soon as it is "strong enough to do so—is the institution of the *law*" (emphasis original). Such impositions of law involved,

the imperative declaration of what in general counts as permitted, as
just, in its eyes, and what counts as forbidden, as unjust: once it has

instituted the law, it treats violence and capricious acts on the part of individuals or entire groups as offences against the law, as rebellion against the supreme power itself... (Nietzsche 1997, bk. II, sec. 11, 75–6)

For our purposes, the often violent expansion of Dominion law defined the forbidden, appropriated disputes from subjects, and disallowed injured parties from pursuing private revenge. It also denigrated any other claims to law, and vilified the idea that Indigenous law might rival its "progressive" jurisprudence (Borrows 2002; Foster 1981; Harring 1998).

In short, from Nietzsche, we may say the "lowly beginnings" of Dominion crime, and the forces that carried it into being, augured around opening moments that claimed a unique capacity to define specific actions and persons as potentially criminal. Usually, such beginnings surfaced through accusations that the sovereign order had been criminally violated—these accusations were crucial to the selective "perception and enforcement of the law" visited upon local subjects and situations. But there is a caveat here—the *lore* of criminal accusation should be distinguished from the *law* of accusatorial procedures, even if both enabled the Dominion's emphasis on criminalizing justice (Pavlich 2006). The lore of criminal accusation, however, was fundamental here, since it deferred to everyday meaning horizons through which specific acts and people could be framed as potentially criminal. That is, through ideas and rituals that made sense of specific events as criminal, accusation played a formative role by opening local relations between subjects to the imposition of criminalizing processes— in our two examples, the latter involved enlarging the Dominion's criminal justice networks.

Initiating Criminal Pathways
Accusation and the Lore of Ordinary Lives

With this broad theoretical approach in mind, the cases reveal something about the very ordinary, initiating moments that founded the force of Dominion law. In Sunday's case, one might imagine a walk home that detoured—perhaps out of curiosity, sociality, etc.—to his neighbour's dwelling. His key opened the door and he helped himself to beans simmering on the stove. A watch chain caught his eye and he removed it from the coat for closer inspection. At that very moment, Rees returned home, his suspicions raised by the strange key in his door. Similarly, a door left ajar interrupted the milk delivery person's ordinary routines, as did the absence of a milk bottle that typically rested on the veranda rail. Though not emphasized in the documents, it was precisely these jarring perceptions that provoked unfamiliar suspicions. They deflected thoughts away from familiar routines, and momentarily suspended everyday horizons of meaning. Unremarkable ways of thinking about the world dissolved into shades of disordering disquietude, as the comforts of taken-for-granted meanings were jolted by experiences of the unfamiliar. In both contexts, an uneasy sense that something was not quite right paved the way to accusations and criminal blame. Living through such moments, Rees's and MacDonald's immediate responses were to reorder unsettled meaning horizons by pondering options and reflecting on "what was going on." Reporting information to legal authorities channelled their disquiet into narratives that centred on providing "information" and "complaints" that crimes had occurred. Reordering disrupted meanings with the help of legal rituals, that is, helped these accusers reframe the complex events through judicial idioms; namely, as offences requiring sovereign redress. But, it should be noted, that option had only recently become possible as the Dominion's sanctioned policing and court institutions were extended westwards.

Regardless, and this is the point, seemingly trivial experiences that prompted accusations of crime were pivotal to contemporaneous forms of criminalization and their symbolic re-orderings. They initiated new chains of signification and unleashed allegations of crime to be dealt with by legal agents. Thus, Rees's surprise at waylaying Sunday with a watch in hand prompted vexed questions that might have resulted in several courses of action—a discussion about divergent settler and Indigenous cultural expectations, even a demand to leave the dwelling and never to return, and so on. Under different historical circumstances, and without the unfolding machinery of Dominion criminal justice, Sunday and Rees may in any case have opted to negotiate misaligned social understandings differently. In the event, however, Rees opted to avow that a crime had taken place, providing information to the recently deployed police force, and accusing Sunday of "unlawfully" breaking into and entering his home (seemingly to steal a watch). His transposed statement of offence declared that both he—Rees—and the Queen's law and peace were aggrieved victims of Sunday's actions. If Rees's decision followed disordering experiences, the latter were assuaged by his accusations to a local constable (and justice of the peace) that Sunday had committed a crime. His actions initiated a criminalizing process that resulted in the accused's apprehension and subsequent journey through the criminal justice system (but eventually resulted in an acquittal).

With Boyle's attempted suicide, we might pause to reflect on social meanings that enabled a milk deliverer to encounter a man in medical distress, offer no immediate assistance, and then decide to move on to his next customers. No doubt, the shock of accosting Boyle's bloodied state would likely have disorientated Macdonald. Yet this kind of jolt indicates precisely the disruptions that push ordinary meaning horizons to disordered confusions, where accusation, allegations of crime, and individual blame might emerge as apposite ways to rearrange scattered experiences. Why would Macdonald's compassion not have spurred him to seek medical assistance? Of course, one cannot answer that question definitively, but the surviving texts suggest that crime-focused legal ideas had become deeply influential amongst settlers, steering this man to the police constable. And again, the commonplace suspicions aroused by an open door, or a missing milk container, led to confusions and a quest to regroup meanings. The latter resulted in the injured Boyle being portrayed, not as someone facing a medical emergency, but as a person whose "criminal" acts warranted police intervention. As such, Macdonald's response to a disorientating situation turned him to the authority of legal forms that only a few decades previously were a distant prospect. Similarly, the constable—even as he noticed an injured Boyle stumbling on the street—opted to approach the police station over the nearby hospital.

In sum, the narratives and actions that flowed from local suspicions suggest how settler-colonial forms of criminalization were initiated within fragile socio-cultural meanings disturbed by local events. In Edmonton, frayed and contested meanings were silenced by naming the events as a break and enter (theft), casting aside the possibility that different meaning horizons might have led Sunday to act as he did. In Nanaimo, we have a distraught man whose life had led to family breakdown, misuse of alcohol, and perhaps a cry for help through the attempted suicide; somehow his tragic decisions and actions were deemed criminal, as an offence against the Queen's order. That either situation should be cast as potentially criminal reveals something of the success in enforcing Dominion criminal law as the sole declarer of "unlawful" acts and persons in context (see also Foster 1994). Here, the legal management of the locally disrupted social meanings perhaps evokes Nietzsche's "lowly beginnings" that created settlers' colonial visions of crime.

Criminal Subjections
Accusers and the Accused

When disrupted socio-cultural meaning horizons led to contacts between local contexts and Dominion law's agents, the result was to generate authorized social entrances that selected potential criminals. No doubt, the imposition of Dominion law had followed—with local modification— English models of justice (Farr 1967). Both framed criminal acts as injuring victims *and* as violating a sovereign's order (Foucault 2015).[9] The two cases at hand also suggest that Dominion law embraced these wider developments by recasting private accusers as witnesses or deponents who merely provided information to state-sanctioned accusers, now authorized to control entry into an expanding criminal justice system. Whatever else, the growth of the Dominion's capacity to criminalize selected subjects relied on locally formed—and fluid—identities of accuser, accused, and mediating authority. Our two cases show how these identities were negotiated through power relations anchored to Dominion versions of crime and criminals.

In unfolding dramas at entryways to criminalization, authorities performed and assigned legal roles to each participant. That is, those who stood before the law with truthful information about a crime were required to adopt legally legible identities as a condition of their participation. For instance, Rees was portrayed as a miner with a fixed abode; these two credentials were decipherable to the law, and enabled him to assume a credible accuser identity. His role as informer became possible once the NWMP had established enough of a presence for authorities to receive, record, and manage information at expanding entrances to a criminal justice system. In swearing an oath that he was telling the truth about a criminal event, Rees participated in a way that not only gave tangible form to a legal entrance, but also shaped his identity as a victim and informant. Equally, Macdonald was seemingly well aware of colonial/Dominion law's expansion over Vancouver Island (Loo 1994b; Parker 2015), and the rise of the British Columbia Provincial Police (Stonier-Newman 1991). Through his decision to report the events to the constable, and so to portray them as potentially criminal, Macdonald took on the role of an accuser who regarded medical assistance as less important than a putative duty to a colonial sovereign in whose name a crime was alleged.

Such accusing identities were, of course, enabled by an unfolding Dominion law seeking to expand its jurisdiction over more areas of society (Foster 1994; Loo 1990; Strange and Loo 1997). Whatever their precise motivations, these subjects were important agents who shaped the creation of crime—where criminal law and society intermingled. They also legitimated, by supplying information, the authorized Crown identities that opened or closed figurative gates to criminal justice networks. Here, the constables were authorized to act on sworn testimony that a crime "against the peace of Our Lady the Queen Her Crown and Dignity" allegedly happened.

Further, authorized government agents decided on whether to admit accused criminals to criminal courts. As indicated by the Edmonton case, where grand juries did not form part of criminal entryways (Parker 2015), decisions on whether to proceed with an accuser's information were granted to justice officials, sometimes with conflicted roles. In this case,

Casey served as a police inspector, but also as a justice of the peace, and then as one of two magistrates who decided to channel the matter further into the criminal justice system. Clearly conflating police and judicial gatekeeper identities, this case highlights how entrances to law initially allowed this designated authority to decide on the validity of his previous decisions. Blurring policing and juridical oversight in this way did little to restrain a potential for capricious and even despotic judgments of criminality (see Macleod 1976). By contrast, the Vancouver Island case relied on different entryway processes; it included a grand jury that indicted Boyle to answer the charges as a "prisoner" at the next convened court competent to hear criminal matters. Even so, in both cases, pivotal decisions required gatekeeping authorities to negotiate identities (e.g., justice of the peace, grand jury member) around legal rituals and assemblies dedicated to deciding whether criminal charges were to be answered in court.

One glimpses here how a newly deployed Dominion law operated through local political arenas, forming legally decipherable identities around allegations of a crime. What then of those key participants who were criminally accused? Their identities were also negotiated through the unfolding situations at hand, out of a politics that recognized limited legal persons from much more complex social beings. We have seen that in a statement of the accused, Sunday seems to have viewed his actions as quite ordinary. Equally, it is doubtful whether Boyle would have described his desperate act of attempted suicide at the end of a protracted alcoholic binge as criminal— worthy of an empathetic response to a clear cry for help perhaps, but not a criminal violation of the Queen's peace. Yet, in its quest to secure a monopoly over criminal jurisdiction, Dominion law silenced any rival ideas about these subjects and their actions; it could not recognize a competing, Indigenous sense of social order, or that a desperately unhappy man who injured himself might not be criminally violating the Queen's order (Foster 1981; Harring 1998). Instead, it shaped accused criminal identities at entryways by allowing limited responses to allegations. In their statements, neither accepted law's imposed identities—Sunday by refusing to view his acts as criminal, and Boyle by electing to say nothing. Both accused criminal identities (a break and enter thief, an attempted self-murderer) were negotiated through ritualized entrances to criminalization with significant implications for people so defined.

To sum up this section, legal agents negotiated the narratives and rituals that formed emerging gateways to criminal justice. Through such processes, socio-political relations that constituted criminalizing entryways shaped fluid identities of witnesses, accusers, accused, and authorities. Indeed, assuming versions of such identities was demanded by the Dominion's unfolding criminal law. By subjecting participants to its enforced rules, this law generated particular kinds of subjects and identities. Yet the latter remained fluid, as they surfaced through the changing responses required by relational complexes at entryways—from the laying of information and complaints, to justice of the peace decisions, to grand jury presentments, and to managed statements from the accused. All played their changing parts in the unfolding dramas that enacted gateways to Dominion legal forms and, in effect, sought to negate rival claims to law in monopolistic bids to criminal jurisdiction.

Avowal at Law's Gates
"Telling the Truth, the Whole Truth and Nothing but the Truth"

This chapter has alluded to broader socio-cultural and political shifts that together with accusation-based subjections shaped particular entryways to Dominion justice. Forging points of contact between criminal law and everyday life, these entryways deployed spaces within which such law could manage avowals of the truth by witnesses, authorities, accusers, and the accused. Foucault's (2014) lectures on avowal noted in the Introduction are useful here. Specifically, historical legal instances required subjects to enunciate truths about themselves in ways that complied with emerging legal rituals (e.g., swearing oaths, referencing science, etc.). Extending Dominion criminal law to the west was accomplished in the first instance by creating entryways with explicit expectations of what could be counted as a legal avowal, and what truth-telling had to involve. For their words to be cast as legal truths, subjects were required to follow legal rituals that supposedly ensured telling—under oath and with God's help—"the truth, the whole truth, and nothing but the truth" in relation to the events at hand. Interestingly, the reference to God was not required of Indigenous persons (Harring 1998). In any case, these sanctioned truth-telling procedures produced particular kinds of subject identities that were shaped by, and yet served as conduits for, opening moments of possible entry to criminalizing processes.

Three aspects of avowal and truth-telling practices are clear from the two cases: the use of uniform idioms to indicate legal truth; an emphasis on so-called factual lexicons to demarcate legal truth; and, the use of transcription to render legal truths available to judicial assessment. Let us explore each in turn. First, as indicated above, testimonies were sworn to under oath, signed by those who testified, and countersigned by law's local authorities—justices of the peace, magistrates, etc. Statements were required to follow idiomatic customs to count as legally valid. Specifically, witness avowals were taken down in writing and represented as legitimate to the extent that they emerged from structured spaces under the directed purview of authorized legal agents. The latter rendered legal narratives in relatively uniform formats considered decipherable to law, and bounded by the threat of perjury charges if deemed false. To ensure that avowed statements were legally decipherable, this law often utilized standardized word patterns set out on forms. The latter recorded information, complaints, witness depositions, indictments, specific bail conditions, statements from the accused, and so on.

Perhaps a good example of such legal lexicons can be gleaned from handwritten (the Edmonton case) or uniformly printed (the Nanaimo case) "Statement of Accused" records. Both solicited contextual avowals through such stock phases and legalese as:

And the said charges being read to the said _____ and the witnesses for the prosecution _____, bring severally examined in his presence, the said _____ is now addressed by me as follows:

Having heard the evidence, do you wish to say anything in answer to the charge? You are not obliged to say anything, unless you desire to do so; but whatever you say will be taken down in writing, and may be given in evidence against you at your trial...[10]

Such prescribed ways of receiving the accused's avowals as countersigned statements indicated that the words were voluntarily offered by the accused after hearing, and being given an opportunity to question, the evidence presented against him or her. In addition, the form required justices of the peace to read the following statement to the accused:

You have nothing to hope from any promise of favour, and nothing to fear from any threat, which may have been holden out to you to induce you to make any admission or confession of your guilt, but whatever you shall now say may be given in evidence against you upon your trial, notwithstanding such promise or threat.[11]

From such phrases, we glimpse this law's attempt to standardize truth-telling practices at entrances to criminalizing rituals, and to generate specific kinds of truth-telling. With the guiding injunctions of uniform language, completed and countersigned forms alleged that avowals conformed to procedural requirements and so could be counted as legal truths. No doubt, comparative assessments of such truths had significant, sometimes violent, effects on people's lives; they were also used to decide on journeys through law—both Sunday and Boyle had to answer charges before so-called competent criminal courts because of legally accepted avowals.

Secondly, the legal genres used in both cases relied heavily on lexicons through which avowals were recorded in a factual, staccato-like style. The countersigned records, for example, presented witness testimony using flattened stylistic formats: "I was away from my house working," "on my return I found the door ajar and some strange keys in the locks which was opened," "I called at the house of William Boyle," "I called out 'Milk' as usual," "his face, neck and hands up to his elbows were covered with blood," and so on. The style of juridical depositions at entryways simply did not allow for complicated argument, proof, convincing prose, or stylistic flair—in law, truth was to appear only as baldly stated fact. Sworn, one-idea statements of facts accrued as "evidence" relating to specified events. Such truth-telling practices served as the basis for decisions on whether to proceed with the case. Indictments further distilled evidence into legally framed allegations to be answered by the accused at a sanctioned criminal court hearing. One senses here a progressive reduction, a filtering, from the sheer complexity of discourses surrounding a contested event, to the simple documents *ex post facto* framed as legal records. Reduced to factual lexicons, complex social events were now presented as sworn truths decipherable to law, and thereby made amenable to legal reasoning and decisions about who to select for potential criminalization.

Thirdly, so-called legal truths and the reductions of fact-based legal lexicons depended on how statements of truth were captured and represented; hence the juridical importance attached to written oral evidence, or *transcription*. An exemplar here might be where a subject—Rees or Macdonald—resolved confusions by orally avowing truths about putative criminal events. Their spoken words were transposed to written legal records by authorized identities; sworn under oath, juridical protocol required that they be signed by the avower, and countersigned by a transcribing authority. Such transcribed documents not only initiated criminalizing entryways, but also became the currency for subsequent juridical governance. It is thus not surprising that attempts should have been made to standardize juridical lexicons through forms and sanctioned traces of putatively criminal events. That is, witness testimonies, depositions, indictments, and judgments enabled a form of legal regulation centred on the creation, control, archiving, and recording of legal documents (Ferraris 2012, 247–49). Coupled with a political capacity to declare these as the privileged (even singular) truths, settler-colonial law's agents could then define particular narratives of events as *the* final truth that was used to govern entryways to criminal justice.

Moreover, legal avowals captured or represented in written documents left documentary traces for subsequent juridical scrutiny and argument. These narrative traces condensed complex events to supposedly factual, legal lexicons, and forged hierarchies of truth amongst written traces, elevating the power effects of certain statements over others (e.g., grand jury presentments over depositions). As the cases suggest, complaints that triggered criminalizing rituals began by filtering compound social relations into narrow legal traces. One might, for instance, imagine the complexity of the interactions between, say, Rees, Sunday, and the justice of the peace, or between Boyle, Macdonald, O'Connell, the doctors, the justices of the peace, and the grand jury. Yet the legally transcribed narratives eschewed any reference to relational intricacy, leaving increasingly condensed traces in the form of staccato-like statements of fact in hierarchically arranged documents, from sworn witness testimony, information and complaints, statements from the accused, indictments, and grand jury presentments.

From the previous section, one glimpses how entryways to criminal justice distilled legal traces in the wake of complicated events. Idiomatic signatures attested to sworn oaths that reduced the nuances of everyday events to transcribed witness statements of fact. Avowed truths written as simple phrases and lexicons were rendered so as to be decipherable to the juridical reasoning of the day. Transposing relational complexity into abridged legal languages compressed pulsing corporeality into muted indictments that alleged clear-cut transgressions of criminal law and the Queen's peace/order. Hence, the heterogeneous meaning horizons surrounding Sunday's excursion into Rees's shanty in search of food (and the ambiguous holding of the watch) were cast as a break and enter with intent to steal. Such juridical reductions of everyday life also enabled the legal silencing of the sheer desperation behind drinking binges that surrounded Boyle's suicide attempt. The archived documents, that is, left legally created traces of abridged stories leading to a simple indictment— a man who committed a crime by cutting and trying to murder himself. The compressions required to render intricacies of social context into legal indictments betrayed a subtle insertion of law as it claimed to offer a privileged, definitive, fact-based, and truthful account of past events. As gatekeepers to criminal justice, Dominion law and its representatives privileged their archived traces in a constrained language of accusation and indictment. The latter alleged that crimes had been committed against the Queen's order, in whose name this unfolding law emerged. It did so by silencing legal pluralism and Indigenous forms of law.

Conclusion

The preceding discussion has interpreted the surviving records of two cases from late nineteenth-century western Canada with an eye to understanding the imposition of criminal law, and specifically the entryways that decided on which acts and persons to criminalize in given circumstances. Having orientated my interpretations around selected comments by Nietzsche on crime, law, and opening moments of criminalization, it highlighted three main themes.

To begin with, the significance of seemingly inconsequential events and perceptions was highlighted—an unfamiliar key in a door, or an open door and an empty bottle not left in a usual spot. Encounters that dislocated socially familiar ways of making sense of the world generated comparable disorder and chaos, leaving the subject open to explanatory tales by which to reorder meaning horizons. In both examples, accusing someone of committing a crime and taking matters to legal authorities reordered moments of disorientating suspicion. At these moments, law and society intermingled and formed entryway mechanisms that sought to impose Dominion law over the west. In other words, settler-colonial law inserted itself into existing social-legal relations as a privileged, ordering force. But such points of contact were also significant in that they initiated the local generation of entryways into Dominion criminal justice, establishing the foundations of the relational hubs from whence its now expansive criminalization derives.

Secondly, these entryways brought several subjects into contact with one another; they shaped identities that performed the roles of informer, accuser, authorized agent, and the accused. Through the limited responses demanded by subjects at entryways, legally legible identities were negotiated, thus restricting the subjects that could be legally recognized. This allowed specific sorts of identities to serve as vehicles for particular entryways to criminal justice. Expanding criminalizing entryways could then insert the Dominion law's recognition rituals into local social relations.

Thirdly, the contact between society and law involved a matter fundamental to settler legal forms: what it means to tell the truth, to avow, in supposedly unambiguous legal ways. Dominion law sought to monopolize its sanctioned ways of telling the truth and so deny an existing (Indigenous) legal pluralism (Nettlebeck et. al. 2016). That monopolization required informers, accusers, and the accused to perform specific rituals to count as speaking "the truth, the whole truth and nothing but the truth." Such juridical truth-telling in the Canadian west at the end of the nineteenth century enlisted particular rituals for swearing oaths, testifying truthfully, signing statements, and countersigning documents. As well, the lexicons for truth-telling practices in law were radically circumscribed by the use of a language that claimed to record the facts in a staccato-like, abbreviated, and reduced fashion. Forms, too, demanded a common language. In other words, oral accounts were transcribed, and indeed translated, into legally decipherable linguistic codes that became the currency for subsequent juridical governance.

By way of conclusion, one might return to a point raised before; namely, the tenacious legacy of imposed criminalizing entryways behind the vast criminal justice networks that confront us today. To be sure, my engagement with a selected past indicates traces of criminal justice that were left behind by settler-colonial impositions of law implied by the cases at hand. But it also implicitly attempts to confront the costly and exclusionary effects of ever-expanding criminal justice networks that have left the law of these cases behind. Even so, crime—no matter where enunciated—is a product of prior criminalizing processes, of legally arranged rituals and practices that constitute entryways used to define specific acts and persons as criminal. Thinking about the enormous criminal justice institutions of our time, and their socially damaging effects, one might come to re-appraise the "lowly beginnings" of crime at the entryways to crime control networks. It may be that such beginnings have been sidelined—even silenced—by the now dominant sense that crime has a fixed being of its own, and that disciplines like criminology can determine its aetiology. But we should recall that the *crimen* of this discipline has etymological links to accusation, suggesting the basic importance of a political logic by which persons come to be accused, and socially called to account for actions (Pavlich 2000). In this sense, the legal creation of crime at entryways could be understood as a pivot for sustaining, but equally for stemming, unequal population flows into criminal justice arenas.

Notes

1. All references to the Edmonton case file may be found in: The Queen v. John Sunday (break and enter), [1888], GR1983.0001, box 1/4, Provincial Archives of Alberta.
2. *The Edmonton Bulletin* (Edmonton, Alberta), March 18, 1888, vol. 1X, no. 20, p. 1; newspaper references may be found at the University of Alberta Peel Library, at http://peel.library.ualberta.ca/newspapers/.
3. *Edmonton Bulletin*, March 18, 1888, p. 1.
4. 1888, p. 1.
5. *Edmonton Bulletin*, May 19, 1888, p. 3.
6. (Form (M) Sec s. 29 for "Indictable Offences").
7. All references to the Nanaimo case file may be found in: Queen vs. Boyle (attempted suicide), [1890], GR-2840.2.16, British Columbia Archives and Museum.
8. He also notes that, "Crime, like other human activities, tends to reflect the predominant social ideas of the era in which it occurs. In the case of the 19th century Canadian West, crime was very closely tied to class and to popular concepts of class. Respectability was the dominant virtue of the middle and upper classes, which meant that criminal activities were associated in the public mind with lower classes.

A middle-class individual who was discovered in some serious violation of the law became almost automatically a social outcast. Everyone expected that the lower orders would break the law. It was one measure of their inferiority" (Macleod 1976, 127).

9. As Farr puts it, "The judicial system of England was used as a model for the administration of justice in the colonies, but the conditions of rough and pioneer territories modified and re-shaped that institution in innumerable ways. The modified system that resulted from these influences was of a different nature in British Columbia than in Vancouver Island, and appeared in a different form in the United colony than in the independent colonies" (1944, 127).

10. The Queen v. John Sunday (break and enter), [1888], GR 1983.0001, box 1/4, Provincial Archives of Alberta.

11. Queen vs. Boyle (attempted suicide), [1890], GR-2840.2.16, British Columbia Archives and Museum.

References

Barman, Jean. 2007. *The West Beyond the West: A History of British Columbia*. 3rd edition. Toronto; Buffalo: University of Toronto Press.

———. 2008. *British Columbia: Spirit of the People*. Madeira Park, BC: Harbour Publishing.

Beahen, William. 1998. *Red Coats on the Prairies: The North-West Mounted Police, 1886–1900*. Regina, Saskatchewan: Centax Books.

Borrows, John. 2002. *Recovering Canada: The Resurgence of Indigenous Law*. Toronto; Buffalo: University of Toronto Press.

Brown, Desmond Haldane. 1989. *The Genesis of the Canadian Criminal Code of 1892*. Toronto: The Osgoode Society for Canadian Legal History.

Chiste, Katherine Beaty. 2005. "The Justice of the Peace in History: Community and Restorative Justice." *Saskatchewan Law Review* 68 (January): 153.

Christie, Nils. 1994. *Crime Control as Industry: Towards Gulags, Western Style*. 2nd edition. London: Routledge.

Dorsett, Shaunnagh, and Shaun McVeigh. 2012. *Jurisdiction*. Milton Park, Abingdon, Oxon, New York: Routledge-Cavendish.

Farr, David. 1944. "The Organization of the Judicial System of the Colonies of Vancouver Island and British Columbia, 1849–1871." Vancouver: University of British Columbia.

———. 1967. "The Organization of the Judicial System in the Colonies of Vancouver Island and British Columbia, 1849–1871." *University of British Columbia Law Review* 3 (1).

Ferguson, Julie H. 2009. *James Douglas: Father of British Columbia*. Toronto: Dundurn.

Ferraris, Maurizio. 2012. *Documentality: Why It Is Necessary to Leave Traces*. New York: Fordham University Press.

Foster, Hamar. 1981. "'The Queen's Law Is Better than Yours': International Homicide in Early British Columbia." In *Essays in the History of Canadian Law: Crime and Criminal Justice in Canadian History*, vol. 5, edited by Jim Phillips, Tina Loo, and Susan Lewthwaite, 41–111. Toronto: The Osgoode Society for Canadian Legal History.

———. 1990. "Long-Distance Justice: The Criminal Jurisdiction of Canadian Courts West of the Canadas, 1763–1859." *American Journal of Legal History* 34 (1): 1–48. https://doi.org/10.2307/845344.

———. 1992. *The White Man's Law in the Far West: Establishing Legal Institutions in British Columbia*. Canadian Legal History Project Working Paper Series, Faculty of Law, University of Manitoba, volume 92, issue 12.

Foster, Hamar, A.R. Buck, and Benjamin L. Berger. 2008. *The Grand Experiment: Law and Legal Culture in British Settler Societies*. Vancouver: UBC Press.

Foucault, Michel. 2014. *Wrong-Doing, Truth-Telling: The Function of Avowal in Justice*. Chicago: University of Chicago Press.

———. 2015. *On the Punitive Society: Lectures at the Collège de France, 1972–1973*. Edited by Bernard Harcourt. Translated by Graham Burchell. London, New York: Palgrave Macmillan.

Gavigan, Shelley A.M. 2012. *Hunger, Horses, and Government Men: Criminal Law on the Aboriginal Plains, 1870–1905*. Vancouver: UBC Press.

Harring, Sidney L. 1998. *White Man's Law: Native People in Nineteenth-Century Canadian Jurisprudence*. 1st edition. Toronto: University of Toronto Press.

Hesketh, Bob, and Frances Swyripa. 1995. *Edmonton: The Life of a City*. Edmonton: New West Publishers.

Innis, Harold A. 2015. *The Fur Trade in Canada: An Introduction to Canadian Economic History*. Toronto: University of Toronto Press.

Komar, Debra. 2015. *The Bastard of Fort Stikine: The Hudson's Bay Company and the Murder of John McLoughlin Jr*. Fredericton: Goose Lane Editions.

Loo, Tina. 1990. "Law and Authority in British Columbia, 1821–1871." PHD diss., The University of British Columbia. doi:10.14288/1.0098760.

_____. 1994a. *Making Law, Order, and Authority in British Columbia, 1821–1871.* Social History of Canada. Toronto: University of Toronto Press.

_____. 1994b. "The Road from Butte Inlet: Crime and Colonial Identity in British Columbia." In *Essays in the History of Canadian Law: Crime and Criminal Justice in Canadian History,* vol. 5, edited by Jim Phillips, Tina Loo, and Susan Lewthwaite, 112–42. Toronto: The Osgoode Society for Canadian Legal History.

Macleod, R.C. 1976. *The North West Mounted Police and Law Enforcement, 1873–1905.* 1st edition. Toronto: University of Toronto Press.

_____. 2004. *North-West Mounted Police.* Oxford: Oxford University Press.

Marquis, Greg. 2015. *The Vigilant Eye: Policing Canada from 1867 to 9/11.* Winnipeg: Fernwood.

Nettlebeck, Amanda, Russell Smandych, Louis Knafla, and Robert Foster, 2016. *Fragile Settlements,* Vancouver: UBC Press.

Nietzsche, Friedrich. 1997. *On the Genealogy of Morals: A Polemic.* Oxford: Oxford University Press.

_____. 2011. *The Will to Power.* New York: Knopf Doubleday.

Palmer, Howard, and Tamara Jeppson Palmer. 1990. *Alberta: A New History.* Edmonton: Hurtig Publishers.

Parker, Nancy. 2015. "Swift Justice and the Decline of the Criminal Jury Trial." In *Essays in the History of Canadian Law, Volume VI: The Legal History of British Columbia and the Yukon,* edited by Hamar Foster and John McLaren, 171–203. Toronto: University of Toronto Press.

Pavlich, George. 2000. "Forget Crime: Accusation, Governance and Criminology." *Australian and New Zealand Journal of Criminology* 33 (2): 136–52.

_____. 2006. "The Lore of Criminal Accusation." *Criminal Law & Philosophy* 1 (1): 79–97.

_____. 2009. "Being Accused, Becoming Criminal." In *Existentialist Criminology,* edited by Don Crewe and Ronnie Lippens, 53–69. London: Routledge.

Reiman, Jeffrey. 1990. *The Rich Get Richer and the Poor Get Prison.* New York: MacMillan Publishing.

Sedgwick, Peter R. 2013. *Nietzsche's Justice: Naturalism in Search of an Ethics.* Montreal: McGill-Queen's University Press.

Stonier-Newman, Lynne. 1991. *Policing a Pioneer Province: The BC Provincial Police 1858–1950.* Madeira Park, BC: Harbour Publishing.

_____. 2006. *The Lawman: Adventures of a Frontier Diplomat.* Victoria: TouchWood Editions.

Strange, Carolyn, and Tina Loo. 1997. *Making Good: Law and Moral Regulation in Canada, 1867–1939*. Toronto: University of Toronto Press.

Taylor, Ian, Paul Walton, and Jock Young. 1973. *The New Criminology: For a Social Theory of Deviance*. London: Routledge.

Wilkins, Charles. 2012. *The Wild Ride: A History of the North West Mounted Police, 1873–1904*. Vancouver: Stanton Atkins & Dosil Publishers.

2

RIGHT TO SPEECH

Accusation, Rhetoric, and Criminal Entryways in BC Colonial Law

MATTHEW P. UNGER

IN 1879, according to the *Daily Colonist,* "the country rang from end to end" upon the discovery of a grisly and tragic murder in Lillooet, British Columbia. This was a particularly spectacular crime that sent shock waves through the community, and appeared to gain national significance.[1] Newspaper articles and witness depositions at the trials devoted to the case speak of several Indigenous people discovering the scene as they approached the Halfway House, a popular roadhouse, hotel, and small store that travellers and gold diggers used as a waypoint through the Cariboo region, then owned by Thomas Poole, a widower with two children. The witnesses recounted encountering the smoldering ruins of a house where they discovered the bodies of Thomas Poole and his daughter, Mary, on a pile of potatoes in the cellar. Upon investigation of the charred remains of the bodies of the victims, the coroner, C. Phair, found gun and stab wounds in both father and daughter. The boy was never found, but it was suspected that other bones and a hat found at the scene were his.

During the course of the trial, several people were accused, both settlers and Indigenous people. The only person actually charged had his sentence commuted. Since the jury accused various people between 1879 and 1891, this case affords a unique glimpse into the accusatory procedures, mechanisms, and practices that were common at the time. These accusatory practices highlight specific contextual aspects: the hierarchical relations between law, settlers, and Indigenous communities in early colonial practices in western Canadian colonies.

This chapter, however, investigates how criminal accusation of the time flowed from: specific forms of knowledge; forging political and legal boundaries between the visible and sensible; who was excluded and included from consideration; and who constituted the proper subject versus the outcast. In concert, these forms of recognition disclose different modes of truth-telling required by colonial dynamics of accusation in Canada's early legal history. The chapter focuses on two main issues. First, it examines the forms of accusation that directed the beginning stages of the trials that reflected close attachments to English Law. One can detect in the original coroner's inquest a poignant example of the rhetorical significance of truth-telling required of this law as it played out in a colonial context. The law restricted who could speak the truth and what kind of speaking was accepted and so was able to be heard by local authorities.

Second, it examines how this context discloses a particular regime of truth predicated on English law and the dispossessions this implied. Through a series of complicated misrecognitions in the encounters between different subjects of this law, the analysis shows how entryways were formed around a contested idea of criminal justice that discloses nascent, but enduring and troubling, colonial dynamics of accusation.

The Accused

On May 4, 1879, two weeks after the bodies of Thomas Poole and his two children were discovered, the police summoned the coroner to hold an inquest over the bodies to determine the nature of their demise. All three people were found to be murdered by gun and knife wounds for the "purpose of plunder."[2] Many people were asked to give their depositions during the several trials associated with this case. While several people were accused during this time, no one was formally charged to the satisfaction of the judges associated with the case.

Through the depositions taken at the initial inquest and in later trials we learn that a fellow named Scotty was instrumental in directing the suspicion of the jury, but also that of the popular media. We read in his depositions two major accusations. The first one is levelled against an Indigenous man named Black Jim, or Yaniew. The second accusation was set against the Chilcotin Indigenous communities, reflecting wide-spread suspicion that they possibly committed the crime. Walter Burgess, a friend of Scotty's, recalled that he had advised Scotty against going after Jim Yaniew (Black Jim). Instead, he suggested going and searching for trails that would lead to tracks from the Tsilhqot'in First Nations. Scotty then recruited thirteen St'át'imc First Nations people from Anderson Lake (N'quatqua) to join him to search for these trails. After a few days, he came back with only evidence of a cow trail. The significance of this accusation is that it reposes upon the practices of dispossession of a settler-colonial society that led to the 1864 Bute Inlet war (Harris 2002; Loo 1994).[3]

Livingston, the constable investigating the crime, collected a series of signatures to indict the individual who had initiated the first accusations: James "Scotty" Halliday. Scotty was named a suspect when evidence and witness statements were brought against him after his initial accusations were not seen as viable. Witness depositions recount the strange ways that he was acting during the Clinton, BC, assize. As part of his initial accusations, Scotty had been asking repeatedly about Poole's character and was seemingly too quick to accuse Yaniew. Hunter Jack's statement gives an interesting account of the accusatory process by following Scotty through the different points at which Scotty directed the attention of the jury and the criminal justice system. We see in this deposition that Scotty was an instrumental part of directing the attention of the criminal justice system. Yet, one thing that drew suspicion onto Scotty was Hunter Jack's state-ment recounting the fact that Scotty had "appropriated" Yaniew's wife and was accusing Yaniew because he was scared of reprisal. Hunter Jack remembered offering a piece of wisdom, stating: "of course you are scared of Black Jim, you are keeping his wife." Hunter Jack had told Scotty that it was "unlikely" that Black Jim committed the crime. After this point, Scotty talked with the justices by whom both he and Hunter Jack were deputized in order to find the trail that led to the Chilcotin Indigenous community and arrest Black Jim. The arrest of Jim Yaniew, however, became harsh, with the men treating Jim terribly, pushing the horses hard with Jim tied on the back of the horse. Jim fell off the horse and was injured.[4]

During the 1879 trial, Scotty was also accused by Scotty's partner at the time, Jenny, previously the wife of Yaniew. She recounted in detail Scotty arriving at their home and how, as they and their neighbours sat down for dinner, she noticed blood stains on his sleeves and on his shoulder; she said he also had a large amount of money in bills and coins, and was acting strangely. The accusation of Scotty inaugurated the first of the major delays in this case, as Scotty was not acquitted until the following year. Scotty was held until the next assize, which was several months away. An article in the *Daily Colonist* from July 15, 1879 deplored the criminal justice system for disenfranchising someone through incarceration who had not been formally charged in prison, and for not prosecuting the first Indigenous person that was accused.

David Skinner levelled yet another accusation against Scotty. Skinner, an African American man from Seattle, had previously lived in the Cariboo region for years and telegraphed several statements between 1881 and 1885 upon learning about the case against Scotty. He recounted a story regarding the time that he lived in Lillooet area in 1869, where he was working as a cook for a Mrs. Schubert, but looking into tending pigs. During this time, he had encounters with Scotty in attempting to acquire pigs both for himself and Mrs. Schubert. During one of the negotiations, Skinner described how Scotty offered him pigs in exchange for killing Poole. Skinner said he refused, and that his business partner Wattie had berated Scotty for offering such a thing. Much of the remaining court and telegraph transcripts of the witness depositions were involved in testing the veracity of his statements.

Other enduring accusations were against other apparent outlaws from the Indigenous communities, Charlie, from Bute Inlet, and Tamio, someone associated with a murder years before of a Chinese person.

Both were rumored to be in possession of items associated with Thomas Poole. Several people were commissioned to search for Charlie and Tamio, neither of whom were actually found.[5]

And finally, in 1891, another Indigenous person, Nemiah, was captured and accused of the crime and charged.[6] He was then sentenced to hang; I have found little information about this particular trial, but his sentence was commuted before the hanging occurred.[7] In my reading of this case, we get further from understanding what actually happened as accusation built upon further accusation, but we possibly get closer to some of the implicit social discourses, presuppositions, and procedures that directed the case.

Accusation, Rhetoric, and Right to Speech

What can be extracted from these complicated accusations is an understanding of the way that law acts as a powerful social discourse that structures relations between people, ways of speaking, and conceptions of truth. The way that the case unfolded evoked several questions for me: What do truth-telling practices tell us about the hierarchies of the day? What rhetorical mechanisms do people need to evoke in order to carry a sense of veracity? What happens to people when they avow some juridical truth? As well, how do these practices recursively construct both the accuser and accused?

Law and the Rhetoric of Accusation

Using the term "rhetoric," through the theories of Michel Foucault (2014) and Pierre Bourdieu (1972), I wish to highlight the foundational accusatory capacities of truth-telling, which renders certain accounts of the social world as decipherable to the legal system. My aim is to examine the conditions of truth-telling practices that produce certain subjects capable of telling the truth, and the agency through which one is able to direct the accusatory gaze of the criminal justice system.

By truth-telling, I mean the ways in which what is said in particular contexts resonates with judicial structures such that it is immediately recognizable as possibly true and can thus direct the gaze of accusatory processes. It appears to me that the first people accused during the course of this case represent an interesting marker of how the criminal justice system at the time functioned, who was able to direct the criminal justice system without resistance, the relations between First Nations and the European settlers, and the way in which English law functioned as it transitioned from the Hudson's Bay Company's frontier-style justice (Gibson 1978, 2015; Loo 1990, 1994).

Michel Foucault's interpretation of the role of truth in juridical practices can help us understand the significance of the statements made during this case, how they were made, and how they were received. The previously mentioned lectures on *Wrong-Doing, Truth-Telling* (2014), describe the transformations that juridical truth-telling underwent beginning with the Greek experience of rhetoric in the Agora; as expressed in the tragedies of Oedipus, in which accusations and truth claims were enunciated in particular ways, directed toward a legitimate audience, and used to have special effects on the audience.

Here, Foucault is interested in the role of avowal in the judicial system—or the transformation from accused to one who tells the truth that brings some danger onto him or herself. This relationship between accusation and truth-telling, according to Foucault, is reflective of a complex of social institutions including the religious, political, and juridical. In this Nietzschean perspective wherein truth functions not merely as correspondence, but as a constructed and taken-for-granted form of currency that shapes and directs individuals and societies, Foucault highlights the need to examine the social conditions of the creation and circulation of the signifiers and discourses that mark the assumed functioning of law. Truth then functions as "a system of ordered procedures for the production, regulation, distribution, circulation and functioning of statements" (1980, 133). It is in this ordered system of procedures that we can see who is able to speak the truth and be heard, whereas those that cannot function as representative of the regime are misrecognized and put at risk.

In the Poole case varying truth claims are judged using different measures. These measures can be analyzed by how the witnesses' statements were immediately apprehended, listened to, or interrogated. These statements on truth may be contextualized through Bourdieu's idea of "right to speech" in his text on power and speech. For Bourdieu, not everyone can speak or be heard equally, but all are judged according to the different forms of capital that they embody and exercise. He writes that "some persons are not in a position to speak or must win their audience, whereas others effortlessly command attention, but also the laws of production of the group itself, which cause certain categories to be absent. These hidden conditions are decisive for understanding what can and cannot be said in a group" (Bourdieu 1972, 648). In the manner that accusation evokes these forms of speech, a complex set of relationships are enunciated and provoke relations between the state and its subjects, and those, then, that have a "right to speech." The hidden conditions of the capacities to elicit forms of speech recognizable to the truth regime of BC colonial law made accusation possible and shaped the direction of the case.

Several interesting aspects of the case stand out as evocative of the way that law provides a powerful social discourse to structure relations between people, ways of speaking, and relations of people to truth. With the many people accused, truth-telling became an important determination of the direction of the case. One might refer to Pavlich's (2007) writing on the "lore of accusation" wherein accusation practices reflect sets of narratives that establish the ethico-political ordering of which the legal system becomes the guarantor. The possible threat to that narrativization of the social order initiates various rituals, structures, and individuals to coalesce and force entryways into the criminal justice system.

Who is Able to Tell the Truth

From the above discussion, we can evaluate how Scotty became the first legitimate speaker able to direct the accusatory gaze. Even though Scotty was accused in the end, it was through the initial grand jury and coroner's inquest that he was able to direct the attention of the criminal justice system in a way that other people in the case were not. He not only acted as a legitimate speaker, but also evoked those who were believably accused of the crime—in particular Indigenous community members. Unfortunately, it did not take much effort for that criminal justice system to grant Indigenous people entry into the legal system. What becomes dramatically clear is that First Nations people were accusable in a way that the European settlers were not.

That accusation is reflective of social discourses privileging certain subjects over others is evinced by the accusations levelled by James Halliday, or Scotty against Jim Yaniew, or Black Jim, and against the Chilcotin First Nations communities. Those enunciated by Scotty influenced the first inquest to commission Scotty to find and arrest Black Jim, but also to take a party of local Indigenous community members to search for tracks in the woods around the Thomas Poole residence. In Scotty's deposition during the initial coroner's inquest, he stated:

> I have suspicions that an Indian is the murderer of Thomas Poole and his two children for the following reasons, that Thomas Poole told me that he was afraid of Black Jim. And I know that Jim bears a very bad character, He has a guilty look, and his actions at the Half Way House were very suspicious since the murder was committed.[8]

The language of accusation in this deposition was based solely on the nebulous characterological judgments of Yaniew. These statements were apprehended as truthful by the jury and worthy of concluding the inquest with a charge set against him. Not only this, the accusation also permitted Scotty to be commissioned to find and arrest Yaniew, which he did, but violently. Because of the violence of Jim's arrest, an Indigenous man named Sheephan, or Hunter Jack, and Scotty were reprimanded by the attorney general for a case of the worst treatments of a prisoner they had seen.[9] Upon testimony, we learn that Yaniew was uncle to Poole's children, his sister being Poole's wife. He recounted that he had intended to visit and stay with Poole and his family the night that they died, and that he went to the house to find the house in ruins and the bodies in the root cellar. He immediately went to the First Nations community at Anderson Lake and assisted in alerting the authorities. Suspicion of Black Jim was formally rescinded and he was released, though media accounts suggest that popular suspicion remained.[10]

In contrast, we can examine how others were not listened to in quite the same way. During the 1879 trial, Scotty was also accused by Scotty's partner at the time, Jenny, previously the wife of Black Jim. She recounted in detail Scotty arriving home on the evening that Thomas Poole was murdered.[11] At the dinner table with five other people, after she had told him to remove his jacket, she noticed the blood stains on his sleeves. As well, she talked of the large amount of money and his strange behaviour, and said that she saw him giving his friend Wattie quite a bit of money. She recounted how Scotty told her to clean his white shirt as he took it off outside, where she received soap from her sister Annie, who lived next door. Despite vivid testimony, her statement was disregarded as the veracity of her statements came under heavy scrutiny. As Scotty had also come back with much flour, the remainder of the court documents that I was able to find focused on whether or not flour burns (since not much flour was left in the ruins of the Poole residence), where Scotty had received the money from, and where the blood-stained shirt had gone to.

A similar effect happened to the testimony of David Skinner. While not giving specific evidence for the crime itself, he gave a testimony that suggests Scotty had been willing to pay him in pigs for killing Poole ten years earlier. What happened with both Jenny and Skinner, then, is that instead of directing the criminal justice system toward Scotty, through their intense interrogation, it is only directed against themselves.

How One Tells the Truth

Another aspect of rhetoric that was significant in this case has to do with evoking proper speech. In David Skinner's statement, the importance and necessity of a certain cultural and symbolic capital in determining entryways into the criminal justice system was made clear. In his testimony, Skinner was forced to represent not just his history as a check to see if he was actually in the area at the time he said he was, but also to account for his character to justify it. In one section of the lengthy interview, the attorney appeared to get the sense that Skinner was fairly eccentric, lived a nomadic lifestyle, and was possibly overstating his position. At this point, David Skinner found it necessary to draw from certain kinds of symbolic capital in order to legitimate his claims. In the interview, he mentioned first of all his connections and the people he knew and met when he was in the Caribou and New Westminster between 1863 and 1880, including such important people as Judge Begbie and Governor Cornwall.[12] The attorney then focused on a section when Skinner, himself an African American, stated:

> The Negroes don't like to see me get along. They'd do anything to get me in the Poorhouse. The colored people in Washington Territory send word round that I'm not blind and tell people not to help me.
> Question: Why do they do that?
> Because they want me in the Poor House and they can get the sway they want.
> Question: What "sway";
> They say they are the noble people and that I'm of no account. They won't believe I had a hand in getting them free.
> Question: How did you get them free?
> I wrote a letter to the Prime Minister Davis and told him that in the letter when Abe Lincoln said if you don't lay down your arms in 90 days I'll set the [n-word] free.

He continued describing how the authorities in Boston and in "Frisco" were after him for writing those letters, and how the African American and Indigenous peoples were envious of him and his influence with the "white people." He continued on to say, "I am a great politician—I closed all the mouths of the colored people by my eloquence at the polls and I got Cleveland elected...by my speaking."[13] However this may have been heard by the court, what this exchange illustrates is the shifting symbolic capital that existed in British Columbia that permitted the production of truthful statements.

In forcing truth-telling, these practices generate and privilege specific types of subjects while denying others. These practices can only be mobilized when specific social and legal apparatuses are already in existence and can be commanded by certain subjects to direct the accusations. On the other hand, marginal peoples who utter accusative speech acts direct the accusatory gaze toward themselves. After these statements, the attorney general sought several statements to verify his claims, but was disregarded even though much of what he said was ratified by other people. In other words, as Foucault discusses with the notion of avowal, there is risk involved in speaking if you are unable to evoke conditions of veracity recognized by the criminal justice system.

Accusability

Another relationship between truth-telling and accusation has to do with the extent to which certain people are more accusable than others. The legitimacy of speech leads to a prefigured accusability of subjects. Hunter Jack, Black Jim, and the Chilcotin First Nations communities were all initially suspect before more plausible subjects appeared to the consciousness of the criminal justice system. How newspapers represented Indigenous people in the course of this case suggests a widespread assumption that most were always already accusable. For instance, a *Daily Colonist* article from 1881 spoke of the procedures of the case during the trial against Scotty as deplorable, since they had arrested first an Indigenous person only to let him go and redirect suspicion toward a settler.[14] Therefore, not only was law differentially predisposed toward internal others through discourses of the day, but more than this, through the mechanisms of truth enunciation, it permitted the production of subjects perpetually under the gaze of the legal system.

As we see in the next section, the differential relation to law is embedded in a particular context that suggests that law is predisposed toward forms of life not seen as its ideal arbiters. Thus, accusation functions not just in the present, but also is prefigured and embodies a teleology. This reflects what Foucault (1977) might call a particular truth regime wherein truth is "produced by virtue of multiple constraints and it induces regulated effects of power." In other words, "each society has its regime of truth, its general policies of truth: that is, the types of discourse which it harbours and causes to function as true; the mechanisms and instances which enable one to distinguish true from false statements, the means by which each is sanctioned; the techniques and procedures accorded value in the acquisition of truth; the status of those who are charged with saying what counts as true." We have seen that being able to direct the criminal justice system in almost an invisible way in the very beginning results in a contingent production of "the techniques and procedures which are valorised for obtaining truth" (Foucault 1977, 112–13).

Indigeneity and Otherness in Accusation

However, we cannot separate this trial and its various accusations from the context of early British Columbian juridical practices and history. If we take into account the context of the relationships between Indigenous peoples and settler-colonial law, we can begin to see some further discourses that directly impacted the case. The different perspectives of justice and interpretations of English law held by settlers and Indigenous peoples seem to have influenced the accusatory process and had a formative effect on entryways into the criminal justice system.

The examination of the relationships between Indigenous peoples and settler-colonial law reveals the circulation of ambivalent and contradictory attitudes, perceptions, and policies that all had an effect on the accusatory process at the time (Harris 2002; Webber 1995). The overall legal policy with regard to Indigenous peoples in the early 1800s was one of a paternalism that believed itself to protect the rights of Indigenous peoples "no less than those of the white man" (Foster 1984). For instance, the first governor of the colony of British Columbia, Sir James Douglas, promised those whom he labelled "children of the forest"—local Indigenous populations—fair treatment, being more sympathetic to their level of dispossession than other colonial officials. Yet, concurrently, "a new problem had already emerged" regarding the disproportionate carceral gaze producing the Indigenous person "as a primary victim of the justice system." It is at this point that "a familiar and distressing pattern had emerged" in the excessive incarceration of Indigenous people (Foster 1984). Despite the ambivalence of colonial discourses, patterns of both geographical and legal dispossession placed Indigenous communities in asymmetrical relationships with a settler-colonial society engaged in nation-building (Barman 2007; Blomley 2003; Harris 2004).

Both settlers and the Indigenous peoples were forced to adopt the increasingly formal form of legal practice after 1870 in British Columbia (Foster 1994, 2001). Prior to this point, scholars suggest that British Columbia held different conceptions of justice based on the different societies that co-existed during the fur trade and gold rush. One of these was a form of justice practiced using the established and democratic Indigenous legal traditions based on community reparation and restitution (Gavigan 2012; Harring 1998; Webber 1995). Colonial forms of criminal justice were often in direct conflict, competition, and tension in encounters with Indigenous law. Accusation was individualistic—directed at specific individuals with specific kinds of speech acts, and with a specific understanding of culpability. So then, a new and more formal language of accusation had to be adopted and employed by both Indigenous peoples and settlers, even if the Indigenous communities saw their form of justice as valid and as non-exclusive of English law (Harring 1998). Despite the increasing marginalization of Indigenous communities in the Northwest Territories, and their highly stigmatized relationship with the law, recent scholars have credited them with much of the enactment of Crown law (Carter 1999). Indeed, "agency and oppression—the twin poles around which much of the writing of the history of so-called 'marginal' groups has been written—were not discrete and exclusive conditions of being, but instead can only be understood in specific contexts of marginalized peoples" (Loo 1995, 150). Significantly, for the Indigenous population, law was experienced, as one might expect, ambivalently—both as something that could be employed in particular ways to assist with the well-being and sustainability of their communities within their own vision of justice and law, but also as an entity that perpetually undermined and disadvantaged them by the disproportionate use of it against their communities. Early Canadian law was explicitly concerned with the social engineering of a Canadian people through moral constraint (Gavigan 2012; Strange and Loo 1997). Thus, law was purposely and differentially directed toward those whose lives were constructed as non-normative. In fact, Indigenous people represented to the Canadian government "potential" to be exploited for the constraint and production of a proper society.

As well, it is important to place the different accusations in the context of the Chilcotin war, or what has previously been known as the Bute Inlet Massacre, and how settler-colonial society viewed Indigenous peoples after the Hudson's Bay Company (HBC) relinquished its claim to British Columbia. In 1864, not far from where the Poole murder took place, an entrepreneur won funding to build a road that would save nearly 200 hundred kilometres of travel over the Caribou wagon road in order to reach gold-mining areas more easily. Two years into the construction, the members of the Tsilhqot'in Indigenous community waged a war against those encroaching in their territory and nineteen road builders were killed by the Tsilhqot'in First Nation's community. The significance of the first accusation by Burgess and Scotty is that it reposes upon the prac-tices of dispossession that settler-colonial society practiced that led to this uprising. Newspaper accounts, witness testimony, and more recent schol-arship has shown that settler perceptions of the First Nations community, were, not surprisingly, not entirely favourable, especially in the wake of these conflicts. Loo (1994) describes the settler-colonial discourses of representation of the Tsilhqot'in Indigenous communities relying on images of savagery and cannibalism. The trauma of the Poole murder might be seen as a traumatic recurrence of the fear mongering and panic that occurred following the Bute Inlet uprising. Thus, we can see that the discourse of law was infused with the power relations of the time, such that Indigenous communities were always already accused and accusable. This can help explain further the commensurability with the initial accusations, and also helps to explain the reference to the newspaper articles that queried whether the incident was by accident or "Indian." This overarching colonial discourse of otherness that settler society held at the time, Loo (1998) suggests, was similar to the British experience of their own internal others. The newspapers documenting the trial confirm Loo's assessment of the creation and enforcement of internal foreigners, which reinforces the ability for people to be seen and heard within the law and may predispose the accusability of Indigenous people. Evidently, the more humanitarian perspectives of Governor Douglas were not so widespread, which is evident in how Indigenous people were treated after Douglas retired (Harris 2002). Tina Loo, examining the ways in which Indigenous peoples were accused of murder in the years that followed the decline of the fur trade, writes that Indigenous engagement with the law in the period after HBC relinquished its claim on BC "was strategic and culturally conditioned," wherein the changing forms of engagement that occurred with changing regimes of justice "structured their choices differently than they had during the fur trade" (1995, 150).

Foster (1984) also suggests that Indigenous people were often amenable to English law at this point when it helped to serve their own ends of justice, but did not see it as superseding Indigenous forms of justice. So, it is not surprising that it was the St'át'imc Indigenous communities from Lillooet and Anderson Lake that helped to mobilize law in this case. We see that the Indigenous people were integral in this case for calling in law and raising awareness of the crime. The Indigenous people who first came upon the ghastly scene and the Anderson Lake community mobilized quickly several parties of disparate locations. Indigenous people not only assisted and helped mobilize, but also led constables toward people that were seen as outlaws.

We may be able to interpret some of the accusations made in the course of the trial as representing the Indigenous attempt to mobilize a law that had invariably marginalized and served to dispossess them of their territory, culture, and livelihood. For instance, previous research had shown that Jenny's accusation could have been because she was being treated poorly by Scotty and needed to find an escape.[15] Furthermore, the various accusations against different people by Indigenous people themselves seemed all to have been against people that were outcast amongst their communities and considered outlaws, according to both the communities and BC law. For instance, in this case, the three Indigenous people that were accused by other Indigenous people had previously committed other crimes, or were people that had contributed to the Chilcotin war, and were seen as disruptive to the community. So quite possibly, as Harring (1998) argues, the criminal justice system was indelibly influenced by the encounter between two different forms of justice, and possibly by the incommensurability between two different forms of accusation. The interaction of two different legal orders—that of Indigenous law and colonial law—still reposed upon a dissymmetry that produced at times a misrecognition of the significance of Indigenous law. He writes that "as colonial and Canadian officials increasingly used their law in ways that affected the lives of Indians, the latter developed strategies for responding" (Harring 1998, 9). However, despite the accommodation that Indigenous people often made for English law, where "Indigenous leaders negotiated, or attempted to negotiate, appropriate compromises between their laws and Canadian ones," Harring notes that "Canadian and colonial officials...did not understand or give legitimacy to Indian legal activity" (1998, 9).

The asymmetrical power structures embedded within Canadian law established the conditions of possibility for truth-telling, what was visible and invisible to the legal structure, and those that could be accused. Even with their increasing marginalization and highly stigmatized relationship with the law, Indigenous peoples' creative use of the law affected the accusatory process and the entryways into the criminal justice system. What

I think then is that accusation and entryways into the criminal justice system were prefigured by the interaction between two different conceptions of law, justice, and accusation that permitted the settler society to enact a certain kind of amnesia around Indigenous law, culture, and traditions.

Law and the Framing of the Social World

By examining how English law was deployed and employed by both the increasing population of European settlers and the Indigenous populations, we can see how law functions as a structuring imaginary that allows certain aspects of the world to be revealed. We might understand the law as a powerful social discourse that produces a picture of the world where some are invisible to the law and others stand in stark relief against the backdrop of the assumed. This picture of the world is one in which certain populations are governed more strictly than others, thus producing social effects of marginalization and geographical and cultural dispossession (Barman 2007; Berg 2011; Harris 2002, 2004; Todd 2006, 2010). This appearance to consciousness is a vital component for entryways into the criminal justice system that work by predisposing certain groups of people, certain forms of life, as subject to the constraining power of law. More than this, the social discourses which predicate these truth-telling practices frame the world as decipherable to people in light of the legal system. However, the new language of accusation within a specific "truth regime" can only heard by those that are representative of colonial power. Legitimate speakers and legitimate speech are what inflects the accusatory process with an immediate veracity not granted to those that fall outside the proprietary consciousness and visibility of the law. As Pavlich writes, the "co-appearance of accuser, accused and authorized selves are fashioned through local rituals that call subjects to avow truths in relation to legally alleged wrongdoing" (2016, 244). Accusation frames and produces, through a politics of recognition, particular subjects that are capable of enunciating forms of speech and rhetoric that recursively reinforce hegemonic images of the world. This, finally, elucidates another aspect of law as a structuring discourse. While producing certain subjects and forms of life that can be invisible to the law, it also produces its own kind of forgetfulness of the people that law is apprehending and shaping— a forgetfulness of the agency of the communities that law marginalizes. The politics of recognition embedded within accusatory practices reflects the kinds of violence that are implicit or explicit, and formal or informal, in the recognition and validation of certain subjects at the expense of marginalized populations and knowledges, such as that of the Indigenous communities, their legal traditions, and their oral histories in British Columbia in the 1800s.

Notes

1. Citations from newspaper sources can be found at: http://www.britishcolonist.ca/.

2. Attorney General, "Thomas Poole," 1879, GR-0431.2.5.3, British Columbia Archives and Museum.

3. Recently, the BC government has exhumed the bodies of the chiefs of the tribe who were accused and subsequently hanged for the Bute Inlet Massacre. It has issued an apology and pardon to the Chilcotin community; see "B.C.'s Apology for Hanging Tsilhqot'in War Chiefs One Step in a Long Healing Process," *The Globe and Mail*, Oct. 24, 2014.

4. Attorney General, "Poole murder," 1881, GR-0429.140, box 1, file 10, British Columbia Archives and Museum.

5. The correspondence recounts how Charlie was always a few steps ahead in this manhunt through the interior BC mountains, which took close to two years. There's an interesting exchange between the Attorney General, L.P. Reed, and the person supposedly commissioned to hunt for Charlie. The commissioned officer wrote to the AG after a year of searching and heading into the mountains where Charlie appeared to have been one step ahead the entire chase. They had to call off the hunt until the following spring when the snow melted. The traverse through the mountains became too difficult. The fellow requested remuneration for the funds that he had to spend up to that point. The AG responded with a stern and curt telegraph suggesting he was not aware of any hunt being carried out for Charlie and replying with, "I am at a loss as to whether the contents of your letter are for my serious consideration or simply an official joke" (Attorney General,

"Chase for Poole murderers," 1883, GR-0429.197, box 1, file 12, British Columbia Archives and Museum).

6. Attorney General, "Capture of Nemiah who killed a Chinese man at Hanceville," 1891, GR-0429.291, box 2, file 4, British Columbia Archives and Museum.

7. Pemberton Museum, correspondence with author, October 28, 2015.

8. Attorney General, "Thomas Poole."

9. H.P.P. Crease, legal papers, "Poole murder case: Clinton evidence," 1879, MS-0054.5.1, British Columbia Archives and Museum.

10. "Not Ready," *Daily Colonist*, July 15, 1879.

11. Attorney General, "Poole murder."

12. "Letter from David Skinner regarding the murder of Tom Poole and his children," 1885, GR-0996.21, file 3, Correspondence inward, British Columbia Archives and Museum.

13. Ibid.

14. "Responsible Ministers and Murders," *Daily Colonist*, May 21, 1881.

15. Pemberton Museum, correspondence with author, October 28, 2015.

References

Barman, Jean. 2007. *The West Beyond the West: A History of British Columbia.* 3rd ed. Toronto; Buffalo: University of Toronto Press.

Berg, Lawrence. 2011. "Banal Naming, Neoliberalism, and Landscapes of Dispossession." ACME: *An International E-Journal for Critical Geographies* 10 (1): 13–22.

Blomley, Nicholas. 2003. "Law, Property, and the Geography of Violence: The Frontier, the Survey, and the Grid." *Annals of the Association of American Geographers* 93 (1): 121–41.

Bourdieu, Pierre. 1972. "The Economics of Linguistic Exchanges." *Social Sciences Information* 16 (6): 645–68.

Carter, Sarah. 1999. *Aboriginal People and the Colonizers of Western Canada to 1900.* Toronto: University of Toronto Press.

Foster, Hamar. 1984. "Law Enforcement in Nineteenth-Century British Columbia: A Brief and Comparative Overview." *BC Studies* 63 (Autumn): 1–24.

———. 1992. "The White Man's Law in the Far West: Establishing Legal Institutions in British Columbia." Working Paper Series, University of Manitoba, Canadian Legal History Project: CLIP-WPS-92-12.

———. 1994. "'The Queen's Law Is Better than Yours': International Homicide in Early British Columbia." In *Essays in the History of Canadian Law: Crime and Criminal*

Justice, Vol. 5, edited by Jim Phillips, Tina Loo, and Susan Lewthwaite, 41–111. Toronto: University of Toronto Press.

⸻. 1995. "British Columbia: Legal Institutions in the Far West, from Contact to 1871." *Manitoba Law Journal* 23 (1): 293–340.

Foster, Hamar, A.R. Buck, and Benjamin L. Berger. 2008. *The Grand Experiment: Law and Legal Culture in British Settler Societies*. Vancouver: UBC Press.

Foucault, Michel. 1977. "The Political Function of the Intellectual." *Radical Philosophy* 17 (13): 126–33.

⸻. 1980. *Power/knowledge*. Edited by Colin Gordon. New York: Pantheon Books.

⸻. 2014. *Wrong-Doing, Truth-Telling: The Function of Avowal in Justice*. Edited by Fabienne Brion and Bernard E. Harcourt. Translated by Stephen W. Sawyer. Chicago; London: University of Chicago Press; [Louvain-la-Neuve]: Presses Universitaires de Louvain.

Harring, Sidney L. 1998. *White Man's Law: Native People in Nineteenth Century Canadian Jurisprudence*. Toronto: The Osgoode Society and University of Toronto Press.

Harris, Cole. 2002. *Making Native Space: Colonialism, Resistance, and Reserves in British Columbia*. Vancouver: UBC Press.

⸻. 2004. "How Did Colonialism Dispossess? Comments from an Edge of Empire." *Annals of the Association of American Geography* 94 (1): 165–82.

Loo, Tina. 1990. "Law and Authority in British Columbia, 1821–1871." PHD diss., University of British Columbia (Canada). ProQuest. doi:10.14288/1.0098760

⸻. 1994. "The Road from Bute Inlet: Crime and Colonial Identity in British Columbia." In *Essays in the History of Canadian Law: Crime and Criminal Justice, Vol. 5*, edited by Jim Phillips, Tina Loo, and Susan Lewthwaite, 112–42. Toronto: University of Toronto Press.

⸻. 1995. "Tonto's Due: Law, Culture, and Colonization in British Columbia." In *Essays in the History of Canadian Law, British Columbia and the Yukon, Vol. 6*, edited by Louis A. Knafla, 128–70. Osgoode Society for Canadian Legal History.

Pavlich, George. 2016. "Avowal and Criminal Accusation." *Law And Critique* 27 (2): 229–45.

Strange, Carolyn, and Tina Loo. 1997. *Making Good: Law and Moral Regulation in Canada, 1867–1939*. Themes in Canadian Social History Series. Toronto: University of Toronto Press.

Webber, Jeremy. 1995. "Relations of Force and Relations of Justice: The Emergence of Normative Community between Colonists and Aboriginal Peoples." *Osgoode Hall Law Journal* 33 (4): 623–60.

"LET THEM LEARN THE LESSON OF THE SEASON"

Suspicion, Habit, and Punishment During the Red River Famine (1825–1826)

AARON HENRY

THE STUDY OF SUSPICION AND ACCUSATION is tied to the formation of bureaucratic social forms. Police depositions and reports, trial transcripts, and *lettres de cachet* reveal the processes of coding and classifying certain forms of behaviour and conduct as "suspicious" and, as such, it is from these documents that one can establish an analytics of accusation/suspicion. While suspicion and accusation have a distinct social form, before the establishment of the legal file these social forms are without a formal "paper trail" to analyze and trace—a consideration which may direct study toward the provenance of the file in the historical constitution of accusation. However, how suspicion, accusation, and punishment were configured before the formation of police bureaus is important in understanding accusation and entryways into regimes of punishment. By reflecting on these earlier modalities, we may better understand the previous moral economies that informed suspicion and also, more importantly, recognize the exposed power relations yet to be cloaked by bourgeois legal forms. In this chapter, I critically examine the relations that connected suspicion to punishment before the emergence of a formal criminal justice system in Canada,[1] by examining the post journal made by Francis Heron, a Hudson's Bay Company (HBC) clerk in charge of Fort Garry during a famine in the Red River colony.[2]

Heron's journal is forty pages in length and is a day-to-day record of events in Fort Garry. The reach of the document is circumscribed by Heron's position as a clerk, but this limitation is also the document's analytical strength. Although the journal initially follows a conventional standard of registration where HBC clerks were asked to record the weather, the activities of company men, and trades, Heron soon veers off course and provides a more detailed account of his attempts to maintain order in the midst of starvation and insurrection. As the chief factor of the district was ill for much of the winter, Heron appears to have had some latitude in how he managed the crisis. He openly recorded his decisions and prejudices about certain populations in the colony and the punitive actions he took against those he suspected were dangerous or disorderly. As such, we may read Heron as a literal gatekeeper: his command of Fort Garry gave him the power to exclude and include certain populations in the colony. How he exercised this power sheds light on the operation of judgment and suspicion without the guidance of law.

In particular, reading Heron's text against late nineteenth-century biopolitical forms of accusation advocated by figures like Cesare Lombroso and Charles Goring (see Pavlich 2009; Walby and Carrier 2010) brings to light the forms of accusation and punishment that operated within the HBC before the advent of a state project of correction. How Heron divided the population of the colony points to a modality of accusation and criminalization that was not productive of individual criminal subjects, but rather an immoral "mob." For Heron, this criminal population was formed in relation to their subsistence habits—settlers who chose to pursue buffalo hunting instead of farming were of particular concern—and whether or not they were capable of self-management, which included working regularly on their crops, paying off debts, and living frugally. It was those who did not live up to these practices who were eligible for Heron's punitive measures. "Improper" habits formed the basis for accusation of wrongdoing or, at least, improper conduct. I argue that punishment was exercised through the fort. In particular, those accused of being indolent were denied aid and shut outside the fort to learn the "lessons of the season." Heron presented this tactic as a reformative type of punishment: those who survived the winter outside the fort without aid would learn "prudence" and engage in more wholesome practices of subsistence in the years to come. Heron's tactics bear some resemblance to what Foucault has referred to as pastoral power as a form of government (Foucault 2007, 168). Pastoral power was not brought to bear on individuals, but rather was aimed at the life, morality, and continuity of the flock or population. As such, pastoral government abided the starvation or elimination of some members for the safety of all. As such, Heron's post journal reveals an episode where punishment was exercised through an alliance between pastoral power and the carceral space of the fort.

I start this chapter with the historical context of Heron's journal. In the 1820s, several years before the famine, the HBC attempted to relocate "dangerous and idle populations" to the Red River colony. The company's discussion of the relocation underscores how subsistence, race, and self-management became the categories that Heron used to anchor his suspicions about the moral conduct of the colonists. Following this, I review Heron's post log. Here, I focus on the emergence of "beggars," "horse-eaters," and insurrections as suspicious figures of the famine that formed in relation to discourses on proper subsistence and self-management. In the third section of the chapter, I place Heron's attempts to teach the colonists the lessons of the season in relation to other historical forms of punishment. I frame this analysis by drawing on two themes from the work of Michel Foucault. First, in trying to unpack Heron's suspicion of wayward colonists and poor self-management, I want to engage with Foucault's work on the formation of "habit" as an allied technique used to stabilize capitalist social relations. Second, I want to interrogate the role the fort played in structuring the punitive measures that Heron utilized, and explore what the prominence of the fort may tell us about Foucault's conception of the carceral archipelago more generally.

Heron's Journal in Context

After a long rivalry, the HBC and rival fur trading company the North West Company merged in 1821. Sir George Simpson took over the reins from HBC governor William Williams and attempted to tighten the company's administrative controls. Simpson, having come from a counting house in London, sought to further improve the company's record-keeping system (Colpitts 2006; Ray 1978; Simmons 2007). The system of management that emerged after the merger rationalized the trade by dividing the fur trade into administrative districts, and chief factors were told to produce more encompassing reports on the districts they oversaw. Simpson proposed that these changes would give the company better records of the credit extended to servants and First Nations hunters, improve receipts for goods as they entered and left districts, and centralize the records under Simpson's authority.

At the end of the summer in 1822, Simpson read letters from the company's board of directors, referred to as the London Council, which had been added to the minutes of HBC's Northern Department .The letters expressed the London Council's concerns over the large "unproductive" populations at HBC forts and outposts. The directors noted, "it has become a matter of serious importance to determine on the most proper measures to be adopted with regards to the men who have large families and who must be discharged and with the numerous half-breed children whose parents have died or deserted them."[3] The company's concerns about the economic costs of these populations stemmed from the fact that it was not uncommon for the company to issue relief to old and infirm hunters, orphans, and widows.[4]

Idle populations of deserted children, "half-breeds," and "indolent natives" "were [deemed] both dangerous to the peace of the country and safety of the trading posts."[5] The council advised that "it was prudent and economic to incur some expense in the removal of these 'dangerous populations' to a place where they may maintain themselves and be civilized and instructed in religion."[6] As it would be "impolite and inexpedient to encourage or allow them to collect together in different parts of the country where they could 'not be under any proper superintendence,' it was decided that 'indolent' Indian men, women, and children, and aged company servants would be removed to Red River colony." The colony was thought suitable for relocation, as it would allow the removed population to be ruled by "a regular police and government by the establishments."[7]

The scheme proposed by the London Council called for the transport of the population to the colony and the assignment of officials capable of supervising the population and "[controlling] their conduct in the first years." While the letters had called for the removal of orphans, widows, "indolent indians" and "superfluous half-breeds," only "men with families" were given the means to settle and cultivate land.[8] That the population would become self-sufficient in procuring its subsistence was imperative as "the settlement [would] not consent to a large population *of this kind* being thrown upon them."[9]

The exact number of people transported from each post to Red River does not appear in the company's records. However, tentative estimates suggest that the population of the colony increased by 350 people from 1821 to the end of 1822, an increase of nearly a third (Gibson 2015, 23). Subsequent minutes from the Northern Department note that Red River remained a repository for infirm company servants as well as First Nation's widows and orphans. In fact, the letters from the London Council suggested that chief factors use measures (including removal) to limit the formation of "dangerous populations" in the future. This process of transporting people to White Horse Plains and Pembina Plains was carried out with the intent that they would farm the land and in turn become "civilized." Simpson's impression of the colony was that it was a "mass of renegades and malcontents" and that the colony "was without law, order, or regularity" (Simpson, as quoted in Gibson 2015, 24). That Heron's account was shaped by the underlying assumption that much of the population was "dangerous" is instructive in approaching how he problematized the settlers during the famine and elected to punish others.

Famine to Insurrection

In dealing with both First Nations traders and settlers, Heron noted that his custom was to ensure that neither party was issued credit for goods that were more expensive than what they could "purchase with the fruits of their own exertions."[10] He also noted the company's success in generating a busy market at the fort, and the efforts to get settlers to regularly trade their grain during the day.[11]

Heron encouraged this regular market activity, as it was both a means to extract grain to support cattle and to grind it for flour for distribution throughout the company during the spring. In addition, settlers were coerced to sell their grain to settle debts owed to the late Earl Selkirk, the first proprietor of the Red River colony. According to Heron's records, during the winter of 1825–1826, half of the grain that each indebted settler produced went directly to the company to settle any debt owed to Selkirk's estate. The settlers were free to use the remainder for both personal consumption and as a means of exchange for any other necessities from the company. Only after receiving half of each settler's crop did the company agree to exchange supplies for the rest. Individuals resisted this provision by giving their grain to those who were not indebted, who would be paid full price for the grain and pass on the share back to the original farmer. The company thwarted these attempts, according to Heron at least, through the use of store records. This restriction was all the more dire given that Fort Garry was the only source settlers and First Nations residents had for clothing. Heron recorded,

> Business recommenced early this morning with the settlers and the
> bustle of buying and selling…many of them sell nearly the whole of
> their grain now so as to purchase clothing for themselves and families
> and trust to labour in the settlement or hunting in the plains for their
> winter subsistence. It is in vain to dissuade them from trusting safety
> to chance. They say it is bad in either case and that it is just as well for
> them to starve to death as to be frozen to death in the winter.[12]

By December 24th, the "quantity [of grain] required by the company" had been reached. Heron noted that the company would now only receive grain to liquidate debt; no goods could be bought with it.[13] Ironically, it was also on this day that Heron received word "from the plains that the buffalo [were] both distant and scarce and the hunters in consequence unsuccessful." By January 2nd, Heron reported,

> *The state of starvation to which the...Indians are thereby reduced*
> *exceeds in extent any thing of the kind ever experienced, at any former*
> *period in this quarter. This unfortunate people have already been*
> *reduced to the necessity of eating their horses, dogs and such parts of*
> *their garments as were of leather; and as these resources have been in*
> *a great measure consumed...the most serious consequences are to be*
> *apprehended should buffalo not soon make their appearance.*[14]

By the end of January, starvation on the plains was no longer just a problem for "Indians." Heron noted, "many of the poorer or rather indolent part of the population of the settlement are also now reduced to the last extremity of want."[15] He concluded that relying on buffalo "for their winter subsistence" rather than producing their own sources of grain was "incautious."[16] With a notable degree of social distance, Heron pontificated that "the experience, however, if experience ever can teach them prudence, of this winter will probably have the effect of causing them hereafter to devote more of their time and attention to agriculture; at least it is but reasonable to think so."[17]

Heron appears unrelenting in his approach. Despite the fact that "the cattle and horses of the colonists [were] dying daily for want of food," Heron refused the requests from the settlers to use some of the surplus hay the company possessed to feed their animals.[18] He remained firm that it was "not the duty of the company to supply them."[19] Rather, his opinion was, had the settlers "the smallest degree of industry" the problem would have been averted. Heron also noted that he had started to sell the grain back to those able to afford it, as it was needed "for subsistence."[20] By the middle of February 1826, Heron remarked that cattle and livestock continued to die for want of fodder. He reasoned,

> *These improvident people incessantly apply to the company not only for food for themselves but for their cattle also. They are in the fort like spoiled children who from the too great indulgence of the parent* are rendered incapable of providing for themselves when left to their own management.[21]

At the end of February, he received word that a twelve-person hunting party in search of bison had died of exposure on the plains. Their deaths intensified the Pembina Plains community's state of extreme starvation.[22] Upon hearing this news, he noted his distrust of those who had opted to pursue the chase rather than apply themselves to their fields. By the middle of March, settler families were travelling by sled to apply for relief at the fort. Heron recorded their arrival by stating "their indolence has brought their present calamities upon them."[23] The company continued to allow settlers to "purchase grain back from the company stores."[24] However, the policy of selling grain back to the settlers that had been appropriated to settle their debts was not well received. At the end of March, Heron noted that the population of displaced settlers around the fort had lost trust in the company and its representatives (himself!) and felt that the company "harbored sinister motives towards them."[25]

In April, news reached Heron that two men from Pembina Plains had resorted to cannibalism and had eaten their families. Despite this grim report, Heron defended his choice to withhold the grain reserves from the starving settlers. As he recorded these events, he also lamented that the colony was on the brink of insurrection. It appears that despite his efforts to keep the company's considerable grain reserves "secret from the public," it had become known that the company was stockpiling grain for its own cattle and for sale as seeds to the colonists in the coming year.[26] News of three different plots to plunder the fort of its reserves reached Heron. Without any police stationed in the colony, Heron noted he could not make use of "physical force or legal measures" to combat the insur-rection.[27] Fearing the worst, Heron shut the gates of the fort and ordered his staff to prepare to defend themselves and "the company's property."[28] He noted that some families and their livestock, i.e., the "wealthier" and "industrious colonists," would be afforded the company's protection inside the fort.

Heron's measures were not without consequence. In one entry, he noted that outside the barred gates of the fort, the people now "prowl[ed] about the settlement in crowds trying by every means in their power...to obtain subsistence."[29] The gates of the fort remained besieged by "beggars and insurrectionists" until May. The scenario came to an end when the Red River burst its banks and flooded the settlement. The settlers were dispersed several miles in various directions in search of higher ground, which effectively attenuated insurrection against the company. Heron and the HBC staff remained in the fort until it flooded. They locked the store-room, took the remaining valuables by canoe to higher ground, and put them under guard. The fort was rebuilt four years later, forty kilometres downstream. Simpson visited the colony personally to enquire about the famine and the flood. Heron was promoted to the rank of chief trader, but by 1840 was reputed to have drunk himself to death.

So, what does this rather curious text offer to us in terms of history of suspicion, accusation, and punitive measures? It is important to recog-nize that we are not only reading an account of a famine, but also a minor history of rioting, insurrection, and looting in a remote colonial fort at the start of the nineteenth century. In this sense, Heron's text offers insight into a period of disorder where behaviour and actions had yet to be clas-sified as "criminal." What needs to be unpacked is how Heron decided who was admitted to the fort and who remained shut outside the fort. Analyzing this question allows us to examine not only the forms of accu-sation that served as entryways, but also might shed light on "where" the entryways of accusation led. Analyzing the form of accusation Heron constructed is important given that he was newly assigned to the post and the population of the colony numbered over a thousand, and so he would not have had extensive knowledge of the families of the colonists under his superintendence. Without any formal criminal classifications or even intelligence to hand, how did Heron decide who belonged outside the walls? I think that by examining his earlier remarks on self-management and subsistence practices, we can unpack the relations between prejudice, suspicion, and exclusion at play.

It can be argued that colonial discourses on subsistence and self-management were heavily linked to Heron's suspicion toward certain colonists. Heron's task of accumulating grain from the colonists for the company's stores is hard to disassociate from his broader judgments about licit and illicit forms of subsistence. Farming is framed in Heron's narrative as a mode of economic activity that is productive and prudent and that encourages industriousness. In contrast, Heron held a low opinion of those who hunted buffalo instead of farming for grain. To Heron, the colonists' decision to "pursue the chase" was indolent and improvident. The buffalo hunt was seasonal and irregular and undercut the company's monopoly on clothing in the colony.

However, when the buffalo failed to materialize, Heron was quick to note that the settlers' "reliance on buffalo for their winter subsistence rather than their own sources of grain was incautious."[30] It is important to note that for many of the newly located colonists, the decision to "pursue the chase" rather than farm the land was probably a wise one. Many of the people on the Pembina and White Horse plains were Métis families that had been relocated to Red River by the company only a few years prior.[31] That some members of this relocated population chose to hunt game rather than farm likely had less to do with industriousness than it did with ability. Those relocated from company forts and posts would have had little experience in farming grain. Hunting buffalo was, in these circumstances, probably the smartest course of action.

Nonetheless, for Heron, the choice to hunt for subsistence rather than tend crops appears to have informed some of his prejudice and later suspicions against certain members of the colony. In this sense, for Heron, both those who had been reduced to begging or had sided with the insurrections were of an indolent and improvident moral character from the outset.[32] In fact, in observing the "wretches" eating the dead and dying horses outside the fort, he remarked that had "they the smallest degree of industry" the entire famine would have been averted.[33] Heron also linked starvation, begging, and disorder, viewing these as evidence of poor self-management. Indeed, if colonists found themselves without enough food to get through the shortage caused by the collapse of the buffalo stock, this was taken as evidence that "they were incapable of providing for themselves when left to their own management."[34] Thus, Heron's judgment of the colonists and setting apart of those who ought to remain outside the walls of the fort and be denied relief were hinged on paired discourses of indolence and improvidence.

As Ute Tellmann (2013) notes, the trope of improvidence in colonial discourses is a well-documented feature in colonial rule, but it was explicitly codified in the HBC's guidelines for punitive measures against its servants. In a memo on how to handle company servants, Simpson noted that Europeans employed by the company were "money making men" and therefore could be ruled "through their fear of fines."[35] Fiscal penalties were enough of a security to maintain the good behaviour of Europeans. "Canadians" and "half-breeds," in contrast, "were more receptive to a blow than a fine."[36] Corporal punishment was not to be used against European servants, but was an acceptable means to discipline Canadian and Métis individuals.[37] The company had inscribed a model of race based on the distinction between the calculating, forward-thinking European who feared financial loss (*instrumental reason*) and the unsophisticated colonial subject who feared pain (*the emotive*) over pecuniary punishment.

In Heron's judgment of the character of the colonists, subsistence and self-management appear to have been used to determine those deserving of support from the fort and those best left on the other side of the wall to "learn the sad lesson of the season." It is also crucial to note that First Nations people remained largely outside Heron's judgment altogether. The "starving indian" is the first subject in Heron's account. They amassed outside the fort. They sought relief. At times, Heron remarked that they, too, were poorly clothed for the conditions, and at times he noted, "[they] are collecting at the fort from all directions." However, Heron freely handed out ammunition, foodstuffs, blankets, and supplies to the First Nations people who visited the fort, and it appears he did so with little concern for improving their capacity for self-management or prudence.[38] Yet, settlers in a state of starvation were chastised for their failure to provide for themselves when left to self-management.

The disparity in Heron's treatment reveals a set of racial assumptions that would later consolidate the liberal subject, and also follows the company's position that it would not pursue law and punishment against Indigenous people unless they committed crimes against "white men." Yet, while Heron considered his decision to let the settlers learn the lesson of the season to be punitive in form, he did not consider it an exercise of law. He confirmed as much in his own confession that he had neither "police nor legal measures" at his disposal. However, legal historians have noted that it was in the years following the famine that Simpson endeavoured with limited success to formalize a court and police system that could try civil and criminal matters in the colony (Gibson 2015, 10). This begs the question, if we read Heron as a gatekeeper in developing entryways into punishment, what were those he accused being entered into?

The legal order of Rupert's Land, the territory granted to the HBC by royal charter for its commercial monopoly from 1670 to 1870, was ideally based on the power conferred to the company by its charter rights. However, the extent to which the charter could be used to draft civil and criminal law was ambiguous. Moreover, there was also a long tradition of the company carrying out punishments—from whipping to exile to execution—in a perfunctory manner without reliance on English courts; in other cases, the company sought to ameliorate concerns from the colonial office by bringing criminals to trial in English courts in Montreal (Hamar 1990, 9). Whether punishment followed the rule of law or not appears to have been discretionary, and based heavily on the social perceptions of incidents and their physical distance or remoteness from established courts of law. As such, one might ask, given the ambiguity of the legal code of the HBC's Charter and the discretionary way in which English law was consulted, how was "justice" administered? Russell Smandych and Rick Linden (1996) have suggested that company factors exercised their own forms of private justice, punishment sanctioned by the personal moral authority of company factors rather than recourse to formal legal codes. What require some illustration are the moral economy and its material underpinnings that sustained this form of private justice during the famine at Red River. In what follows, I trace out this moral economy by examining how accusation and suspicion were articulated through a notion of "habit" and how Heron's system of punishment was operationalized through the logics of the fort. The interesting point that arises from this is that "private justice" relied heavily on pre-bourgeois models of social control, such as banishment.

Habit, Suspicion, and Accusation

Near the end of his lectures *On the Punitive Society*, Foucault turned his attention to the change in political fortune that habit experienced between the eighteenth and nineteenth centuries. In the eighteenth century, habit had functioned as a rhetorical technique used by the bourgeois to criticize tradition and rituals in law, politics, and economics advanced by an aristocratic class. By the nineteenth century, habit was "used prescriptively: habit [was] what people must submit to" (Foucault 2015, 238). Habit became "a technique to bind those who [were] not property owners to an apparatus they [did] not own" in a form of moral regulation that bound individuals to the instruments of production and "a political order" (Foucault 2015, 239). According to Foucault, the rise of habit as a political technique was part of a shift away from sovereign power to a form of power intended to normalize social life through the inculcation of habit; the human sciences played a key role in this deployment. Yet, there may also be a potential alliance amongst habit, suspicion, and criminal accusation in liberal rule. If this is the case, that in the nineteenth century "habit" became a prescriptive measure to inculcate certain forms of economic and moral conduct, then it also produced normative thresholds of behaviour. In terms of criminal accusation, the identification of those who are of poor habit becomes one means of locating individuals who are worthy of suspicion, and thereby forms part of the modality for criminal accusation.

Foucault's analysis of habit sheds some light on the dynamics of suspicion and accusation in Heron's text. Habit features in how Heron understood his role of superintendence at Fort Garry as being to help encourage settlers to engage in "business transactions throughout the day."[39] Tasked with overseeing and promoting regular market exchange, Heron encouraged settlers to be mindful of paying their debts to the colony, and to tend their crops rather than hunt for subsistence. All of these productive habits can be read as ways in which colonialists and newly arrived populations were bound to the political and economic order of the colony. The inculcation of good economic and moral habits was a mode of moral regulation that the company sought to exercise over the settlers. However, the other way in which habit makes its appearance in Heron's account is in the moralization and suspicion of those who did not heed what the company thought was desirable economic conduct.

As noted, Heron made repeated inferences to the "poorer improvident settlers" who did not lay down sufficient reserves to withstand the winter. His discourse linked the failure of settlers to maintain these habits to their experience of famine. Those who were a threat to the colony and those who were not worthy of assistance were identified largely in terms of their habits. Did they take up the habit of cultivating their fields, managing their affairs, and clearing their debts? Or, did they pursue the irregular practice of chasing buffalo, which encouraged an irregular attention to their land? The line Heron drew between the indolent and the industrious related to the formation of proper, industrious habits—to the extent that, in Heron's mind, the failure of most of the colonists to pursue proper habits was linked to disorder and a new collapse of the political order of the colony. For Heron, "had they applied a small share of the industry" or had they adopted a habit of "frugality" and "not exchanged grain for ammunition," the famine and subsequent fall into insurrection could have been avoided.

The Colony Fort and Punitive Measures

This account is confined to Heron's text and what he thought fit to record. Consequently, it is easy to overlook the material conditions and circumstances that surround the text. One such circumstance that structures both Heron's narrative and his subsequent punitive action is the fort itself. As I have argued elsewhere, in many ways the HBC fort was implicated in two very different regimes of power and sovereign command during the eighteenth and nineteenth centuries (Henry 2017). The eighteenth-century HBC fort operated on a model of permanent enclosure and exclusion. In policy, First Nations traders were forbidden from entering the fort and company servants were confined to the fort and could not leave without written permission from the fort governor (Mackay 1936, 220).

By the turn of the eighteenth century, the company had remodeled the colony fort to support greater circulations of people and goods. In fact, starting with a design implemented at York Factory, an HBC trading post, First Nations traders and other individuals not employed by the company were admitted into the fort. By the nineteenth century, the stockades and numerous external walls were removed or reduced and replaced by a singular fortified keep at the centre of the establishment. In short, the HBC fort shifted from a site of exclusion and wealth extraction to a site intended to support economic circulation. This shift entailed the development of more detailed systems of documentation and surveillance to keep tabs on the populations around the fort, with particular attention being devoted to developing dossiers on the moral conduct of male First Nations hunters.

Thus, the fort shifted from a site of enclosure to a site of inspection and classification. Good habits, moral conduct, and effective economic control were furnished by managing economic exchange and circulation through the creation of dossiers on individuals and records of the movement of goods in and out of the fort. Heron's narrative of the famine reflects this process. His account opens with a review of his artful economic management of economic exchange and trade, but by the end of the narrative, the fort features as a site of containment and security. The gates were closed, the defences prepped, and outside of the walls were hordes of "beggars" and "insurrectionists." There are two points that can be drawn from the role the fort played in structuring the dynamics of exclusion.

First, it is hardly novel to suggest that illiberal social forms accompany capitalist or even semi-capitalist forms of exchange. As Valverde (1996) argues, liberalism functions through a dialectical relation to despotic practices. Practices of ruling colonial subjects and also practices of self-mastery, the restraint of vice and passion, no doubt hallmarks of liberal rule, are in fact despotic techniques (Valverde 1996, 370). This despotic relationship has been chronicled in European history. Police, prisons, workhouses, and asylums have come to bear the emblems of liberal bourgeois society, yet function through despotic forms of rule. The HBC reveals the place of the fort in structuring the dialectical between liberalism and despotism in the colonial theatre. In the early pages of Heron's account, the fort is a site of commerce; but once indolence and improvidence threaten the property of the company, rule retreats to the keep and shifts from the liberal form of incentives to governing through despotic means. The architecture of the fort itself appears conditioned by this "economy" of liberalism. The liberal freedoms of exchange and the pursuit of free enterprise are inaugurated and annulled by the mere opening and closing of gates; with similar ease, one shifts from being a rational economic subject to a subject worthy of suspicion that can now be subjected to drastic and injurious methods of reform by being "left out in the cold."

Second, in Heron's narrative, the fort has the dual function of shutting out the poorer members of the settlement, while keeping the crowd of beggars swarming around the walls of the keep and effectively spatializing dissidence. Ann Stoler noted, "the colony does more than criminalize dissidence. It *produces* enemies within and without and anxiously awaits their moments of capture" (2011; emphasis added). The penal colony, military colony, and trading colony are architectural configurations that are productive of social enemies, or, at least, of strangers. Curiously, Foucault analyzed the formation of criminological thought and punishment in a similar way. Foucault noted that a decisive moment in nineteenth-century criminological thought was the creation of an alien and wild population existing within the very nation-state of the bourgeoisie (2015, 164). Foucault linked the production of this alien population to the growth of punitive power. Crucially, for Foucault, this carceral geography informed by a constellation of disciplinary institutions—schools, hospitals, prisons, asylums—was distinct from the earlier archipelagos of colony-spaces—forts, penal colonies, military colonies, agricultural colonies—dispersed within and on the borders of empires. Yet, the earlier archipelago of colonial spaces formed the templates for the "barricaded security regimes of empire" and geopolitical technologies that "endure in the distribution of protected spaces and sites of containment today" (Stoler 2011; emphasis added).

Arguably, Heron's post log points to the materiality of the fort in structuring logics of exile in the first two decades of the nineteenth century. This is of interest for two reasons. First, I think perhaps we are under the impression that, by the nineteenth century, the logics of exclusion, what Foucault famously termed "leper games," had given way to the legal-medical classification and confinement of "dangerous individuals" (Foucault 1978). It appears, though, that in British North America the distinction was not so hard and fast and the fort perpetuated the logics of exclusion. Second, Heron's logics of exclusion were not without a reformative impulse. To discontinue relief and to shut individuals outside the gate also, in Heron's mind, became a project that taught indolent settlers prudence and to engage in more regular farming "habits." Heron's narrative reflects a unique episode where the reformative arc of disciplinary power and what was purported as an earlier form of sovereign rule premised on exclusion coalesced.

Conclusion

In this chapter, I tried to examine a few ways in which we can start to think about judgment, suspicion, and punishment in a situation of disorder that was without legal authorities and legal categories to draw upon.

Given that the situations that remain outside the legal codifications of the liberal bourgeois state produce little criminological documentation, these historical episodes are as important as they are difficult to study. Perhaps, unsurprisingly, the case of the famine in the Red River colony reveals the linkages amongst prejudice, judgment, and suspicion. As such, it directs our attention to the power of moralization in producing the "social enemy" embodied in Heron's text as the "beggars" and "insurrectionists" that were put outside the fort. There should be little surprise that Heron's judgment of the moral character of the population relied so heavily on discourses of industrious/indolent forms of subsistence and prudent/improvident modes of self-management. Subsistence has long been a conduit through which moral assessments become codified as legal-criminal types, a point Marx (1842) touched on long ago in his analysis of the theft of wood.

However, in thinking about the entryways through which individuals are entered into a system of punishment, be that punishment delivered by a modern criminal justice system or meted out by a minor colonial official in charge of a fort, these moral economies are crucial in understanding the various ways in which something as personal and seemingly intangible as "suspicion and accusation" is constituted differently in certain social formations. As I outlined earlier, one analytical technique for understanding how individuals come to be determined as suspicious may be a study of "habit." If it is the case that habit made its emergence in the nineteenth century as a prescriptive and normalizing project, then it is the deviation of habit, in which individuals fall under a form of moral gaze, that takes on the power to accuse when it doubles as a legal gaze. Though this pulls away slightly from the focus of this chapter, there is perhaps a double movement of "the unusual" in the process of criminal accusation. To arouse suspicion, one must first notice something out of the ordinary: hence, "did you notice anything unusual?" The successful inculcation of a social habit as an innate personal disposition gives rise to whole series of habitual, "regular" micro-practices of behaviour, ranging from how we move through doorways, to how we greet one another, or even park our cars.

In this sense, once habit becomes generalized and has the social appearance of "regular personal conduct," it becomes possible to see the deviation of these habitual patterns as a cause for suspicion, concern, or judgment. The second movement of "the unusual" in this process is historically contingent on the legal-psychiatric power to assign external manifestations of unusual or irregular actions and behaviour to the psyche of the individual as either evidence of guilt or "abnormality." Hence, unusual or irregular has a double existence as that which alerts attention and that which is then fixed within the subject to justify said attention *post festum*. Of course, because of circumstances and the relative historical period in which Heron drafted his account, he does not afford an example of this process. However, the way in which habit and suspicion feature in his account principally as prejudice and moral judgment is instructive of future lines of inquiry.

In particular, one way to analyze how suspicion has been constituted in bourgeois civilization might be to consider if there are nineteenth-century contact points between medical discourses on psychological abnormality and moral discourses on habit and regularity. If such contact points can be found, they may disclose how legal-police-medical discourses came to operate by linking externally visible, unusual or irregular behaviour to internal unusualness under the sign of disorder or criminality. It seems that an "Art of Suspicion" operates by ensuring that unusual behaviour is not only readily visible to us as a deviation of habit, but also by calibrating the legal apparatus—through witness statements, police reports, and psychological assessments— to seek the effective relocation of this "external deviation" to an individual's "interior" as a sign of guilt, disorder, or abnormality—s/he acts strangely because s/he is guilty and we know s/he is guilty because s/he acts strangely.

My last point is that the role the colonial fort played in rendering visible and spatially fixing "social enemies" or "alien populations" in British North America has been understudied. Although it is interesting to note how exile and reformative action were exercised through the fort, I think future research would do well to consider the fort in the history of punishment and dissidence in Canada. The disappearance of the fort as a site of power in British North America may not only have to do with changes in settlement size and immigration, but might also be a marker of a shift in the logics of punishment and political sovereignty. As such, the colonial fort may be a site from which we can study shifts in punishment from exclusion and spectacle to confinement—a history that may in fact have depended on different actors and a later historical period than those featured in the transformation from exile to confinement in European societies.

Notes

1. There has been some excellent work on prelaw institutions and practices, though these tend to focus more on British Columbia and western Canada than on the institutional conducts and practices of the HBC (see Foster 1996, 1984; Harring 1998; Symandych and Linden 1996).

2. Francis Heron's Post Journal, 1825–1826, Microfilm reel, 1M153, B235/a/7, Archives of Manitoba (hereafter cited as Heron's Post Journal).

3. HBC Northern Department Minutes of Council, August 12, 1822, 1M814 B.239/k/1, 1821–1831, Archives of Manitoba.

4. Christopher Hanks touches on this point more thoroughly in his account of the HBC's attempts to rationalize the costs of operation, both by limiting the debt issued to individual hunters in a bid to limit economic liability, and in the company's attempts to discourage polygamous marriage in a bid to limit the size of the families that would need support if hunters died or became injured (1982, 104–05).

5. HBC Northern Department Minutes.

6. Ibid.

7. Ibid.

8. Ibid.

9. Ibid; emphasis added.

10. Heron's Post Journal, 1826, 27.

11. Ibid., 28–29.

12. Ibid., 29.

13. Heron's Post Journal, 1825, 32.

14. Heron's Post Journal, 1826, 34.

15. Ibid., 38.
16. Ibid.
17. Ibid.
18. Ibid., 39.
19. Ibid., 40.
20. Ibid.
21. Ibid., 41; emphasis added.
22. Ibid., 43.
23. Ibid., 46.
24. Ibid., 47.
25. Ibid., 48.
26. Ibid., 54–56.
27. Ibid., 56.
28. Ibid., 54.
29. Ibid., 55.
30. Ibid., 38.
31. "Minutes on the Assiniboia District," 1823–1824, 3M43/D/4/87, Archives of Manitoba.
32. Heron's Post Journal, 1826, 41.
33. Ibid., 38.
34. Ibid., 41.
35. George Simpson's Letter from Norway House to London Council, June 23, 1823, Resolution 160, 3M43/D/4/87, Outward correspondence, Archives of Manitoba.
36. Ibid.
37. Ibid.
38. Heron's Post Journal, 1826, 46, 56.
39. Ibid., 29.

References

Colpitts, George. 2006. "Accounting for Environmental Degradation in Hudson's Bay Company Fur Trade Journals." *The British Journal of Canadian Studies* 19 (1): 1–32.

Deidre, Simmons. 2007. *Keepers of the Record: The History of the Hudson's Bay Company Archives*. Montreal: McGill-Queen's University Press.

Foster, Hamar. 1984. "Law Enforcement in Nineteenth-Century British Columbia: A Brief and Comparative Overview." *B.C Studies* (Autumn): 3–28.

———. 1990. "Long-Distance Justice: The Criminal Jurisdiction of Canadian Courts West of the Canadas, 1763–1859." *The American Journal of Legal History* 34 (1): 1–48.

_____. 1996. "British Columbia: Legal Institutions in the Far West, from Contact to 1871." *Manitoba Law Journal* 23: 293–340.

Foucault, Michel. 1978. "About the Concept of the 'Dangerous Individual' in 19th-Century Legal Psychiatry." Translated by Alan Baudot and Jane Couchman. *International Journal of Law and Psychiatry* 1 (1): 1–18.

_____. 2007. *Security, Territory, Population.* London, New York: Palgrave Macmillan.

_____. 2015. *On the Punitive Society, Lectures at the Collège De France, 1972–1973.* Edited by Bernard Harcourt. Translated by Graham Burchell. London: Palgrave Macmillan.

Gibson, Dale. 2015. *Law, Life and Government at Red River, Volume 1.* London, Toronto, Chicago: McGill-Queen's Press.

Hanks, Christopher. 1982. "The Swampy Cree and the Hudson's Bay Company at Oxford House." *The American Society for Ethnohistory* 29 (2): 104–05.

Harring, Sydney. 1998. *White Man's Law: Native People in Nineteenth-Century Canadian Jurisprudence.* Toronto: Toronto University Press.

Henry, Aaron. 2017. "Fortification and the Fabrication of Colonial Labour." In *Destroy, Build, Secure: Readings on Pacification,* edited by Tyler Wall, Parastou Saberi, and Will Jackson, 107–25. Ottawa: Red Quills Press.

Mackay, Douglas. 1936. *The Honorable Company.* Indianapolis: Bobbs-Merrill Company.

Marx, Karl. 1842. "Debates on the Law on Thefts of Wood." Translated by Clemens Dutt. *Rheinische Zeiung* Nos. 298, 300, 303, 205, 307 (October).

Pavlich, George. 2009. "The Subjects of Criminal Identification." *Criminology and Criminal Justice* 10 (3): 171–90.

Ray, Arthur. 1978. *Give Us Good Measure.* Toronto, Buffalo, and London: University of Toronto Press.

Smandych, Russell, and Rick Linden. 1996. "Administering Justice Without the State: A Study of the Private Justice System of the Hudson's Bay Company, to 1800." *Canadian Journal of Law and Society* 11 (1): 21–61.

Stoler, Ann Laura. 2011. "Colony." *Political Concepts: A Critical Lexicon* 1 (Winter).

Tellmann, Ute. 2013. "Catastrophic Populations and the Fear of the Future: Malthus and the Genealogy of Liberal Economy." *Theory, Culture and Society* 30 (2): 135–55.

Valverde, Mariana. 1996. "Despotism and Ethical Liberal Governance." *Economy and Society* 25 (3): 357–72.

Walby, Kevin, and Nick Carrier. 2010. "The Rise of Biocriminology: Capturing Observable Bodily Economies of Criminal Man." *Criminology and Criminal Justice* 10 (3): 261–85.

4

ENTRYWAYS TO CRIMINALIZATION

Cases of HIV Prosecution in Canada

AMY SWIFFEN & MARTIN A. FRENCH

Introduction

This chapter examines criminalization of activities related to HIV/AIDS
in Canada, specifically in cases of persons alleged to have not disclosed
their HIV status to a sexual partner.[1] It analyzes how health information
is used in criminal prosecutions for these types of offences. Health information appears in two forms. As medical information pertaining to the
health status of the individual and as epidemiological information, which
is aggregate health data that applies to populations. A distinguishing aspect
of the criminalization of HIV/AIDS in Canada is the way that courts have
taken up both medical and epidemiological information as a form of
evidence derived from individual blood samples. Because the aggregate
data is generally not personally identifiable, its uptake by courts is typically
not seen as ethically problematic. In this chapter, however, we analyze the
use of population-level information from another perspective. The chapter
considers what role population health information has come to play in the
forms of legal reasoning underpinning HIV criminalization. With a focus
on convictions for HIV non-disclosure in Canada and concentrating on three
important cases in particular, we analyze how the uptake of epidemiological

information by courts creates an entryway into the criminal legal system for those with HIV.

The first section of the chapter provides a brief discussion of the type of health information that has been taken up by courts in Canada in the context of HIV non-disclosure prosecutions. The second section contextualizes this uptake in relation to the phenomenon of HIV criminalization in general and the legal principles and precedents used to justify prosecution in such cases. The third section looks at how this legal reasoning has incorporated the interpretation of health information in three cases: *R. v. Mabior* [2012], *R. v. Aziga* [2007], and *R. v. Ngeruka* [2015]. The fourth section of the chapter draws on the concept of biopolitics to argue that the link between individual health information and epidemiological information is a point of entry for individuals to a medico-legal space in which medical treatment is linked to legal liability determined by the body's biological status.[2] The final section of the chapter suggests that this type of entryway to criminalization corresponds to a form of governmentality in which the life of the population and the individual overlap at the level of blood, and in which control of blood plays a double role in shaping juridical interpretations of the legal subject and creating new classes of criminal life.

Repurposing of Epidemiological Information

Since 1998, the Public Health Agency of Canada (PHAC), under the direction of Health Canada, has conducted routine surveillance to track patterns in HIV-1 subtypes and HIV-1 transmitted drug resistance in the Canadian population through what is known as the Canadian HIV Strain and Drug Resistance Surveillance Program (SDR Program). Provincial partners in the SDR Program send blood samples originally taken for diagnostic testing from individuals newly diagnosed with HIV or from those who have never received treatment for HIV to the PHAC, where strain analysis and drug resistance genotyping is conducted (PHAC 2012, 2). For each sample submitted, a substantial amount of personal health

information is sent, specifically what is known as "non-nominal" epide-
miologic information, which includes "CD4 count,[3] viral load at diagnosis,
and previous HIV testing history," as well as information collected
on national and provincial HIV case reporting forms (PHAC 2012, 2).
Moreover, although the information forwarded to the PHAC is non-
nominal, it remains connected to individual donors through unique
identifying numbers. This is to allow for analysis of patterns of HIV transmission and drug resistance across the population, and to correlate these
patterns to best health practices and forms of medical intervention.

However, a novel use was devised for the program in 2004 when
Health Canada was approached to assist in a criminal investigation into
whether or not a Canadian man had intentionally or recklessly infected
his sexual partners with HIV. Health Canada made specimens from the
accused and the complainants available for forensic analysis from the
SDR Program, and a report was provided to the court responsible for adju-
dicating the trial by Dr. Paul Sandstrom, Director of the National HIV
and Retrovirology Laboratories, which is a partner in the SDR Program.
The man in question was ultimately convicted of two counts of first-
degree murder and ten counts of aggravated sexual assault. In 2007, he
was also classified as a dangerous offender and he remains incarcerated
for an indefinite period of time.[4] The epidemiological evidence was not
necessarily determinative of his guilt, but, as demonstrated below, it is
significant how the court integrated it into its legal reasoning as a circumstantial piece of evidence. In so doing, a medico-legal space is crested that
acts as an entryway into the criminal legal system for those with HIV.

The prosecutorial use of the Canadian SDR Program's data raises a
number of ethical questions, specifically whether it is appropriate to use
individuals' blood for purposes to which they did not consent, in particular if it could end up being part of evidence used against them in a future
criminal trial. On the one hand, one could argue that such use is justified if the prosecution of individuals who do not disclose their HIV status
genuinely protects public health. If this were the case, the privacy and
confidentiality rights of donors may be superseded by the responsibility of

the state to protect public health.[5] However, there are some problems with this reasoning. One is that there is no evidence that prosecuting individuals for HIV-related offences actually protects public health, and, in fact, there is reason to wonder if it will actually have the opposite effect.

Critical public health researchers and HIV advocacy groups have argued that criminalization could end up harming public health for several reasons. One reason is that personal health information is used as evidence in criminal prosecutions for HIV non-disclosure, and some argue that this may transform the conditions of HIV counselling in ways that undermine the work of HIV prevention (French 2015; Mykhalovskiy 2011, 2015; Sanders 2015). Another concern voiced by critics is that criminal prosecution for HIV non-disclosure will discourage people from getting tested. Wilful non-disclosure of HIV status is rare and most transmissions occur because someone is not aware of their infected status. However, one of the main reasons people do not get tested for HIV is a fear of stigmatization (Burris et al. 2007; Klemm 2010). If criminalization of HIV-related offences contributes to the stigmatization of HIV, it is reasonable to imagine that it could make people less likely to get tested, which would end up harming public health (Mykhalovskiy 2011). From this perspective, some have wondered if the criminalization of HIV could end up functioning as "a perverse incentive not to find out one's disease status" (Fan 2012, 572). For these types of reasons, the use of the Canadian SDR Program's data in cases of HIV non-disclosure has been seen as questionable from a public health perspective. This is simply because there is no evidence demonstrating that criminalization protects public health and there is reason to think it might have the opposite effect.

Another issue, however, is the link between individual blood samples in developing the population health information that is later used to interpret individual medical evidence in criminal prosecutions against someone whose blood information made the population health information possible in the first place. How does the link between medical information and population health information translate in criminal law and what are the consequences for those living with HIV? In what follows, we attempt to answer by analyzing the ways that health information has been used in criminal trials in three different cases. First, however, it is important to understand the broader context of HIV criminalization and the legal framework that the health information has been translated into.

Fraud Vitiating Consent to Sexual Relations

HIV criminalization is a broad term that describes the criminal accusation of persons with HIV in instances of transmission, exposure, and non-disclosure. In recent years, several countries have created specific criminal laws that target individuals with HIV in these situations, while others have applied existing criminal laws to situations involving HIV transmission and non-disclosure (Grace 2015; Secretariat, Global Commission 2012, 20). The Global Network of People Living with HIV (GNP+) has documented hundreds of cases around the world of individuals being convicted under either HIV-specific or general criminal laws (GNP+ 2010; see also Secretariat, Global Commission 2012, 20). Recently, GNP+ and the HIV Justice Network identified Canada as a criminalization "hot spot" along with Austria, Australia, Finland, New Zealand, Norway, the United States, Singapore, Sweden, and Switzerland (HIV Justice Network 2013, 7). Canada seems to be a leader in this group, since as of 2011 it had "convicted more people (a disproportionate number from minority ethnic, especially African and Afro-Caribbean, communities) for HIV exposure and transmission offences than all the other countries of the world combined" (Mykhalovskiy 2011, 20; see also Symington 2009).

The situation in Canada exists in part because Canadian jurisprudence has developed to include not only the transmission of HIV, but also the non-disclosure of HIV status, which is what the majority of the criminal prosecutions involve. These are cases in which people are accused of crimes even if no HIV transmission takes place. Transmission and non-disclosure have been prosecuted under different charges, including common nuisance, sexual assault, aggravated assault, aggravated sexual assault, administering a noxious substance, attempted murder, and murder. The first cases occurred in 1989, and in them HIV non-disclosure tended to be prosecuted under the less serious charges of common nuisance and administering a noxious substance. As time has gone by, however, individuals have tended to be charged with more serious offences, such as aggravated sexual assault. Critics have expressed alarm that this approach (criminalizing non-disclosure) has resulted in countless criminal investigations and growing rates of charge and conviction (Mykhalovskiy, Betteridge, and McLay 2010).

The legal principle out of which this phenomenon has emerged is known as "fraud capable of vitiating consent to sexual relations." Its history begins in the nineteenth century with cases reflecting a view that failing to disclose that one has a serious sexually transmitted disease could constitute fraud vitiating a partner's consent to sexual relations. Rather than defining the meaning of "fraud," courts extended the definition on a case-by-case basis in a way that centred "the right of the woman involved to choose whether to have intercourse or not."[6] For instance in R. v. Flattery [1877], the Court upheld a conviction of rape for a man operating a booth at a fair who had sex with a woman under the pretext of a medical procedure. It held that the victim had consented to medical contact, not a sexual act. Thus, her consent was vitiated by the man's fraud. What emerged out of this approach in early case law is the idea that fraud about one's identity and about the nature of the activity itself could vitiate a partner's consent to sexual relations.[7] Courts at this time also recognized that concealment of venereal disease could constitute fraud vitiating consent to sexual relations. For example, in R. v. Bennet in 1866 and in R. v. Sinclair in 1867, it was found that the non-disclosure of venereal disease amounted to criminal fraud, as the complainant "would not have consented if she had known," thus "her consent is vitiated by the deceit practised upon her."[8]

The approach of the courts began to change into the late nineteenth century as courts incorporated Victorian notions of sexual morality into their reasoning.[9] A case that announced the change was Hegarty v. Shine [1878], which was a civil tort. Shine was the master of a house and had sexual relations with a servant who became pregnant, and both she and the child were infected with syphilis. The court dismissed the case for damages against Mr. Shine on the basis of a legal concept known as *ex turpi causa non oritur actio*, which translates as "from a dishonorable cause an action does not arise." The court essentially decided that the woman was the victim of her own immoral act and would not condone it by bringing a judgment against Mr. Shine. As it explained, "In the case before us the plaintiff actively consented to the very thing, that is to say, sexual intercourse, with full knowledge and experience of the nature of the act."[10] In other words, it was the complainant's decision to engage in morally questionable sexual relations and thus she was morally responsible for the consequences, which included the possibility of sexually transmitted infections (STIs). At the time, the transmission of STIs was seen as a moral phenomenon as it was seen as being caused by immoral sex (e.g., adultery, prostitution). Thus, the court was asking who was morally blameworthy for the complainant's infection and was less concerned with the right to refuse sexual relations.

The *Shine* precedent was solidified in *The Queen v. Clarence* [1888], which is the first case in which a court explicitly limited the definition of fraud in the context of sexual relations to reflect the dominant morality of the time.[11] The facts were that a husband contracted gonorrhoea and did not disclose it to his wife, and subsequently transmitted the infection to her. He was charged with assault and unlawful infliction of bodily harm. However, the opinion of the court was that the victim consented to the sexual act and was not deceived as to the identity of the accused; therefore, she could not claim that her consent was obtained through fraud. In this way, the *Clarence* decision limited fraud capable of vitiating consent to sexual relations to two types: where an individual is deceived as to the nature of the sexual act and/or the identity of the partner.[12] Legislation passed by Parliament after the *Clarence* decision seemed to reflect this narrower view as well. The first Canadian Criminal Code defined fraud for purposes of rape and indecent assault as "false and fraudulent representations," and excluded the omission of information, i.e., non-disclosure

(s. 259(b)). Under the *Clarence* test, therefore, if an individual consented to a sexual act with a given person, that person could not be convicted for the act no matter the deceit involved. Needless to say, cases where an individual consents to sex but does not realize it is sex, or that their partner is a person impersonating someone else are rare.[13] Therefore, in all but rare cases, fraud could not vitiate consent to sexual relations.[14] Thus, what we see in the late nineteenth century in Canadian criminal law is a narrowing of fraud as an entryway to criminalization in the context of sexual relations.

After the implementation of the Charter of Rights and Freedoms in 1982, however, Canada entered a new "post-*Clarence* era" and a more contextual approach to the determination of fraud emerged.[15] Parliament undertook a reform of the Criminal Code aimed at bringing it into conformity with the Charter. In 1983, the law on sexual offences was amended by removing the qualifying phrase "false and fraudulent representations" (s. 265(3) (c)). The Canadian Supreme Court (SCC) has interpreted this change as reflecting Parliament's will that fraud in the context of sexual relations be understood more broadly than in the past, and that the omission of information in some contexts could amount to fraud vitiating consent to sexual relations.[16] Despite the legislative change, courts did not explicitly repudiate the more restrictive *Clarence*-inspired interpretation of fraud until 1998 in the *Cuerrier* decision, which involved an accusation of HIV non-disclosure. In that case, the SCC found that being unknowingly exposed to the HIV virus is profound enough that it fundamentally alters the "nature and quality" of the sexual act that is being consented to. It affirmed that,

> *...consent to sexual intercourse can properly be found to be vitiated by fraud under s. 265 if the accused's failure to disclose his HIV-positive status is dishonest and results in deprivation by putting the complainant at a significant risk of suffering serious bodily harm.*[17]

In other words, the non-disclosure of HIV status may constitute fraud that vitiates a partner's consent to sexual relations depending on contextual factors. The Court characterized this decision as guided by the legislative changes mentioned above, noting that "it is clear that Parliament intended to move away from the traditional approach to fraud as it relates to consent in sexual assault offences."[18] In subsequent decisions, the SCC has also aligned this re-broadening of the concept of fraud with Charter values, which require "full recognition of the right to consent or to withhold consent to sexual relations" and "an understanding of sexual assault based on the preservation of the right to refuse sexual intercourse."[19]

In a sense, the *Cuerrier* decision was a return to the pre-*Clarence* approach to fraud in that the meaning of the term was once again left undefined and amenable to a case-by-case approach. However, there are some key differences as well. The older jurisprudence reflected a more paternalistic attitude toward women and the transmission of STIs had an assumed moral significance, rather than a medical and scientific one. In contrast, the contemporary jurisprudence reflects an attempt to shift away from moral standards in favour of harm and risk-based assessments. The SCC specified in *Cuerrier* that the legal duty to disclose only applies if the non-disclosure exposes an individual to a "significant risk of serious bodily harm."[20] The "fraud" of non-disclosure is not subject to criminal liability because of moral notions of truth-telling, but because it exposes an individual to a serious potential health risk without their consent.

However, the difficulty that became quickly apparent with the *Cuerrier* standard was that determining what amounted to a "significant risk" of transmission proved challenging. This becomes clear if we consider how the criminalization of HIV has developed since *Cuerrier*. To that end, the next section will analyze three cases: *R. v. Mabior* [2012], *R. v. Aziga* [2007], and *R. v. Ngeruka* [2015]. In each of these cases, health information was integral to the court's reasoning and determination of criminal conduct, although in different ways. At the same time, given the legal principles described above, each case also demonstrates how the link between

individual health information and epidemiological information broadens
the entryway to criminal accusation for individuals with HIV.

Case I
R. v. Mabior [2012]

While the *Cuerrier* decision defined a standard for HIV non-disclosure, it
did not explore the question of how to assess in a specific case whether a
risk of transmission constitutes a significant risk. It did not define what
would precisely constitute a "significant risk" of HIV transmission and
whether and how it could be mitigated. As a result, there was a lack of
clarity as to when individuals with HIV had a duty to disclose their status
to sexual partners, due to differing interpretations by police, prosecutors,
and lower courts (Mykhalovskiy 2011). For instance, some judges placed
significant weight on condom use (e.g., *R. v. Agnatuk-Mercier* [2001]; *R. v.
Edwards* [2001]; *R. v. Smith* [2007]), while others found culpability even
when a condom was used (e.g., *R. v. JT* [2008]). There were calls for the
courts to more precisely define "significant risk" of HIV transmission in
the context of sexual relations, and in so doing clarify the duty to disclose
(Grant and Betteridge 2011; Mykhalovskiy 2011).

The SCC had an opportunity to do just that in 2012 in *R. v. Mabior*. In
Mabior, an accused was charged with nine counts of aggravated sexual
assault for not disclosing his HIV status before engaging in sexual relations with nine complainants. It was found at trial that, at the time of the
incidents, the accused had an undetectable HIV viral load and he had used
a condom with three of the complainants. He was therefore convicted on
only six counts and acquitted on three. The court held that because he had
an undetectable viral load and used a condom with three of the complainants that made the risk of HIV transmission negligible, and therefore
relieved him of the duty to disclose in those cases. In other words, in this
case, both factors together (condom use and an undetectable viral load)
were deemed necessary to absolve the accused of the duty to disclose his
HIV status. Thus, the *Mabior* decision put forward the idea that sex with

a condom when one's HIV viral load is undetectable is required in order to mitigate the "significant risk of serious bodily harm," the standard required by *Cuerrier*. On appeal, the defence in the case argued that the *Cuerrier* standard was too high and that either an undetectable viral load *or* condom use could negate significant risk of transmission and therefore the duty to disclose. The court of appeal agreed with the defence and reduced to two the counts on which the accused could be convicted, while entering acquittals on the four remaining counts.

The Crown appealed the court of appeal's decision and the SCC heard the case in 2012. In its decision, the Court affirmed the principle in *Cuerrier* that the duty to disclose should apply in contexts where HIV non-disclosure puts a sexual partner at a "significant risk of serious bodily harm"; however, it specified that a "significant risk" of bodily harm in the context of HIV means "a realistic possibility" of transmission of HIV.[21] To determine what qualifies as a "realistic" possibility of HIV transmission, the Court turned not to notions of sexual morality, but to notions of health risk. In particular, the Court drew on epidemiological information offered in a report on male to female sexual transmission of HIV, prepared for the Court by an expert physician who also testified about its contents. During his testimony, the doctor stated that the baseline risk of HIV transmission per act of vaginal intercourse with an infected male partner ejaculating without a condom ranges from 1 in 2000 to 1 in 384. He also stated that having an undetectable viral load lowers this risk by at least 89 percent and that condom use lowers it by an additional 80 percent.[22] Based on this population-level health information on HIV transmission risks, the SCC determined that individuals have a duty to disclose their HIV status unless they have an undetectable viral load *and* a condom is used. That is, there is no duty to disclose HIV status if a condom is used and the viral load is undetectable. In this way, health information was integrated into the determination of fraud in the context of sexual relations at the level of the individual and at the level of the population. This represents a shift in legal reasoning away from the Victorian approach that explicitly framed STIs as a moral phenomenon and toward a focus on health status and risk. In the next case, we discuss how this shift plays out when the risk of transmission becomes real and results in actual transmission.

Case 2
R. v. Aziga [2007]

The accused in the *Aziga* case was a Ugandan-born Canadian charged with two counts of first-degree murder and thirteen counts of aggravated sexual assault for allegedly engaging in sex without a condom and without disclosing that he had HIV with thirteen sexual partners. Of the thirteen, seven contracted HIV and two died as a result of the transmission. The Crown argued that the accused was responsible for the death of two complainants and the transmission of HIV to five others, and that he exposed the remaining six to significant risk of HIV transmission through his non-disclosure. To help make its case, the Crown relied on information from the SDR Surveillance Program. This was the first time that the program was involved in trial proceedings. The goal was to assess the genetic similarity between the subtype of HIV infecting the accused and that infecting the complainants. A report presented to the court indicated that the accused and the complainants shared a specific form of the HIV virus that is rare in Canada but prevalent in Uganda. The lawyer for the accused objected to this evidence, likening it to racial profiling, but this argument was dismissed by the court, which pointed out that the epidemiological information could not be used to conclude where the shared virus came from or if a man from Uganda had indeed transmitted to the complainants. It "in no way refers to criminal activity attributed to an identified group in society on the basis of race or colour."[23] Thus, it found there was no evidentiary foundation for the claim that the report was racial profiling.

Indeed, the report did not say anything about the accused's behaviour or draw any probabilistic conclusions based on his race or national origin. It simply implied that he was amongst a relatively small cluster of individuals in Canada with the same subtype of HIV as the complainants.[24] The court is correct that such phylogenetic analysis cannot indicate anything about the path of transmission in a specific case. It pertains to molar categories, such as age, sex, and race/ethnicity, and molar disease categories, such as influenza, HIV/AIDS, and malaria, which are treated as social facts irreducible to their individual component parts (see Fenton and Charsley 2000). At the same time, however, these categories are laden with "specific social and cultural values" that are rarely interrogated in epidemiological discourse (Namaste et al. 2012). Considering this, the question is what exactly is the significance of epidemiological facts in the context of criminal accusation? How does population-level knowledge function in legal forms of reasoning that apply to individuals and their conduct? Consider the hypothetical claim that "a higher proportion of African, Asian and people of mixed ethnicities may be infected with non-B HIV-1 subtypes than Caucasians"—made in the context of an epidemiological report in which the racial categories are taken as molar categories for the purposes of understanding health patterns in a population. However, in juridical contexts, the meaning of such epidemiological information becomes circumstantial evidence about an individual's conduct. In the context of a criminal trial, an epidemiological fact attributed to a molar group can function as powerful circumstantial evidence when an accused is a member of that group. This becomes even clearer in the third and final case discussed below, where the molar category in question was not only defined socially, but also by bodily health status.

Case 3
R. v. Ngeruka [2015]

The *Ngeruka* case occurred in 2015. The accused was charged with aggravated sexual assault for having sexual relations with a complainant without disclosing to her that he had HIV. She was subsequently diagnosed with HIV. At trial, the accused accepted responsibility for the non-disclosure, but he would not admit responsibility for transmitting the virus to the complainant. However, evidence provided by two HIV experts convinced the Court beyond a reasonable doubt that the strain of the HIV virus that infected the accused was so similar to the one that infected the complainant that there almost certainly must have been a sexual connection between them. One expert witness, a specialist in infectious disease and HIV care in the Yukon, was the treating physician for both the complainant and the accused. Dr. Barbara Romanowski testified that a "clade" is a specific strain of HIV and that an individual's clade is determined when they are tested for HIV drug resistance. Only individuals who have a detectable viral load can be resistance tested. Dr. Romanowski indicated that of the sixty-two HIV-positive individuals that she had seen in the Yukon, thirty had been resistance tested. Of these thirty, three were Clade A, twenty-five were Clade B, and two were Clade C. Since both the complainant and the accused had been resistance tested, Dr. Romanowski was able to say that the accused was Clade A-1 and the complainant was Clade A. Further, she stated that Clade A-1 and Clade A are very similar strains of the HIV virus. She was also able to determine that the accused had been infected first.[25]

The second expert, Dr. Mark Wainberg, director of the AIDS Centre at the Jewish General Hospital at McGill University, was called by the Crown to provide evidence in the areas of microbiology and immunology. He testified that different types of the HIV virus (i.e., clades) can be distinguished on the basis of the sequencing of the nucleic acids of the viruses. However, if an individual transmits HIV to a second individual, there is a high likelihood that the two viruses will resemble one another; further, if an individual transmitted HIV to a second individual who then transmitted the virus to a third individual, it would be likely that all three viruses would strongly resemble each other. Therefore, if there is a strong degree of similarity between viruses in two individuals, there is a high probability that the viruses are of common origin. Dr. Wainberg was provided with blood samples from both the accused and the complainant to conduct his analysis. He concluded that the viruses were "very closely and strongly related."[26] However, he also stated it is not possible to determine the direction of transmission. It could be that either one of the two individuals infected the other, or that one individual infected another person who in turn infected the second individual, all within a relatively short period of time. While the viruses were related, Dr. Wainberg could not say whether the accused infected the complainant or whether he infected an intermediary individual in a transmission cluster that included the complainant. Nonetheless, based on the testimony of both experts, the court was convinced beyond a reasonable doubt that the complainant had contracted HIV from the accused, who ultimately pled guilty and was sentenced to thirty months in prison.

Health Information as an Entryway to Criminal Accusation

All three of the cases examined above show that while courts are aware of the differences between epidemiological facts and legal proofs, and of the limits of drawing conclusions about individual conduct from population-level health information (see Christoffel and Teret 1991; Schauer 2012), such awareness does not stop epidemiological information from working as a powerful form of circumstantial evidence of individual wrongdoing depending on one's blood status. In the Canadian context, information derived from the SDR Program and other epidemiological sources has factored into the legal reasoning of courts on various levels. The reason an individual patient's blood ends up in the SDR Program is originally medical in nature, as the donors are those seeking HIV testing and medical care. In a criminal trial, however, one's own blood and its link to the material in the SDR Program can become a liability. In this sense, to receive an HIV diagnosis in Canada today is to become embedded in a complex assemblage of health professionals, public health institutions, and now the criminal legal system.

This link between medical and legal space is consistent with Michel Foucault's notion of biopolitics as developed in the first volume of *History of Sexuality* ([1976] 1990) and in his lectures at the Collège de France. Therein, Foucault describes how juridical power manifested historically in localized displays of spectacular violence, such as public executions. These manifestations started to decline in frequency in the modern era at the same time as the value of the life and health of the population became a concern of the state. Concomitantly, a form of "biopower" develops that involves managing the life of the "species body" (i.e., the population) through disciplining individual bodies and fostering different forms of life (Foucault [1976] 1990, 139). In his historical analyses, Foucault describes various techniques of biopower as they are taken up in juridical realms through interventions and regulatory controls aimed at governing and shaping the life of the population by mastering "all the conditions that can cause these to vary" ([1976] 1990, 139).[27] As Lemke notes, Foucault was referring to "the emergence of a specific political knowledge and new disciplines such as statistics, demography, epidemiology, and biology," which "make it possible to analyse processes of life at the level of popu-lations," which then inform the government of individuals through "practices of correction, exclusion, normalization, disciplining, thera-peutics, and optimization" (2011, 5). Within this paradigm of biopolitical forms of governance, the life of the population and the health of the indi-vidual body overlap materially at the level of blood.

For individuals living with HIV, the incorporation of health informa-tion into legal reasoning has opened up a medico-legal space within which they are faced with a requirement of perpetual surveillance of their blood status and an ethic of continual disclosure that serve both health purposes and legal purposes. The health status of the individuals involved in partic-ular cases and their status in relation to characteristics of population health have also been incorporated into the legal reasoning. In this sense, the initial taking of blood for a medical diagnosis becomes a material and practical link between systems of individual medical health care, systems of public health, and systems of criminal punishment. This chapter focused on the way that jurisdiction over blood links these systems and acts as an entryway to criminal accusation for individuals living with HIV.[28] Moreover, the epidemiological information that informs the legal reasoning underpinning HIV criminalization is made possible by individ-uals freely giving their blood for medical care. This blood then becomes a powerful force shaping the judicial interpretation of individual conduct and moral responsibility when it is analyzed in relation to a population. Attention to the role of epidemiological information in enabling HIV criminalization isolates the law's jurisdiction over blood as it circulates through individuals and the population, which in turn links the health of the population to individual bodies through medico-legal forms of governance. This is one reason why the courts in Canada have shifted away from moral criteria to notions of harm and risk, and why epidemiological information is appearing in criminal law contexts, and why blood comes to function as both a material and normative threshold through which legal liabilities are determined. The circulation of blood that links the individual body and the health of the population also materializes the link between the species body and individual bodies constitutive of biopolitical forms of governance.

Conclusion

The goal of this chapter was to analyze the role of health information in the criminalization of HIV non-disclosure in Canada. It provided examples of the types of medical and epidemiological information that have been taken up by Canadian courts in the context of HIV non-disclosure cases, and explained how this information was made possible by virtue of people consenting to give their blood for purposes of medical care. It explored the fundamental issue of how epidemiological information is shaping traditional forms of legal reasoning, including criminal law hermeneutics of individual responsibility and moral blameworthiness. Through a brief genealogy of the legal principle of fraud vitiating consent to sexual relations, it was argued that the courts have re-adopted a more flexible interpretation of fraud in the context of sexual relations, and that notions of sexual morality have been replaced by epidemiological determinations of health risk. One of the consequences of this intersection is the creation of a medico-legal space for individuals living with HIV in Canada. Through three case studies of individuals charged with HIV-related offences, we demonstrated how accessing medical care for HIV acts as an entryway to criminal accusation through the mediating effect of population-level knowledge. The concluding discussion of biopolitics showed the double role of blood in constituting medico-legal entryways, and more generally, how jurisdiction over blood in biopolitical forms of governance creates an entryway into the criminal legal system for those living with HIV.

Notes

1. This chapter is the outcome of research conducted using The HIV Criminal Convictions and Sentencing Database. With financial support from the Government of Quebec and under the direction of Amy Swiffen, a digital database has been built that collects all available judicial decisions in cases of individuals who have been convicted of, or pled guilty to, HIV-related offences in Canada. The database is organized to include all legal actions related to an individual's case, which means appeals and sentencing decisions. All of the cases in the database have been coded with qualitative and quantitative information, one of which is health information.

2. For a discussion of the idea of a "medico-legal borderland," see Timmermans and Gabe (2002).

3. CD4 is a glycoprotein found on the surface of immune cells.

4. Individuals convicted of violent offences can be designated a "dangerous offender" during sentencing if a sentencing court is satisfied that the offender constitutes a threat to the life, safety, or physical or mental well-being of the public. An offender who is designated a dangerous offender may be sentenced to an indeterminate term of imprisonment (Public Safety Canada n.d.).

5. This line of reasoning is suggested, at least, in the way that bioethicists have described, for example, the justification for "overriding rules of privacy in order to protect other moral objectives" (Beauchamp and Childress 1989, 323).

6. R. v. Mabior, [2012], SCC 47, para. 31.

7. R. v. Dee [1884]: "Whether the act of consent be the result of overpowering force, or of fear, or of incapacity, or of natural condition, or of deception, it is still want of consent, and the consent must be, not consent to the act, but to the act of the particular person—not in the abstract, but in the concrete" (para. 598).

8. R. v. Mabior, para. 29. See also R. v. Bennett (1866): "An assault is within the rule that fraud vitiates consent, and therefore, if the prisoner, knowing that he had a foul disease, induced his niece to sleep with him, intending to possess her, and

infected her, she being ignorant of his condition, any consent, which she may have given, would be vitiated, and the prisoner would be guilty of an indecent assault" (para. 925).

9. R. v. Mabior.

10. Hegarty v. Shine, [1878], 14 Cox C.C. 124 (H.C.J. Ir. (Q.B.D.)), para. 130, as cited in R. v. Mabior.

11. R. v. Mabior.

12. See R. v. Mabior.

13. Though not unheard of: see R. v. Harms [1943]; Bolduc v. The Queen [1967]. In R. v. Crangle [2010], a man was convicted of sexual assault on the basis of fraud vitiating consent when he initiated sexual contact with his twin's brother's wife without disclosing he was not her husband but in fact his twin.

14. See R. v. Mabior.

15. R. v. Mabior, para. 43.

16. See R. v. Cuerrier, [1998], SCC 2 R.C.S., and R. v. Mabior [2012]. See also R. v. Petrozzi, [1987], 35 C.C.C. (3d) 528 (B.C.C.A.); R. v. Lee, [1991], 3 O.R. (3d) 726 (Gen. Div.); R. v. Ssenyonga, [1993], 81 C.C.C. (3d) 257 (Ont. Ct. (Gen. Div.)).

17. R. v. Cuerrier, para. 373.

18. Ibid., para. 381.

19. R. v. Mabior, para. 43, 45.

20. R. v. Cuerrier, para. 373.

21. R. v. Mabior, para. 93. The SCC further suggested that, "as a general matter, a realistic possibility of transmission of HIV is negated if: (i) the accused's viral load at the time of sexual relations was low *and* (ii) condom protection was used" (para. 94).

22. This evidence was accepted alongside the testimony of a Manitoba public health nurse, who stated that the baseline risk of HIV transmission per unprotected act of vaginal intercourse is 1 in 1000; (see R. v. Mabior, para. 97).

23. R. v. Aziga [2007], para. 16.

24. This point was acknowledged by the court: "The evidence in question relates to the identification of a subtype of the HIV virus and the determination as to whether there is any relationship between the specimens obtained from the applicant and the seven complainants infected with HIV. That is, there is no conclusion in the report to indicate where the shared virus came from or that the complainants were infected by a black man from Uganda. The conclusions in the report merely indicate that the applicant accused and the infected complainants share

a particular virus which is a rare clave in Canada but prevalent in Africa" (R. v. Aziga, para. 13).

25. R. v. Ngeruka, para. 16–30.

26. R. v. Ngeruka, para. 35.

27. In *Security, Population, and Territory*, Foucault defines biopower as "the set of mechanisms through which the basic biological features of the human species became the object of a political strategy, of a general strategy of power, or, in other words, how, starting from the 18th century, modern Western societies took on board the fundamental biological fact that human beings are a species" (2004, 1).

28. Consider, for instance, Waldby and Mitchell's argument that blood donation "would appear to be an exemplary act of imagined community in Anderson's terms, a gift of health to an unknown other with whom one has nothing in common other than the shared space of the nation" (2006, 4).

References

Burris, Scott, Leo Beletsky, Joseph Burleson, Patricia Case, and Zita Lazzarini. 2007. "Do Criminal Laws Influence HIV Risk Behaviour? An Empirical Trail." *Arizona State Law Journal* 39 (2): 467–519.

Beauchamp, Tom, and James Childress. 1989. *Principles of Biomedical Ethics, Third Edition*. Oxford: Oxford University Press.

Canada, Public Health Agency of. 2012. *HIV-1 Strain and Transmitted Drug Resistance in Canada: Surveillance Report to December 31, 2008*. Ottawa: Centre for Communicable Diseases and Infection Control, Public Health Agency of Canada.

Christoffel, Tom, and Stephen Teret. 1991. "Epidemiology and the Law: Courts and Confidence Intervals." *American Journal of Public Health* 81 (12): 1661–66.

De Keijser, Jan, and Henk Elffers. 2012. "Understanding of Forensic Expert Reports by Judges, Defense Lawyers and Forensic Professionals." *Psychology, Crime & Law* 18 (2): 191–207.

Fan, Mary D. 2012. "Sex, Privacy, and Public Health in a Casual Encounters Culture." *U.C. Davis Law Review* 45 (2), 531–96.

Fenton, Steve, and Katharine Charsley. 2000. "Epidemiology and Sociology as Incommensurate Games: Accounts from the Study of Health and Ethnicity." *Health* 4 (4): 403–25.

Foucault, Michel. [1976] 1990. *The History of Sexuality: An Introduction, Volume I*. New York: Vintage Books.

———. 2004. *Security, Population, and Territory*. Lectures at the Collège de France 1977–1978. New York: Picador.

Global Network of People Living with HIV (GNP+). 2010. *The Global Criminalisation Scan Report: Documenting Trends, Presenting Evidence*. Amsterdam: GNP+. Online. http://www.HIVpolicy.org/Library/HPP001825.pdf.

Global Network of People Living with HIV (GNP+) and HIV Justice Network (HIVJN). 2013. *Advancing HIV Justice: A Progress Report of Achievements and Challenges in Global Advocacy Against HIV Criminalisation*. Amsterdam and London: GNP+ and HIVJN. Accessed January 11, 2014. http://www.HIVjustice.net/wp-content/uploads/2013/05/Advancing-HIV-Justice-June-2013.pdf.

Klemm, Sara. 2010. "Keeping Prevention in the Crosshairs: A Better HIV Exposure Law for Maryland." *Journal of Health Care Law & Policy* 13 (2): 495–524.

Lemke, Thomas. 2011. *Biopolitics: An Advanced Introduction*. Translated by E.F. Trump. New York: New York University Press.

Mykhalovskiy, Eric. 2011. "The Problem of 'Significant Risk': Exploring the Public Health Impact of Criminalizing HIV Non-disclosure." *Social Science & Medicine* 73 (5): 668–75.

———. 2015. "The Public Health Implications of HIV Criminalization: Past, Current, and Future Research Directions." *Critical Public Health*, 25 (4): 373–85.

Mykhalovskiy, Eric, Glenn Betteridge, and David McLay. 2010. *HIV Non-Disclosure and the Criminal Law: Establishing Policy Options for Ontario*. Toronto: A Report Funded by a Grant from the Ontario HIV Treatment Network. Accessed January 11, 2014. http://www.catie.ca/pdf/Brochures/HIV-non-disclosure-criminal-law.pdf.

Namaste, Viviane, Tamara Vukov, Nada Saghie, Robin Williamson, Jacky Vallée, Mareva Lafrenière, Marie-Josee Leroux, Andre Monette, and Joseph Jean-Gilles. 2012. *HIV Prevention and Bisexual Realities*. Toronto: University of Toronto Press.

Ontario, Inquiry into Pediatric Forensic Pathology (The Goudge Inquiry). 2008. *Inquiry into Pediatric Forensic Pathology in Ontario, Report: Volume 2 Systemic Review*. Toronto: Ministry of the Attorney General.

Public Safety Canada. n.d. *Dangerous Offender Designation*. http://www.publicsafety.gc.ca/cnt/cntrng-crm/crrctns/protctn-gnst-hgh-rsk-ffndrs/dngrs-ffndr-dsgntn-eng.aspx.

Schauer, Frederick. 2012. "Lie-Detection, Neuroscience, and the Law of Evidence." *Virginia Public Law and Legal Theory Research Paper*, No. 2012-09.

Secretariat, Global Commission on HIV and the Law. 2012. *Global Commission on HIV and the Law: Risks, Rights & Health*. New York: United Nations Development Programme (UNDP). Accessed December 9, 2013. http://HIVlawcommission.org/index.php/report.

Symington, Alison. 2009. "Criminalization Confusion and Concerns: The Decade Since the Cuerrier Decision." *HIV/AIDS Policy & Law Review* 14 (1): 1–10.

Timmermans, Stefan, and Jonathan Gabe. 2002. "Introduction: Connecting Criminology and Sociology of Health and Illness." *Sociology of Health & Illness* 24 (2): 501–16.

Waldby, Catherine and Robert Mitchell. 2006. *Tissue Economies: Blood, Organs, and Cell Lines in Late Capitalism*. Durham, NC: Duke University Press.

Cases

Bolduc v. The Queen [1967] S.C.R. 677

Hegarty v. Shine [1878] 14 Cox C.C. 124 (H.C.J. Ir. (Q.B.D.))

R. v. Agnatuk-Mercier [2001] O.J. No. 4729

R. v. Aziga [2007] O.J. No. 4965, 164 C.R.R. (2d) 122; 75 W.C.B. (2d) 6732007 CanLII 56095 (ONSC)

R. v. Bennett [1866] 4 F. & F. 1105, 176 E.R. 925 (West. Cir.)

R. v. Crangle [2010] ONCA 451

R. v. Cuerrier [1998] SCC 2 R.C.S.

R. v. Dee [1884] 15 Cox C.C. 579 (Cr. Cas. Res. Ir.)

R. v. Edwards [2001] NSSC 80, [2001] N.S.J. No. 221

R. v. Flattery [1877] 13 Cox C.C. 388 (C.C.A.)

R. v. Harms [1943] 81 C.C.C. 4 (Sask. C.A.)

R. v. Lee [1991] 3 O.R. (3d) 726 (Ont. Gen. Div.)

R. v. Mabior [2012] SCC 47

R. v. Ngeruka [2015] YKTC 10

R. v. Petrozzi [1987] 35 C.C.C. (3d) 528 (B.C.C.A.)

R. v. Sinclair [1867] 13 Cox C.C. 28

R. v. Smith [2008] SKCA 61

R. v. Ssenyonga [1993] 81 C.C.C. (3d) 257 (Ont. Ct. (Gen. Div.))

The Queen v. Clarence [1888] 22 Q.B.D. 23 (Cr. Cas. Res.)

Legislation

Criminal Code of Canada, S.C., 1892, c. 29

FROM SCIENCE TO SLUGGING

Foucault, Law, and Truth in Prize Fighting

BRYAN R. HOGEVEEN

Introduction

In 2003, Jay Chang was charged with "promoting, permitting and encouraging" prize fighting after he organized what *CBC News* called an "extreme fighting championship."[1] Chang advertised the September 27, 2002 event by distributing leaflets, tacking up posters, and taking to the internet. Unfortunately for Chang, the event was so widely publicized that the police were alerted and not only attended the event, but video recorded the proceedings. Audience members who paid an admission fee were treated to several matches where combatants were using acts "of punching, kicking, pushing, kneeing, lifting, elbowing and wrestling," which some witnesses referred to as a "mixed martial arts (MMA) contest."[2] Although Chang arranged for referees to officiate the matches, his event was not sanctioned by the province of New Brunswick. On the basis of the video recorded evidence and eyewitness testimony presented before the court, Jay Chang was convicted.

In Canada, prize fighting that has not been sanctioned by an athletic commission is illegal and subject to criminal prosecution. Citizens turned promoters cannot simply decide to host an event by putting together a fight card, booking a venue, and hiring referees. They must first receive permission from an athletic commission to host mixed martial arts or boxing events. The Canadian government has downloaded the responsibility to form athletic commissions to the provinces. In almost every case, the province holds this function and regulates combative sports that occur in its jurisdiction. In a limited number of other spaces, such as in Alberta, the province has delegated municipalities this responsibility (e.g., Edmonton). When combative sports events are held in places without a provincial or municipal athletic commission, they are, as a result, unsanctioned and the pathway is cleared for prosecution.

As we can see in the case of *R. v. Chang* [2003], what constitutes prize fighting and how the accused becomes subject to law is relatively straightforward and clearly spelled out. Today, Section 83 of the Criminal Code of Canada exempts fighters from the law and from prosecution. According to the Criminal Code of Canada (s. 83 (2)):

> prize fight *means an encounter or fight with fists, hands or feet between two persons who have met for that purpose by previous arrangement made by or for them, but does not include (a) a contest between amateur athletes in a combative sport with fists, hands or feet held in a province if the sport is on the programme of the International Olympic Committee or the International Paralympic Committee and, in the case where the province's lieutenant governor in council or any other person or body specified by him or her requires it, the contest is held with their permission.*

While today the matter of the prize fight seems relatively settled, this has not always been the case.[3] Before accusations of prize fighting could be made, the truth of the conduct needed to be fixed. Prize fighting is indicative of a particular set of actions that were, at a particular point in time, grouped under this legal category. Throughout the early twentieth century, as we will see below, legal professionals established the truth of the prize fighting prohibition in law by differentiating it from more acceptable combative forms (i.e., sparring, exhibitions, and jiu-jitsu).

Identifying subjects as those who have violated the law turns on establishing what exactly constitutes a prize fight. That is, the truth of what is,
under law, a prize fight. Without first producing this truth, the prohibition
is illusory. In this way, prize fighting law does not repress, or only repress
and silence, but creates the thing itself. In his interview with Pasquale
Pasquino and Alesandro Fontana in 1977, Michel Foucault maintained that:

> the notion of repression is quite inadequate for capturing what is
> precisely the productive aspect of power. In defining the effects of
> power as repression, one adopts a purely juridical conception of such
> power, one identifies power with a law that says no—power is taken,
> above all, as carrying the force of prohibition. (Foucault, 2000a, 120)

Insertion into the criminal justice process hinged on the response to
the question, "what is a prize fight?" Only when the truth of what constituted such an encounter was established could the law intervene. I am not
saying that "prize fighting" was discovered at a particular instance, but
that there was a need for, or will to, discovery. A desire to form a truth
that would submit violators to an apparatus of punishment and discipline.
Foucault (2000a) carefully set out how the will to truth constitutes objects
and subjects of discipline. Thus, law not only fashions the metaphors and
aphorisms that constitute the truth that is prize fighting, but also sets
the conditions of penalty. Judge Snider, who we will meet again later in
this chapter, explained that those found to be guilty of prize fighting were
liable to be punished with "imprisonment for a term not exceeding twelve
months and not less than three months, with or without hard labour."[4]
Thus, as Foucault has clearly articulated, "the exercise of power perpetually creates knowledge and, conversely, knowledge constantly induces
effects of power" (1980, 51–52).

During the early twentieth century, the particular standards and metaphors detailing what exactly constituted prize fighting lacked clarity.
What was considered prize fighting and boxing, a legal pastime that was
not only permissible but encouraged toward bolstering the nation through

the cultivation of manliness, was tremendously uncertain. Consider, for example, the following language employed by a *Globe* reporter:

> *The attention of the Attorney-General's Department having been called to the fact that a prize-fight between two professionals...was advertised to take place at Fort Erie on May 16, instructions were immediately sent to the Chief of Police to investigate...If a prize-fight is contemplated it will be stopped, but the regular boxing competition scheduled to take place at Fort Erie next week will not be interfered with.[5]*

At what moment does the regular boxing competition become a subject of and to law? Over what threshold does the event or occurrence need to pass to be entered into the criminal justice domain for prosecution and punishment? To this end, what *truth* needs to be established and who is required to do the truth-telling? I begin to address these important questions through the theoretical wisdom of Michel Foucault's (2000b) lecture series on "Truth and Juridical Forms" and his interview "Truth and Power."

In this chapter, I am not solely concerned with the formation and formulation of a law that accuses, but also with the performativity of the accusation—"a performance with effect" (Butler 1997, 7). Accusations not only say that some conduct is "out of joint" with contemporary standards, but that the performance has implications beyond the pronouncement of a future to come (Derrida 1993). Increasing numbers of scholars interested in elaborating a more nuanced understanding of law and its effects have engaged Judith Butler's (1997a) elaboration of performativity (MacGregor 2015; Passavant and Dean 2001; Race 2011; Schuster 1999). Ken Race, for example, in an article written about HIV and law states that "to ask about the performativity of the law is to ask a series of questions about whether and when the law does what it says" (2012, 330). In this way, law is not simply a noun referring only to what is codified. It has effects. Performative accusation is the keystone in the criminal justice arch. Entryways into the criminal justice nexus through accusation by police or other extra-legal officials are not simply the function of the identification of the guilty, but a "conventional bearing that interpolates and constitutes a subject" (Butler 1997a). As we will see, individuals accused of prize fighting are displaced by and situated within the discursive boundaries of the performatory accusation and thus subject to an uncertain future within the criminal justice process (Passavant and Dean 2001).

After an overview of these important works, and through an examination of several legal cases and newspaper reports from the early twentieth century, I highlight how prize fighting was fashioned in and by law and how those who were accused of this crime were entered into the criminal justice process.

Foucault, Truth, and the Juridical

In late May of 1973, Foucault delivered five lectures to an audience eager to hear him speak. The lecture series was held at the Pontifical Catholic University of Rio de Janeiro and translated for the third volume of *The Essential Works of Foucault (1954–1984)*, edited by Paul Rabinow and appropriately titled "Power" (2000b). In his 2013 discussion and reflection, Alan Hunt calls these lectures a "stimulating and original account of the place of law in modern society" (2013, 64). These lectures were not meant to provide an overarching and totalizing examination of the history of law, but rather "working hypotheses, with a view to a future work" (Foucault 2000b, 1). As far as I can discern, Foucault never harvested this potentially rich soil. His interlocutors are now left to this task. My intention is not to provide a detailed overview of the lectures delivered in Rio. Rather, I want to present some ideas that inform the following discussion and that might stimulate future investigations.

Foucault's first lecture in the series had a historical trajectory in the sense that he was exploring the following question: "How have domains of knowledge been formed on the basis of social practices?" (Foucault 2000b, 1). His objective in this session was to highlight how "social practices may engender domains of knowledge that not only bring new objects... to light, but also give rise to totally new forms of subject and subjects of knowledge" (Foucault 2000b, 2). That is, to examine how subjects and things become constituted and established through and in that which is juridical. Foucault (2000b) was convinced that what happens in and through the juridical is amongst the most important social practices employed toward purposefully establishing the truth about a thing or a subject, not in terms of true and false, but in relation to the formation of objects and subjects. Indeed, his objective was to show "how certain forms of truth can be defined" and to develop the general theme of "juridical forms and their evolution in the field of penal law as the generative locus for a given number of forms of truth" (Foucault 2000b, 4; see also Hunt 2013).

To this end, drawing on the work of Nietzsche, Foucault wanted to develop a historical examination of the politics of truth. For Foucault, knowledge is always a "strategic relation." It is never neutral, but rather creates things by subjecting them to, and carving them, via social practices like law. In this lecture series, then, Foucault intended to tackle "the problem of the formation of a certain number of domains of knowledge on the basis of the relation of force and the political relations in society" (Foucault 2000b, 15). The latter are fundamental to the development of Foucault's understanding of truth and truth relations.

Jumping ahead to the fourth lecture, we now see Foucault analyzing, much like he did in *Discipline and Punish* (1979), the emergence of the disciplinary society in the late eighteenth and early nineteenth centuries. In this discussion, he considers the "reform or reorganization of the judicial and penal systems in the different countries of Europe and the world" (Foucault 2000b, 52). But perhaps more importantly, he highlights how (amongst other items) "what forms of knowledge [*savoir*], types of knowledge [*connaissance*], and types of knowledge subject [*sujet de connaissance*] emerged, appearing on the basis of—and in the space of—the disciplinary society" (Foucault 2000b, 52). This is the problem I have set out for this chapter. How was the prize fighter, as a subject of law, formed? What knowledges and discourses were established that set conditions for his/her entry into the criminal justice system?

These lectures go some distance in helping us to see how and that Foucault was very interested in how law constitutes subjects through truth. He was convinced, as we have already seen, that power produces and creates subjects and things. Equally important is how truth underlies power and is produced in and through institutions like law (Foucault 2000a, 132). "'Truth' is...a system of ordered procedures for the production, regulation, distribution, circulation and operation of statements [and] is linked in a circular relation with systems of power" (Foucault 2000a, 133). Truth produces and establishes how we come to know and relate to the things in our world.

Law thus establishes the truth and produces the standards and subjects for entry into the criminal justice system and process. In the remainder of this chapter, I will demonstrate how truth as a collection of statements and aphorisms about prize fighting was fashioned by law and, as such, produced the prize fighter. Regulation pertaining to prize fighting, in other words, is connected to the organization of knowledge centred on this subject, but it is also a series of contemporary social and political processes. This is not to say that prize fighting is solely the artifact of law, but that the game of truth in which prize fighting is invested is linked to "games and institutions of power" (Foucault 1989, 445). For Foucault, games of truth are not about saying that nothing exists, but rather that it is "a question of knowing how madness, under the various definitions that have been given, was at a particular time integrated into an institutional field that constituted it as a mental illness" (Foucault 1989, 446). It is not, then, that we are interested in what is valid and counterfeit, but, rather, in the various definitions and qualities that have been assigned and give meaning to the category of prize fighting. Truth carves the entrance to law and being accused of prize fighting thus subjects offenders to the power of law.

It is imperative that we further elaborate, in the same instance, the performativity at play when the other is accused of prize fighting and thereby entered into the criminal justice network by actors delegated by the state. Allow me to set the stage. Two individuals are in a boxing ring, circling each other and looking for an opportunity to score a blow on the other. At some point in the proceedings, a police officer under orders from her/his supervisor jumps into the ring and calls a halt to the proceedings and accuses the combatants of prize fighting. From where do the orders emerge? On what or whose authority? And, more to the point, what are the effects of this performance? In her 1993 book *Bodies that Matter*, Butler maintains that "performative acts are forms of authoritative speech. Indeed, it is through the invocation of convention that the speech act of the judge derives its binding power" (225). Here, the officer has the authority to intervene as a condition of both the discursive constitution of prize fighting law, and the fact that she/he is legally bound to inscribe ritualistic and binding conventions in which the violation occurs. Whether or not the accusation will be taken seriously depends primarily on the "convention-ally sanctioned authority of the executor, and therefore upon the social and institutional context" (Boucher 2006, 126). Accusations of prize fighting and the subsequent entryway into criminal justice processes are constituted through discourse buttressed by institutional authority. Well formulated accusations are speech acts that emerge in the appropriate circumstances and are articulated by sanctioned officials.

Butler (1997a) deploys Althusser's (1974) concept of interpolation to maintain that it is the performance of the accusation that establishes the subject. Although Butler never weighed in on the topic of prize fighting, her work is instructive. When the police officer claims that what s/he observes is a prize fight, the accusation is the performative act. Such performances are reliant upon prior discursive assemblages, wherein the fabricated assemblage governs the subjects transgressing its boundaries. And here the performance of law is constituted by not only the language of law, but also the manner and subject of accusation, which interpolates the perceived wrong-doer (Butler 1997b). Accusing individuals of prize fighting enters them into the institution of law, which depends both on a prior enunciation of what that constitutes and an authority who performs the accusation. The accusation emerges through the performance of the officer in announcing that the conduct transgresses the law and registers and initiates future consequence. But it is the inaugural performance, a speech act, that accuses and serves as the conduit into the criminal justice process. Accusation, then, emerges as the "apparent effect of a performative act" (Butler 1997b, 11). Nevertheless, this entry into law made by its officials is informative to the extent that it foreshadows subsequent conditions and actions. A spectator mentioning that the scene they are witnessing is a prize fight has limited future implications for those in the ring. Butler states that not all performances "have the power to produce the effects or initiate a set of consequences" (1997b, 16). However, when the body performing the accusatory speech act is informed and sanctioned by the law, the accusation initializes an event horizon brought about by the discourse that gives meaning to the scene. For Butler, "the act 'works' in part because of the citational dimension of the speech act, the historicity of convention that exceeds and enables the moment of its enunciation" (1997b, 33).

The linguistic scene I have been laying out starts with subjects who, because of the stage upon which they are operating, possess a psychic disposition to be moved to respond to the official's accusation, much in the way of Althusser's (1974) person on the street who is hailed by a passing police officer (Butler 1997a). A passerby accusing two children arguing over a sandbox toy of prize fighting is not only disingenuous, but absurd. There would be no sound reason for such an accusation to be taken seriously by the children or the parents who are attempting to separate their children. Indeed, Butler maintains that, "if the one who delivers it [the accusation] does not author it, and the one who is marked by it is not described by it, then the workings of interpolative power exceed the subjects constituted by its terms, and the subjects so constituted exceed the interpellation by which they are animated" (1997b, 34). Effectiveness of the performatory accusation relies on the presence of specific and relevant circumstances, actors, psychic dispositions, conditions, and environments that frame the scene in which the accusation is inserted. The accusation of prize fighting by state officials, then, constitutes and fixes its subject for entryway into the criminal justice process.

Law, Truth, and Prize Fighting

In the early twentieth century, the law established that a prize fight was "an encounter or fight with fists or hands between two persons who have met for such purposes by previous arrangements made for them."[6] Understandably, citizens and criminal justice officials found this conception frustratingly vague and sweeping. It provided very little guidance as to *what* exactly was being created and governed. As it stood, this understanding could have rendered all combative sports, including sparring in boxing gyms, illegal throughout Canada. However, as we will see later, the politicians and legal authorities of the day were interested in regulating something altogether different.

Sparring is a significant and fundamental part of training for boxers. Pugilists employ this form of training to improve their timing, hone new techniques, and work out new positions and footwork in a "live" environment—though the practice is not limited to these. Although the intensity involved in sparring is most often scaled back, these sessions often descend into more intense encounters where participants get physically injured. Bloody noses and black eyes are common sights around many boxing clubs. Strict application of the Criminal Code could have thus made sparring illegal.

The question of what constitutes a prize fight, or what elements differentiate such an encounter from sparring or a mere "exhibition," was front and centre in the 1911 case of *R. v. Wildfong and Lang.* This case was contested in the first division court of Wentworth, Ontario, and came to police attention when the Hamilton Bowling and Athletic Club employed eight skilled boxers to give what they called a "boxing exhibition" to its members. Those attending the exhibition paid a small entry fee from which the pugilists were to be compensated. For the audiences' entertainment and education, Mr. M.M. Robinson, a club member, arranged for four bouts between boxers of varying levels of skill and experience. The first three matches went off without incident, but the fourth was stopped even before any punches were thrown, because,

*the chief of police, acting on instructions from some person whom he
saw fit to obey, announced some days before the time fixed for the
event that he would arrest these men at once on their appearance. It
was thereupon arranged that these men should appear on the stage
ready to give their exhibition, and be then arrested.*[7]

The fighters were subject to the law, not for what they had done, but
for what they had agreed to do—to fight. The ten-round affair, 6-ounce
gloves, and the fact that the combatants were more than "ordinarily
skilled in the science and [we]re paid to give scientific boxing exhibitions"
provided the police sufficient evidence that this was going to be more than
a mere exhibition of boxing—it would be a fight.[8] The question for Judge
Snider, who presided over the case, came down to this: "is a 'boxing exhibition' a 'prize fight' within the meaning of the Code?" He first conceded
that there did not have to be a prize offered or won in order to violate
the prize fighting section of the code. Snider noted that, "in the common
acceptance of the words 'prize fight' it would mean a 'fight' for a prize, but
there needs to be no prize to constitute an offence."[9]

Let us more fully examine the language of the law, which will help
determine the threshold or entryway for and to the law and penality.
When we look further, we see that there is an additional requirement,
that is, there must be an encounter or fight. Snider was convinced that
the requirement of an "encounter" between bodies was self-evident and
unnecessary. Since any time novice boxers meet in the gym to train there
is an encounter, but not a violation of the law, he was of the mind that
this was a meaningless distinction. For him, the whole matter came down
to "looking on at two persons having an engagement" and determining
"whether or not it was a 'fight.'"[10] But what elements and conditions
would constitute a fight?

In evidence, the deputy chief of police, who was touted as having much
experience in these matters, suggested that there is definitely a "distinction between a 'prize fight' and a 'boxing exhibition'—that one is blows,
the other is simply scientific boxing."[11] An obvious attempt is being made

in this case to distinguish between fighting and boxing. But *R. v. Wildfong and Lang* was not the first occasion where legal officials gestured toward distinguishing between what might be constituted as a prize fight and sparring. Snider was following the precedent set in the case of *R. v. Orton* [1878], where the trial judge found that: "A mere exhibition of skill in sparring is not illegal. If, however, the parties meet intending to fight till one gives in from exhaustion or from injury received, it is a fight and a breach of law."[12] In the *Orton* case, the lawyers involved paraded the bloodied gloves used by the combatants in front of the jury, who concluded that "although the appearance was of an organized boxing match, such was the severity and intensity of the blows that the nature of the fight clearly went beyond that which would *normally be expected* of a gloved sparring exhibition of fixed duration."[13]

Discerning what would be normally expected goes some way in helping to understand what characteristics or qualities judges like Snider employed in the game of truth that solidified the prize fighting prohibition. What other qualities or metaphors were employed to this end? What other standards provided evidence that an event was more than a mere exhibition or sparring match? In 1912, Toronto Police, with the aid of the morality squad, accused James Fitzgerald of promoting a prize fight. On January 17th, 1500 spectators paid the $2 admission fee to watch the event that was held at the Riverdale arena in Toronto. According to the newspaper report of the court case, the Crown "contended that the sole object of the contestants was to knock the other out" and that the matches were "more like a barroom fray" than a sparring match or exhibition.[14]

In sparring, like in football, lacrosse, and hockey, the intention is not to maim or injure. Rather, honing one's skills or, in the case of the exhibition, showcasing expertise is its objective. According to early twentieth-century legal officials, the word "fight" evidences and is founded upon a much different truth. Whereas sparring is conducted toward a creative end (developing skill and fostering acceptable masculinity), fighting finds its end in the destruction of the other. Snider concluded that, in a prize fight, each individual's primary purpose is to "so injure the other that he [sic] cannot or will not continue the contest."[15]

In the case of *Steele v. Maber* [1901], the event was advertised as a "Grand Athletic Exhibition between 'Shadow Maber,' champion of Canada" and William Henessey of Boston. The bout was held on March 20, 1900, in a public hall in Farnham on a roped-in platform. After the combatants were introduced by the referee, Maber proclaimed to the audience that he would "knock this gentleman out in fifteen rounds or forfeit his money."[16] After a relatively pedestrian first round, true to his word, Maber knocked Henessey down in the second. The latter lay "moaning and twisting as if in great pain," while Maber played to the audience and boasted that he would "knock him out" should he get to his feet. While Henessey was able to continue to fight, the bout soon came to a violent conclusion. In the third round, Maber made good on his promise and knocked Henessey out cold. The latter was subsequently carried away from the ring on a stretcher. In this instance, there was no pretense to an exhibition or sparring demonstration. No attempt was made during the bout to count points. Magistrate Mulvena remarked in his ruling that "it was merely, first, a knock down, and then a knock out" and sentenced Maber to "3 months in jail at hard labor."[17]

Entry into the criminal justice nexus was predicated on coordinating and tallying the event with the attributes of what had been established as a prize fight. To this point, we have seen that this meant the match was akin to a "barroom fray," featured "blows," and was severe, intense, and at variance with what would normally be expected. In his fourth lecture in Rio, Foucault argued that law must "represent what is useful for society" (Foucault 2000b, 53). Through law and by shunting conduct deemed offensive into the criminal justice process, society is inter alia defining what it tolerates and what it disavows. Foucault maintained that law "defines as reprehensible that which is harmful to society, thus defining, by negation, what is useful to it" (Foucault 2000b, 53).

We begin to get an even more acute sense of what legal authorities were attempting to negate and to produce when we return to the case of *R. v. Wildfong and Lang*. In this case, Judge Snider was very clear that it was not the roughness of the sport, or the potential for someone to be knocked unconscious that was at issue for him or legal authorities. Snider noted, following the deputy police chief, that in sparring someone may be knocked out, but that this would be "accidental and not intentional."[18] He conceded that hockey, football, and lacrosse are similarly rough sports, but are not the subject of law. Players may be knocked out from a body check in hockey or may be seriously injured from a slash across the arms in lacrosse. For Snider and the legal authorities of the day avowed that there was a significant difference between prize fighting and these mainstream sports. He was convinced that in the latter sports injuries are incidental, rather than the very intention of the undertaking. Mere intensity or roughness were not what was at issue. In his decision, Snider insisted that tough sports were fundamental to fostering manliness and virility in young men and boys, and was reticent to legislate against such dangerous sports. He concluded his decision by citing Bramwell's contention that: "I have no doubt but that the game was in any circumstances a rough one, but I am unwilling to decry the manly sports of this country."[19]

Judges, police, and magistrates in the early twentieth century were anxious to suppress prize fighting, but were reticent to abolish every boxing encounter. They were very clear that boxing had its place amongst men in the developing nation (Weiner 2004). Judge Fitzpatrick, for example, was cited in the *Dawson Record* in 1903 as saying he would not be "stampeded into doing away with these honest manly contests with gloves...which are conducive to a great deal of good to those who use them properly."[20] Because they purportedly developed character and manliness in those who participated, sparring and exhibitions in boxing were not only to be tolerated, but encouraged.

In the July 29, 1903 edition of *The Globe*, the editor was adamant that prize fighting should be abolished since its character is "brutal and brutal-izing."[21] However, they were insistent that boxing and sparring should be preserved. To wit, they argued that "no reasonable objection can be offered to 'honest, *manly* contests with gloves, such as take place every day in gymnasiums.'"[22] At the turn of the twentieth century, combative training between males under controlled circumstances was seen to fashion appropriate forms of masculinity and manliness—especially for men of the working classes. Sparring encouraged the characteristics that *fin de siècle* Canadians valued and aimed to foster in men. Prize fighting, by contrast, represented the underbelly of society and the extreme hegemonic masculine qualities of men (Weiner 2004). Toward fabricating acceptable masculinity, Canadian legal officials eschewed the violence and brutality they associated with prize fighting as being harmful to not only young men, but to the nation.

Sparring and boxing forged men, whereas prize fighting, by contrast, was not only injurious to the individual, but ruinous of the developing nation. In the same article, the editor praised the House of Commons for amending the Criminal Code definition of prize fighting and "making contests 'with or without gloves' against the law."[23] Significant in this distinction is that this modification (with or without gloves) held the potential to open the category of prize fighting to a new class of combatant. Here I am referring to those trained in judo, catch-as-catch-can wrestling, and jiu-jitsu, who travelled the world giving exhibitions of their skill and earning money through demonstrations of their abilities against local toughs who were sufficiently bold as to accept their challenge. For example, Mitsuyo Maeda, who famously taught the founder of Brazilian Jiu-Jitsu, Carlos Gracie, the intricacies of Japanese Jiu-Jitsu, travelled the globe conducting exhibitions and fighting for money against men who were trained in a variety of martial arts, including boxing. As far as I can discern, he was never convicted of prize fighting despite the intensity and severity of his matches.

An exhibition akin to that in which Maeda would have participated was held in Hamilton, Ontario, on June 8, 1907, without incident or legal intervention. S. Karp and Charles Conkle agreed to give:

an exhibition of jiu-jitsu...before a fair sized audience. It was agreed
that the men should continue until one gave up...After three quarters of
an hour of very rough work, Karp cried quits and Conkle was declared
the winner. When they started they wore kimonos [similar to a karate
gi], which were in a short time torn to shreds. The men tried hard to

choke each other with the torn kimonos...Conkle several times threw
Karp from the platform and, after one of these exhibitions, Karp
complained that his ankle was injured.[24]

This description echoes the qualities of prize fighting that legal officials abhorred, including its severity, intensity, bearing of a striking resemblance to a barroom fray, and that it was conducted without gloves and at odds with what was normally expected. Despite being publicized in the newspapers of the day, this event was ignored by legal officials and allowed to continue untouched by law. Aficionados of contemporary MMA would be quick to point out the eerie similarities between what is being described here and inaugural events in their sport. Until 2013, when the House of Commons passed Bill S-209, MMA was (technically) illegal across Canada. However, unlike the provincial authorities in the case of *R. v. Jay Chang*, early twentieth-century criminal justice officials looked the other way.

Canadian legal experts had little difficulty accepting this kind of exhibition, and did not agonize over the deleterious influence of jiu-jitsu on the nation or its young males. However, when it came to prize fighting, they were not nearly so reticent or apprehensive. For example, on July 26, 1904, what *The Globe* deemed a "real prize fight" was promoted and ensued in Fort Erie, Ontario.[25] Fort Erie, for those unacquainted with the geography of Southern Ontario, is located on the Niagara River adjacent from Buffalo, New York. Proximity made Fort Erie attractive to American promoters, in whose country prize fighting was strictly illegal save for a few select municipalities. One newspaper report expressed the citizens' worry that the town was "becoming the red light district of Buffalo."[26]

Many Canadians abhorred prize fighting. A *Globe* commentator referred to such events as a "relic of Canadian barbarism, and it is not gratifying to our national self-respect."[27] So-called upstanding citizens connected it with savagery and the worst characters of society—many of whom, they were certain, were American. American prize fighting fans and promoters coming to Canada to indulge their favourite pastime has a long history. Although prize fighting was prohibited under Canadian law, many American enthusiasts were under the impression that the law was not strictly enforced. One late nineteenth-century commentator on the subject bemoaned the fact that "among the pseudo-sporting classes in American cities," in order to "indulge in their amusements...they had nothing to do but to cross the line in force and set at defiance Canadian laws and the Canadian authority."[28] These early observers were convinced that turning a blind eye to these bouts was a blight on the national character. For example, *The Globe* opined, "if civilization in this country has not advanced beyond the stage in which alien prize-fighting is countenanced and protected, let us cease talking about Canadian nationhood and go back to learn some of the primary lessons in fundamental morality and social dignity."[29]

Important in this analysis is how we once again witness the productive force of law as a strategic relation. Regulation of prize fighting not only negates and says no, but in the effort cultivates the image of the developing nation. By defining what was opposed to the national character—the savagery, gambling, and brutality they associated with prize fighting—and what should therefore be suppressed through legal intervention, these commentators and the legal authorities that enforced the prize fighting prohibition were in the same instance setting out what was advantageous to the social world.

In 1904, the main event in Fort Erie pitted Kid Fredericks against Curley Supples, who were reportedly evenly matched and vaunted for their ability to "knock men senseless." Even though, as the *Globe* reporter noted, these were not heavyweights in the truest sense of the term, he was certain that the "contest was intended as a prize fight pure and simple." The writer was convinced that the number of rounds for which the bout was scheduled (twenty), and the proclivity of the combatants in rendering opponents unconscious provided sufficient evidence that this was to be "practically a fight to the finish." Despite early warnings and evidence that it might be something other than a sparring demonstration, the fight was allowed to commence. According to *The Globe*:

The men began sparring smartly, Supples being the aggressor, and
Fredericks...received a short arm blow in the fall and appeared to be
dazed, and raising his gloved hands shielded his face from the blows
that Supples began to rain in on him, and although the fight had gone
only thirty seconds it looked as if a knockout would come, when a little
man climbed through the ropes, and passing before the referee, stepped
between the men and stopped Supples in the moment of his victory.[30]

Much to the dismay of the crowd and the victor, Inspector William Greer
of Toronto (who was the little man referred to above) was in attendance
on the orders of the Ontario attorney general and had been instructed to
"stop the fight, if fight there was," which he carried out.[31] Greer, by stepping in and halting the bout, employed the standards of truth contained in
the prize fighting prohibition to disavow and accuse the other of violating
the law. His proclamation is constitutive of the truth within the confines
of the law, which is performed for an authority. The act of stepping
between Supples and Fredericks interpolated the subjects and defined the
conduct as conduct that runs counter to law.

Truth imbricated in the prize fighting law informed Greer's accusatory performance. He had been instructed by an authority to step in and
halt the event should it coincide with the verity of prize fighting. Calling
a halt to the event was an accusatory act that interpolated the fighters as
those who had transgressed the law. Greer's performance was sanctioned
by a conventional authority and relied on the prior discursive assemblage
as existing internal to the prohibition and thus as subject to sanction.
Stepping in marks the moment of accusation as it halts the proceedings and impels the subjects to respond to the address (Althusser 1974).
Accusations of this sort interpolate the subject as one to whom the address
applies, but, as Butler maintains, "perhaps most important to consider is
that the voice is implicated in a notion of sovereign power, power figured
as emanating from a subject, activated in a voice, whose effects appear to
be the magical effects of that voice. In other words, power is understood
on the model of the divine power of naming, where to utter is to create the

effect uttered" (1997b, 32–33). Accusation, then, materializes through the performance of the authority recognizing and halting the act. What Greer accomplished in his accusatory performance was to constitute the boxers as legal subjects (because their conduct aligned with the prohibition) and pave the way for their entryway into the punitive criminal justice state.

Greer's intervention is instructive for what it reveals about the performativity of law, truth, and fighting. Although Canadian legal officials encouraged boxing for developing the nation and masculinity, they abhorred the brutality and destruction associated with prize fighting. A fight to the finish, where one individual was no longer physically able to continue, represented the wretchedness of the nation and was not only to be abhorred, but negated. At the same time, and as we have seen, the regime of truth invested in prize fighting was produced in and through law, which manifested and buoyed what was valuable for the social world. Bouts like the one between Supples and Fredricks were entered into the Canadian criminal justice system not only because their event countered appropriate *fin de siècle* masculinity and the national character, but also because their conduct dovetailed with the metaphors and standards associated with—the truth of—prize fighting prohibitions.

Conclusion

Two months later, the Fort Erie group was back and promoting what they were certain was a "strictly amateur boxing tournament" that boasted twenty matches.[32] Inspector Greer was once again on hand to enforce the law and step in to "prevent slugging."[33] On this occasion, he was accompanied by seven members of the provincial police whose aggregated weight was reported by *The Globe* to be 1680 pounds. *The Globe* reporter recounted that Inspector Greer stopped four matches by indicating to the referee to stop the fights because they had lapsed from "science into slugging." Another bout was called a draw when Greer passed word to the referee to "stop the fight because *it was clearly moving in the direction of becoming illegal.*"[34]

Through his accusatory performance, Greer brought law into force, and through this game of truth, fashioned an entryway for the combatants into law and its regime of punishment. Interrupting the event to invoke the law thereby revealed the truth of the law and the definitions, metaphors, and qualities that had been assigned and gave meaning to the category of prize fighting. The performative force of his accusation depended on this truth and thereby affirmed the conduct of combatants as being the subject of and subject to law.

Witnessed in such an address of the other is the affirmation of the subject as one whose conduct coordinates with the qualities of the prohibition against prize fighting, and, in the same instance, the other is affirmed as a subject of law. When Greer intruded into the space of the match some*thing* was being performed for an authority. Accusing combatants is a form of address for someone who is other and who is in authority. Through this accusatory performance, Greer entered the offenders into the criminal justice process, which has the final say in the matter.

Whatever the ultimate outcome of the trials, the cases discussed here reveal law's Janus face. On the one side, through prohibition, it negates and disavows individual conduct. On the other, law is a nodal point through which a regime of truth determines and produces conduct that Canadian society values and holds in high regard. Truth that is produced through and spawns law is a strategic relation that oscillates between renunciation and advocacy, between repudiation and promotion, and that serves as the entryway into the criminal justice system.

Notes

1. "Promoter Found Guilty," CBC News, New Brunswick, August 28, 2003.
2. R. v. Chang, [August 22, 2003], New Brunswick Provincial Court, para. 7.
3. I use the term "relative" here because section 83 of the code is still not exact and clear as to the extent to which Muai Thai kickboxing and kickboxing are permissible.
4. R. v. Wilfong and Lang, [January 1, 1911], Ontario Court of Justice (General Division), s. 6.

5. "Must be no Prize Fight: Attorney General's Department Takes Steps to Prevent Advertised Combat," *The Globe*, May 12, 1904.

6. Steele v. Maber, [April 15, 1901], Magistrate's Court, District of Bedford, Quebec.

7. R. v. Wilfong and Lang, para. 253, Ontario Court of Justice (General Division), para. 253.

8. Ibid.

9. Ibid.

10. Ibid.

11. Ibid.

12. R. v. Orton, [1878], Cox Criminal Cases, para. 227, as cited in Anderson 2014, 63.

13. R. v. Orton, para. 226, as cited in Anderson 2014; emphasis added.

14. "Boxing Contest a Prize Fight," *The Globe*, January 30, 1912.

15. R. v. Wildfong and Lang, para. 256; see also R. v. Littlejohn, [September 13, 1904], St. John County Court, N.B.

16. Steele v. Maber, s. 5., Magistrate's Court, District of Bedford, Quebec, s. 5.

17. Ibid., s. 6 and s. 15.

18. R. v. Wildfong and Lang, para. 255.

19. Ibid.

20. "Canada May Stop Prize Fights," *The Dawson Record*, August 12, 1903.

21. "Prize Fighting and Parliament," *The Globe*, July 29, 1903.

22. Ibid.; emphasis added.

23. Ibid., 6.

24. "Wrestling: Rough and Tumble Exhibition," *The Globe*, June 8, 1907.

25. "Fort Erie Prize Fight Stopped," *The Globe*, July 26, 1904.

26. Ibid.

27. "Prize Fighting in Canada," *The Globe*, July 14, 1903.

28. "The Baffled Prize Fighters," *The Globe*, May 19, 1880.

29. "Prize Fighting in Canada."

30. "Fort Erie Prize Fight Stopped." *The Globe*, July 26, 1904.

31. Ibid.

32. "No Prize Fighting: Tame Boxing Bouts Pulled Off at Fort Erie," *The Globe*, September 5, 1904.

33. Ibid.

34. Ibid.; emphasis added.

References

Althusser, Louis. 1974. *Ideology and Ideological State Apparatuses*. London: Verso.

Anderson, Jack. 2014. "The Right to a Fair Fight: Sporting Lessons on Consensual Harm." *New Criminal Law Review* 17 (1): 55–75.

Boucher, Geoff. 2006. "The Politics of Performativity: A Critique of Judith Butler." *Parrhesia* 1 (1): 112–41.

Butler, Judith. 1997a. *The Psychic Life of Power*. Stanford: Stanford University Press.

———. 1997b. *Excitable Speech: A Politics of the Performative*. New York: Routledge.

Foucault, Michel. 2000a. "Truth and Power." *Power: Essential Works of Foucault 1954–1984*. Edited by Paul Rabinow. New York: The New Press.

———. 2000b. "Truth and Juridical Forms." *Power: Essential Works of Foucault 1954–1984*. Edited by Paul Rabinow. New York: The New Press.

———. 1989. "Ethics of the Concern for Self." *Foucault Live: Collected Interviews, 1961–1984*. Edited by Sylvere Lotringer. New York: Semioext(e).

———. 1980. "Prison Talk." *Power/Knowledge: Selected Interviews and Other Writings (1972–1977)*. Edited by Colin Gordon. New York: Pantheon Books.

Hunt, Alan. 2013. "Encounters with Juridical Assemblages: Reflections on Foucault, Law and the Juridical." In *Re-Reading Foucault: On Law, Power and Rights*, edited by Ben Golder, 64–84. New York: Routledge.

MacGregor, Casimir. 2015. "The Right to Life: Human Life, Bio-Power and the Performativity of Law." *Journal of Sociology* 51 (1): 47–62.

Passavant, Paul, and Jodi Dean. 2001. "Laws and Societies." *Constellations* 8 (3): 376–89.

Race, Ken. 2012. "Framing Responsibility: HIV, Biomedical Prevention and the Performativity of Law." *Bioethical Inquiry* 9 (3): 327–38.

———. 2011. "Drug Effects, Performativity and the Law." *International Journal of Drug Policy* 22 (4): 410–12.

Schuster, Heather. 1999. "Reproduction and the State: Between Bodily Performance and Legal Performativity." *Angelaki: Journal of the Theoretical Humanities* 4 (1): 189–206.

Weiner, Martin. 2004. *Men of Blood: Violence, Manliness and Criminal Justice in Victorian England*. Edinburgh: Cambridge University Press.

Cases

R. v. Chang [August 22, 2003] New Brunswick Provincial Court.

R. v. Littlejohn [September 13, 1904] St. John County Court, N.B.

R. v. Orton [1878] Cox Criminal Cases.

R. v. Wildfong and Lang [January 1, 1911] Ontario Court of Justice (General Division).

Steele v. Maber [April 15, 1901] Magistrate's Court, District of Bedford. Quebec.

IMPRISONED AT LARGE

The Perpetual State of Accusation

DALE A. BALLUCCI

CHANGES IN CRIMINAL IDENTIFICATION technologies, and strategies to monitor offenders are recurring themes in both the contemporary
and historical literature on governance. Scholars have documented shifts
in state practices used to maintain social order through the regulation of
those that do not adhere to the status quo (Garland 2001; Haggerty and
Ericson 2000; O'Malley 2004; Pavlich 2007; Simon 2007). Risk assessment
techniques, for example, reflect a move toward monitoring not only those
that violate norms, rules, and laws, but also those with the potential for
future criminality. The precautionary nature of risk assessment witnessed
in the 1990s continues to flourish and expand. Some scholars describe
the current governing regime as a form of "threat control" (Jochelson,
Kramar, and Doerksen 2014). Under this regime, offenders do not need to
actually commit a crime, but can instead be surveilled for merely having
the potential to commit a crime. This significantly alters the entryways to
crime control, and the kinds of accusatorial techniques used to target new
subjects of such regulation.

The latter operate more and more through the construction of fluid
categories and individual identities, facilitated by criminal identification
techniques that provide justification for crime control initiatives. Several

commentators have drawn attention to various aspects of such changes (see Diab 2011; Haggerty 2009; Zedner 2009). What is less documented, however, are empirical practices of state agency initiatives that operate in light of what can be described as the "policing of possibility." Moreover, few show how state programs identify and facilitate offenders' entry into the criminal justice system. Here, I contribute to this lacuna by examining a set of policing practices that target the potentiality for crime, showing how this changes the way offenders enter and re-enter an altering criminal justice system. My case example provides further support that current governing practices focus on managing the possibility of crime and criminality (see Haggerty 2009; Jochelson et al. 2014), and details one of the many ways that offenders enter and re-enter the criminal justice system, placing them in what I call a perpetual state of accusation.

In this chapter, using a case study approach, I discuss the operational process and objectives of a target offender management system in a Canadian province that identifies "prolific" (or "chronic") offenders. The process of identifying and managing prolific offenders, as with pre-existing criminal identification initiatives, is rooted in discourses of neutrality and objectivity. As such, identifying prolific offenders involves crime analysts who extract and make sense of individuals' information generated from police databases. These approaches operate on the expectation of a person's future criminality (based on their criminal histories), and justify monitoring would-be re-offenders prior to an actual offence occurring. Hence, the foundation of the prolific offender initiative reflects a pre-crime agenda that justifies policing the possibility of criminality. Describing these strategies also reveals how entryways into the criminal justice system can be created. I not only show how prolific offender programs are viewed as a legitimate form of governing offenders that have not committed a crime, but also how they increase the potential for individuals to enter into the criminal justice system. I show, and problematize, the fact that contemporary practices, embraced by prolific offender initiatives, are founded on the dominant typology of the criminal. The label of "prolific" not only generates suspicion of future criminality, but also justifies surveillance practices' and the "hegemonic hold of criminal identification" (Pavlich 2009, 183). An empirical case study reveals actual governing practices, effects, and their respective power-knowledge relationships (Ratner 2006). These select offenders remain the subject of inquiry and live under the gaze of the state well after release. To this end, I argue that prolific offender programs effectively reproduce and sustain criminal identities, placing individuals in a state of perpetual accusation.

I have organized the chapter into three sections. In the first section, I briefly discuss the long-standing practice of criminal identification as a mechanism to populate entryways to criminal justice. This highlights the operational premise of criminal identification, providing a context for prolific offender programs. In the second portion of this chapter, I analyze the interviews from an empirical case study that examines how prolific offenders are identified in a Canadian province. With this data in mind, I discuss the importance of crime analysts as gatekeepers, as well as the objectives and effects of the label "prolific" being used for offenders. In particular, I illustrate that being "prolific" creates the conditions for a perpetual state of accusation and an increased probability of "re-entry" into the criminal justice system.

Identifying "Criminals" at Crime Control Entryways

Several scholars illustrate the relevance and impact of criminal identification and bio-criminality theories (Carrier and Walby 2015; Pavlich 2009). Some of the most exemplary historical figures in the field of criminal identification include Bertillon (1877), Galton (1977), and Lombroso (2006). Although different, these approaches are all premised on the notion that physical, biological, or genetic characteristics can identify who is most likely to be a criminal. Bertillon's writings in the 1870s paved the way for criminal identification thinking in his study to determine the distinct physical features of criminals. The proliferation of Bertillon's work is evidenced in its initial implementation in France (Pavlich 2009) and other parts of the world (Rhodes 1968), as well as in contemporary policing practices (Cole 2001;

Saferstein 2004; Sengoopta 2003). Galton, also renowned for his work on criminal identification, developed a "generic type." Like Bertillon, Galton incorporated photography in order to capture the physical details of his subjects to better predict who is most likely to engage in criminal activity. Galton's work echoed Lombroso's conception of "atavism" that also further supported the development of a nineteenth-century figure: the habitual offender. These key figures introduced and developed a form of thinking about how to manage and identify offenders that remains present in contemporary society.

The attention to physical or biological characteristics in the field of criminology is not simply an idea of the past. Today, we continue to see scholarship that aims to bridge these two fields. The concept of "cross fertilization" (Carrier and Walby 2015) has led to heated debates in the literature concerning the role of biology in both understanding and devising solutions to criminality. Walsh and Wright (2015), for example, assert that a very clear link exists between human beings and biological nature. Wright (2009) argues that the complex relationship between the environment and the individual is unpacked though the lens of a biosocial approach. In contrast to this view, Carrier and Walby (2015) write that biosocial criminology embraces a limited view of the Lombrosian conception of the criminal. The existence of these debates further shows the vibrancy of criminal identification in various venues (Garland 1985; Spencer and Fitzgerald 2015). Although today there is a move away from primarily focusing on biological factors in criminal identification, the late nineteenth and early twentieth centuries' quest to use scientific methods to study and prevent crime and criminality has persisted (Garland 1985).

Criminal identification as a form of crime control was largely developed around the creation of typologies. Risk assessment tools exemplify how the imputed characteristics of particular offenders licenses the justification of particular control mechanisms. Such initiatives have a widespread appeal. Fears amongst the general public often decrease with an increase in the use of technology and science, which have enjoyed a long-standing reputation as a means by which offenders can be identified and truths discerned. As Hulsman (1986) reminds us, when it comes to crime reduction, both reform and policy need to fit within the limits of what "public opinion" deems acceptable. The need for science to deal with rising crime rates and public fear (Radzinowicz and Hood 1990) is justified under the rubric of crime reduction and public safety. The implementation of prolific offender programs reflects such reasoning. The programs in this case study, similar to other programs in Canadian police agencies, were implemented under the crime prevention strategy (Interviews).[1] For police, employing criminal identification practices (such as identifying prolific offenders) rooted in objectivity and (loosely defined) scientific methods, reflects a non-partisan, objective practice that effectively assists in their primary goal—crime reduction.

Although modified, the principles that underlie criminal identification remain today, and support a policing the possibility of crime agenda. Criminal identification and monitoring techniques operate by assessing individual characteristics and histories. Such knowledge is used to both identify and manage offenders, reinforcing the notion that criminality is an individual problem, and may facilitate conditions for governing through crime (Simon 2006); but it also changes crime control entryways by nurturing a context where potential offenders confront a perpetual state of accusation. This kind of accusation, however, does not simply involve a public allegation. Instead, the conditions for perpetual accusation assume that criminality is an individual problem, such that a person's past actions are framed in such a way as to justify the suspicion that they should be considered irredeemable recidivists. Zedner's (2009) concept of pre-crime offers support for this claim. Features of a pre-crime society include an increase in practices that pursue security to reduce criminal activity. The creation of a prolific offender program reflects a preventive approach to crime control aimed at regulating the threat of criminality. It is this very objective that provides the conditions for groups of offenders to remain in a perpetual state of accusation.

Problematizing the Identification of Prolific Offenders

Criminal identification methods rely on the classical formulation of the criminal—that offenders choose to engage in criminal behaviour and should therefore be punished to reduce recidivism and increase public safety. In opposition to this perspective is the work of several scholars who challenge the idea that the individual should be the main object of inquiry to understand criminality. Nietzsche (1901, 1968), for example, examined crime as a complex problem that can only be understood in relation to the multifaceted aspects of social life. He is not alone. Drawing from his work, Pavlich problematizes responding to criminality as the product of individual actions. Specifically, he brings our attention to the differences between "being" and "becoming" a criminal in his work on the processes of accusation (Pavlich 2007). Pavlich argues that the creation of the criminal is a product of political alliances and strategies that are solidified in various governing apparatuses such as law and policing practices. A central tenant in this work is to highlight the importance of understanding how modern approaches to crime are rooted in the politics of exclusion. As Pavlich reminds us, "the reality of crime is also very much the product of other cultural practices that organize signs: media portrayal, television dramas, crime fiction, electioneering, and just plain gossip" (2000, 142).

By examining the process of accusation, the limitation to modern criminal identification techniques (Pavlich 2000), techniques of governance, and their presumptions and limitations are made evident. The process of accusation

> creates other identities from a given present, and so consolidates the limits of patterns of associations. By creating excluded subjects, it is involved in supporting specific boundaries around given collective identity formations. Through its exertions of other news, accusation helps to support a given status quo. (Pavlich 2000, 144)

Accusation involves a process of judgment with an actionable outcome. It operates using techniques that exclude and differentiate subjects. A successful accusation involves the deployment of objective techniques that creates typologies, which implies that the category of criminal pre-exists. Examining this process demonstrates that defining an offender as prolific involves a process of "becoming" that is produced through various power relations, rather than an ontological discovery revealed by objective forms of assessment. This is especially so with prolific offenders. An empirical examination of accusation demonstrates the limitations of these forms of governance, particularly how they isolate the individual and de-politicize crime (Pavlich 2007). Building on this work, my analysis of the assumptions and objectives of prolific offender typology provides an empirical example of the accusation process that highlights how offenders remain an object of inquiry and the consequences of this practice.

Critical criminologists continue to make the claim that the homogenization of "the criminal" through typologies, risk tools, and other scientific forms of objectification presents particular limitations. The most long-standing, and arguably the most important, of these arguments is the idea that human beings are complex (Hulsman 1986; Pavlich 2000; Taylor et al. 1973). As simple as this argument may seem, some policing initiatives do not necessarily reflect such sentiments. Prolific offender programs rely on technology and are founded on "knowing" the individual in order to manage their risks. Risk-based analysis, for example, which is the foundation of several management regimes, is founded on the premise that similarities exist between aggregate groups to the point where individuals can be represented as sums of the parts. It also assumes that characteristics and histories are significant indicators of future activities. Techniques to identify sex offenders, violent offenders (Spencer 2009), and, as I will show below, prolific offenders, are rooted in similar ideas. The ways by which science and technology (including statistics) are used in correctional management reduce the problem of criminality to an individual level and continuously depoliticize crime (Hulsman 1986). Focusing solely on the individual's characteristics, outside of his/her environment, displaces the power-knowledge relations that make up the criminal (Pavlich 2009) and reproduces the socio-political status quo.

A Case Study

In the following sections, I discuss the objectives and features of prolific offender programs to show how offenders are identified, and specifically, how this process creates what I call a perpetual state of accusation at changing entryways to crime control. These arguments are made using research from a Canadian case study on prolific offender programs. I use interview data gathered from a case study to understand the broad role of crime analysts and prolific offender management techniques and strategies. I draw on this data, derived from interviews with crime analysts in one Canadian province, to learn how prolific offenders are defined and managed. In an effort to understand the management process, I interviewed all of the crime analysts tasked with determining which offenders are deemed prolific. I also interviewed administrators of the units who were responsible for overseeing, designing, and implementing these programs. Semi-structured interview data were gathered over several months in 2013. Although several themes and topics were discussed in these interviews, for this chapter, I focus on those that illuminate the objectives and assumptions in the process of identifying and managing prolific offenders.

Prolific Offender Ideology and Typology

Prolific offenders by definition are known to the police and the criminal justice system. Offenders that are potentially eligible to be labelled prolific are actively involved in the criminal justice system and some also have long criminal histories. These characteristics are central to the typology of prolific offenders and illustrate how such a label creates a perpetual state of accusation. The assumptions upon which this typology are built create conditions and justifications for making an offender known within the system, and justify increased supervision and monitoring.

Creating a typology of a prolific offender is challenging, and scholars have shown that defining the characteristics of a prolific offender is rife with complexities and ambiguities (Ballucci n.d.; Blokland, Nagin, and Nieuwbeerta 2005). Yet, one consistent characteristic remains: the criminal activity of these offenders accounts for over half of all crimes committed (Mawby and Worrall 2004; Skardhamar 2009; Wolfgang, Figlio, and Sellin 1972). Interviewees, when asked how they defined a prolific offender, had several responses that, although thematically consistent, were often equally vague. Analysts described prolific offenders as those that "are the most [criminally] active," "have the most calls for service," or "for whom crime is a way of life" (Interviews). In more general terms, this group is "known to police," has a "long criminal history," and is "currently criminally active." Encapsulating the sentiments about these offenders' commitment to criminality, one analyst explained that "it's not a matter of whether or not they will commit crime, it's a matter of when" (Interviews). The crime analysts' descriptions reflect the dominant ideology of crime and criminality. This includes the notions that: 1) offenders are responsible for their predicament; 2) an offender's past activity is a strong indicator of future activity; and 3) an offender in contact with the law denotes a problematic individual. From these features, it is the notion that these offenders will commit a crime again that defines them as a group, and that justifies both the label of prolific and the need to be more proactive in reducing their ability to commit future crimes.

Although the details concerning the characteristics and boundaries of prolific offenders are not clearly articulated, the notion that these offenders are likely to commit crime again provides a foundation for the initiatives. The justification for this category of offenders is rooted in the notion that offenders with high and/or consistent amounts of criminal activity have the potential to commit crime in the future. The prolific offender is one who is not only active, but also identifiable.

Identification Process: Justifying the Possibility of Recidivism

Following the trends in criminal identification management (Pavlich 2009), prolific offenders are identified using a pre-determined formula. Reflecting the ideas discussed above, the cornerstone of all practices involved in determining which offenders fit the prolific typology centres on determining which offenders are most active. Crime analysts, who in this case study are responsible for identifying prolific offenders, identify potential candidates by querying their database (which operates under various names) that records all "occurrences" at their respective police service. This involves placing values on an offender's criminal history (how far back analysts went also varied) that vary based on offence type and severity (see Ballucci n.d., for more details). This calculation creates a ranking of offenders from lowest to highest. The top scoring offenders' profiles are often vetted to pare down the list to a manageable number of offenders for each police service to monitor. The goal of this process is to identify which offenders have the most convictions, arrests, and calls for service. Although each police agency has its own formula and approach with which to evaluate offenders, what is common in all of them is the goal to make the most active offenders known.

What do the definition and process undertaken to define this group tell us about the typology of the prolific offender? The methodological process demonstrates that the criteria for this label focus solely on individual characteristics, voiding all social context and state responsibility. A prolific offender's activity (current and historical) is constructed as the most influential indicator of their failure to engage in transforming the self, justifying exclusion (cf. Cruikshank 1996) and the need for greater police attention. The high volume of activity deems prolific offenders (as opposed to non-prolific offenders) as not only distinct from law-abiding citizens, but also from other offenders. In this process, the social conditions in which the offender has committed these crimes are excluded from the equation. Instead, what is prioritized is counting and weighing the evidence that these individuals have chosen to break social norms, rules, and laws. This typology—that is entrenched in the notion that prolific offenders will continue to commit crimes—creates the conditions for information to be shared and the justification to employ strategies that focus on preventive crime approaches that do not require crimes to occur, but rather justify increased surveillance and control on the basis of the possibility of criminality (see Diab 2011; Jochelson et al. 2014; Zedner 2009). Being identifiable creates the conditions for the possibility of accusation—that, in turn, facilitates re-entry into the criminal justice system.

Spreading the News: Crime Analysts as Gatekeepers of Information

Identifying and sharing the names and details of the offender deemed prolific facilitates an offender's potential to re-enter the criminal justice system. The designation of prolific has little impact on those identified unless the information is shared. Once the crime analysts have applied their methodology and produced a prolific offender list, the names of those offenders are made known to police officers. The most common ways to communicate this information are by emailing the list to all police officers, posting the list in the common meeting rooms, and reviewing the list at shift-change meetings. The information shared goes beyond the offender's name to include a synopsis (produced by the crime analyst) of what is known about each offender. This includes the offender's image, date of birth, last known and previous address(es), and any current court activity or conditions on which they are listed (Interviews). The role of the crime analyst in sharing information is reflected in the description provided by one analyst concerning how the names of prolific offenders are shared. She explained,

> I distribute it to the members...I update the [database] files. If someone from outside our jurisdiction, for example if someone from...police would arrest him [sic] if they check his [sic] CPIC [Criminal Record Check] they would see [me] to advise me if they have dealt with him [sic]. I get some information from other...police departments. I also check them every once in a while to see if they are still at the same address. If they have conditions, I update them if they change. I keep track of their court dates so if they go for trial and are found guilty and sent to prison I will update the list and let the [officers] know. Every two weeks I update the [officers] through a bulletin on what kind of contact we've had with them, if we've received any information that

they've left a place or if we had calls about them so that every member
in the district is up to date on our offenders.

In this comment, the analyst describes several practices used to both make the offender known and to ensure that what is known is accurate and current, demonstrating the important role of the crime analysts—they are the gatekeepers of knowledge and information sharing.

Crime analysts share information in various formats, and with varying levels of detail. For example, one analyst explained that she shares the information via a computer drive that all officers can access. Not only does she provide information, but she also instructs and monitors the officers' surveillance of those on the prolific offender list. She told me:

I do a calendar every month with the names, like from the 1st to the
31st, and it tells members, "okay, this guy [sic] with certain colours, I
need to check him once this week." If it's in yellow, it's three times per
week, if it's in red, it's every day. They go and if they do check on the
2nd, they write their initials. The next member who comes in the next
night goes in and he [sic] says, "okay, they asked for one curfew check
during that week and did it on Monday, so I don't need to go, [instead
the] next week I'll go."

In some agencies, police officers received additional "analytic" products (Interviews). One analyst described what these materials might look like. She explained that:

[they] could be something as simple as a hot spot map....So we've had a
real hot spot of break and enters, I'll print them out a map or whatever
and provide that to them, so that if they're running [they know]
whether to turn left or turn right when they leave the detachment,
[and] hopefully that b and e hotspot will encourage them to turn right.

In other words, crime analysts are responsible for disseminating who is on the prolific offender list, and what information is known about their criminal activity. As seen from these various examples, crime analysts take seriously the need to provide up-to-date information to the officers. What is the importance and relevance of both knowing about the offender and sharing information with police officers when it comes to the role of accusation?

Having knowledge of an offender (common crimes and motivations) not only allows crime analysts to inform police officers of which offenders to monitor more closely, but it also places them in the position to make claims about who might have committed a current crime being investigated. Put another way, it provides them with the credibility to initiate the accusation process. The ways in which this occurs are seen in the relationships between analysts in their district and across the province and country. Analysts describe the importance of communication to assist in tracking offenders who are often mobile within their province and sometimes across Canada. The example below from the same analyst best exemplifies this process:

> ...a couple of my offenders moved into [L]'s area. The analyst emails me: "I got a few break and enters, it's a weird MO, they're breaking the screen this way, do you know anything?" I said, "I know exactly who it is." And I said, "You might want to consider these people as persons of interest." They did some surveillance, caught them red handed. So there's a lot of that, but it comes after you've identified them as [part of] getting to know your offenders.

As demonstrated by this comment, the crime analyst's knowledge of prolific offenders' criminal history creates suspicion. Her position as a crime analyst and her knowledge of a prolific offender's past not only makes her a source of knowledge, but also legitimizes the information she provides. The analyst's knowledge concerning the similarities between a specific prolific offender's criminal tendencies and the crime in question legitimizes her claims. The similarities between the characteristics of crimes are presented as causal links to guilt, or at the very least as enough to sustain an accusation. The fact that an offender is known has more immediate effects on the accusation process than information revealed from an investigation. This example alerts us to the power of being known to police. Arguably, these examples suggest that the designation of prolific, in many ways, holds similar weight to that of genetics evidence in the early nineteenth century. The information shared concerning an offender's whereabouts and most common criminal activities extends the gaze of the state and allows for the conditions for the "accusation moment" to occur.

Show Cause Packages

Another responsibility of the crime analyst that makes offenders known is to prepare a "show cause package." The package provides a detailed history as well as current information to the courts in cases where an offender has re-offended and is facing the court for violating his/her parole conditions. This package not only provides information about the offender, but also gives credibility to the analyst's assessment. Police officers, and crime analysts, are granted a certain level of credibility that is reinforced by their specialized knowledge of the offender, exemplified in various documents including a "show cause package." This tool was described in interviews as follows:

> [police obtain the] show cause folder from the analyst, take it down to the judge, and this will contain everything about their history: their criminal record, all their prior violations, anything that indicates that they're a flight risk, or that they have previous fail to attends, breaches of probation. Pretty much anything that says, "This person should be locked up." And say, "Here you go." Just to increase the likelihood that these people will be kept in jail. Crime analysts discuss this part of the process as an effort to increase knowledge of the offenders' history [and provide it] to the courts with ease.

In addition to providing a synopsis of an offender's known criminal history, crime analysts also provide evidence as to whether an offender might cause harm to a community. This package is presented to the judge once an offender has been brought to court for breaking any conditions. The rationale for the show cause package is that it highlights an offender's history, rather than having the current charge be the focus. One analyst interviewed explained:

> with prolific offenders that meet that criteria of—if they are released, they are going to continue committing crimes and that's the angle that you are trying to go with, saying if you release them, maybe it was just a minor offence, but there's 25 entries before that one so it's a high cost to society.

The sharing of this information is described as important and beneficial because it provides the judge with a synopsis of the offender's history and contextualizes the charge at hand. It was also communicated to me that show cause packages are efficient for the judges because they provide quick and easy access to information. Again, the crime analyst's role as a gatekeeper is exemplified with the show cause package. The information the analyst provides can impact the outcomes of decisions.

The types of conditions that are recommended provide insights on the typology of a prolific offender in these cases. This type of offender is constructed as one-dimensional—a criminal. One crime analyst's description and rationale for conditions that she often recommends work to illustrate the strength of this typology. In her interview, she stated:

> Yeah, usually the most common ones are a curfew or house arrest. If they're not working, then, and we know they're committing crime, well, don't let them out of the house. There's no need for you to leave the house. Or, [it] could be a no-contact order. So if we know that they're on a crime spree with a couple of their criminal associates, we'll put a no-contact order there. If it's drugs that...we have one offender that generally gets into trouble whenever he drinks so we'll, we can put that condition on him: No drugs and alcohol. And these are

*pretty standard conditions that the court requests. The thing is that
we'll try to make sure that they're there, especially the curfew one. The
curfew one we've had wonderful success with.*

Within this quote, the line "there is no need for you to leave the house"
requires further discussion and thought. The comment demonstrates the
specific and different expectations for offenders deemed prolific. Although
these offenders have completed their sentences, they are not expected, or
deemed able, to re-engage in a non-criminal lifestyle (such as attending
social events, going grocery shopping, and engaging in hobbies or activities). A prolific offender remains a criminal—someone who only knows
how to violate social norms and social order, and who does not possess the
abilities to engage in "normal" day-to-day activities. It is such presumptions that do not allow for a different vision of the offender, crime, or
alternative solutions for dealing with criminality (Pavlich 2009). Again,
these comments demonstrate how the power of the prolific offender
typology can place offenders under a constant state of suspicion, and leave
little space for new identities and possibilities for change.

Effects of the Prolific Offender Designation

Curfew Checks and Verifying the Typology

Thus far, I have described a prolific offender typology, and how the crime
analysts interviewed in my case study typically share what is known about
these offenders. These discussions lay the groundwork for this next section,
which describes the consequences of this label. As will be shown, the prolific
offender typology and knowledge of the offender are key justifications for
why, and how, offenders should be heavily surveilled. Frequent surveillance techniques are applied to monitor prolific offenders—all of which
are justified on the assumption that criminal activity is imminent, only
further demonstrating how these offenders live in a perpetual state of
accusation.

Crime analysts make these offenders known (to officers and other analysts) to ensure that offenders are effectively and frequently monitored. One of the most common surveillance techniques deployed by police includes compliance checks that verify that offenders are following the condition of their court or their release. These orders require offenders to follow a curfew, refrain from using alcohol and/or drugs, and commonly list people they are not to associate with. The frequency of these checks vary for offenders generally, but for those who are named prolific they occur more frequently (Interviews). One analyst explained,

I think if you are on the list you're gonna get a lot more police attention in the sense...that if you're on a curfew, your curfew will be checked regularly. If you're arrested, as per policy, we have to attempt to remand you. So it's more that kind of attention. Whereas if you just did a mischief, you know, we're gonna try to remand you, that kind of stuff.

Other crime analysts who described curfew checks as extremely useful echoed the above sentiment. The justification for this strategy is rooted in the assumption that criminal activity is imminent for all those deemed prolific. One of the crime analysts explained that prolific offender programs are beneficial precisely because they allow officers to catch offenders in the act. She stated,

it's worth it because we know they are still active, we know they are still stealing and we just can't prove it. At least with conditions we can go check him [sic]. If there's a crime that's happened, or if there is a break and enter, they can go check his [sic] curfew and if he's [sic] not home and if he's [sic] the type to do this offence, while they might be more included [sic] to check if he [sic] did the break and enter, for example.

Central to the success of these initiatives is the idea that offenders will commit future criminal acts. Officers catching offenders violating conditions or committing new crimes reaffirms the typology—and the accuracy of the prolific offender identification process. Another analyst shared an example of how an offender's criminal history is a strong indicator of the potential to recidivate.

> *Whenever they're put on curfews, we'll actually go and knock on their door...And it's not only prolific offenders that we do it for. But there's a noticeable drop in negative police contacts when they're on curfew. If you can compare, kind of, the six months before to the six months after, it's huge...It's just enormous. Numbers like thirteen offences six months before down to like one six months after whenever they're on curfew. So it's huge, right. And that could be just because they're caught. One could make that argument. But we've also seen it where six months before they do a whole bunch of crime, we catch them, they're on curfew for whatever, some court-imposed house arrest. So when they're on that, basically no criminal activity. As soon as they're off it, away they go. The data is there to support that.*

Again, in this example, the importance of the typology of the prolific offender is made evident. In this example, curfew checks are not only effective as a control mechanism, but also necessary to catch the prolific offender who will commit crimes again. The only way to curb the effects of prolific offenders' determination and desire to commit a crime is to place them under the gaze or watchful eye of the police. The presumed effectiveness of the prolific offender program is captured in the example provided below. One analyst explained:

> *That one day, the officer went over to them, say it was five o'clock in the evening and he was there and he played the part and it was all good, everything was fine. The officer went back about 20 minutes after the person's curfew, knocked on the door and there is no answer. He went upstairs and there was a neighbour apartment, who said the guy left in a red car. The officer kind of parked out of sight and [was] waiting for another hour and a red car shows up. Here was a bad guy*

getting out of the passenger seat. What you have right there, right
away, is a breach of his conditions—"you are under arrest, let's go to
jail." Why is that? It's because of this program.

For this crime analyst, the knowledge that an offender had been deemed prolific provided the officers with a justification for returning to the house after the offender's curfew time had passed. Being known as a prolific offender to police also widens the net of surveillance. One officer explained that, armed with such information, police are likely to recognize prolific offenders while conducting street checks and patrolling neighbourhoods. When observed, the whereabouts of such offenders is documented—the information gathered from random sightings was viewed by some analysts as useful for later investigations. This allows police to verify or discredit the offender's whereabouts, which assists them in building a case to accuse the offender of particular crimes. The knowledge gained from curfew checks and general policing and patrolling provides the means to gather evidence or corroborate the offender's criminal history. An offender's status as "prolific" legitimizes the gaze of the state, turning these offenders into perpetual targets for accusation.

Conclusion
Living Under the Gaze of Accusation

In this chapter, I have shown that prolific offenders' identities are presented as static ones. Through a discussion of prolific offender management practices, I have alluded to the ways that those so identified must confront a state of perpetual accusation. An offender's past history is used to justify monitoring and surveillance. These types of programs reflect a larger governing trend that is precautionary, preventive, and proactive in terms of dealing with those who are deemed risky. Although these trends are not new to policing, examining this particular type of programming and doing so with a focus on how it provides little room for offenders to deviate from this label is somewhat novel.

In the case of prolific offenders, the criminal identification and accusation process is somewhat unique, but the components of this practice are nevertheless similar to other forms of criminal accusation. Unlike classic methods of criminal identification that apply theories of physical features and genetic disposition, the practice of identifying prolific offenders focuses on the individual offender's criminal activity (current and historical). Also unique to this process is that surveillance ensues and continues based on the presumption of imminent criminal activity. Prolific offenders are monitored and watched after having completed their sentences for previous crimes. Police actions are justified, not based on a criminal offence occurring, but rather on the possibility of future activity—a growing governing strategy (see Jochelson et al. 2014; Zedner 2009). This ideology is supported through the prolific offender typology that constructs offenders as "lifetime criminals." Intense surveillance techniques are used to monitor and control this group. Such strategies both assure that these offenders, when released, are not free from the gaze of the state, and greatly increase the possibilities for future accusation— or, put another way, place offenders in the constant state of accusation.

The goal of this chapter is not to criticize policing practices, but rather to challenge wider ideas about crime and the criminal. Prolific offender management programs allow us to see clearly, and consequently think about, the processes of creating criminality at the entrances to today's crime control practices. Such programs are predicated on the notion that criminal activity is an individualistic, rather than societal, problem. As such, they focus on individual action as a basis for social exclusion. Whether intentional or not, prolific offender programs immobilize the potential for offenders to deviate from or move beyond this identity. The surveillance and monitoring of individual offenders, without taking socio-economic relations into account, removes responsibility for crime away from society. These types of programs also enable the potentially far-reaching idea that it is not only the actual commission of crime, but the potential for criminality, that ought to be governed. Aside from radically altering entrances to criminal justice, the very label of "prolific offender" creates the impression of a fixed identity who must face new controls. The latter not only places such offenders in a state of "perpetual accusation," but also diminishes our potential to consider alternative forms of justice.

Note

1. All interviews for this case study were conducted in confidentiality between 2013 and 2015, and the names of interviewees are withheld by mutual agreement.

References

Ballucci, Dale. Under review. "Making the List: Who is a Prolific Offender?"

Bertillon, Alphonse. 1977. *Alphonse Bertillon's Instructions for Taking Descriptions for the Identification of Criminals, and Others.* New York: AMS Press.

Blokland, Arjan A.J., Daniel S. Nagin, and Paul Nieuwbeerta. 2005. "Life Span Offending Trajectories of a Dutch Conviction Cohort." *Criminology* 43 (4): 919–54.

Carrier, Nicolas, and Kevin Walby. 2015. "Crime, Criminalization, and the Poverty of Biosocial Criminology." *Journal of Theoretical & Philosophical Criminology* 7: 73–82.

Cole, Simon A. 2001. "Fraud, Fabrication, and False Positives." In *Suspect Identities: A History of Fingerprinting and Criminal Identification,* edited by Simon A. Cole, 259–86. Cambridge, Mass.: Harvard University Press.

Cruickshank, Barbara. 1996. "Revolutions Within: Self-Government and Self-Esteem." In *Foucault and Political Reason: Liberalism, Neo-liberalism, and Rationalities of Government,* edited by Andrew Barry, Thomas Osborne, and Nikolas S. Rose, 231–52. Chicago: University of Chicago Press.

Diab, Robert. 2011. "Sentencing for Terrorism Offences: A Comparative Review of Emerging Jurisprudence." *Canadian Criminal Law Review* 15 (3): 267.

Galton, Francis. 1877. "Address by Francis Galton, FRS." *Nature* 8 (August 23), Section D, Anthropology section: 344–47. Available at www.galton.org.

Garland, David. 1985. *Punishment and Welfare: A History of Penal Strategies.* Brookfield, VT: Gower.

———. 2001. *The Culture of Control: Crime and Social Order in Contemporary Society.* Chicago: University of Chicago Press.

Haggerty, Kevin D. 2009. Forward: Surveillance and Political Problems. In *Surveillance: Power, Problems and Politics,* edited by Sean P. Hier and Josh Greenberg, ix–xviii. Vancouver, BC: UBC Press.

Haggerty, Kevin D., and Richard V. Ericson. 2000. "The Surveillant Assemblage." *The British Journal of Sociology* 51 (4): 605–22.

Hulsman, Louk H.C. 1986a. "Critical Criminology and the Concept of Crime." *Contemporary Crises* 10 (1): 63–80.

———. 1986b. "Critical Criminology and the Concept of Crime." In *Towards a Non-Repressive Approach to Crime*, edited by H. Bianchi and R. Van Swaaningan, 25–42. Amsterdam: Free University Press.

Jochelson, Richard, Kristen Kramar, and Mark Doerksen. 2014. *The Disappearance of Criminal Law: Police Powers and the Supreme Court*. Halifax: Fernwood Publishing.

Lombroso, Cesare, Mary Gibson, and Nicole Hahn Rafter. 2006. *Criminal Man*. Durham, NC: Duke University Press.

Mawby, Rob C., and Anne Worrall. 2004. "'Probation' Revisited: Policing, Probation and Prolific Offender Projects." *International Journal of Police Science & Management* 6 (2): 63–73.

Nietzsche, Friedrich. 1968 [1901]. *The Will to Power*. New York: Vintage Books.

O'Malley, Pat. 2004. "The Uncertain Promise of Risk." *The Australian and New Zealand Journal of Criminology* 37 (3): 323–43.

Pavlich, George. 2000. "Forget Crime: Accusation, Governance and Criminology." *The Australian and New Zealand Journal of Criminology* 33 (2): 136–52.

———. 2007. "The Lore of Criminal Accusation." *Criminal Law and Philosophy* 1 (1): 79–97.

———. 2009. "The Subjects of Criminal Identification." *Punishment & Society* 11 (2): 171–90.

Radzinowicz, Leon, and Roger G. Hood. 1990. *A History of English Criminal Law and Its Administration from 1750*. Oxford: Clarendon Press.

Ratner, Robert S. 2006. "Pioneering Critical Criminology in Canada." *Canadian Journal of Criminology and Criminal Justice* 48 (5): 647–62.

Rhodes, Henry Taylor Fowkes. 1956. *Alphonse Bertillon, Father of Scientific Detection*. Toronto: Harrap.

Saferstein, Richard. 2004. *Criminalistics: An Introduction to Forensic Science*. Upper Saddle River, NJ: Prentice Hall

Sengoopta, Chandak, 2003. *Imprint of the Raj: How Fingerprinting Was Born in Colonial India*. London: Macmillan.

Simon, Jonathan. 2007. *Governing Through Crime: How the War on Crime Transformed American Democracy and Created a Culture of Fear*. New York: Oxford University Press.

Skardhamar, Torbjørn. 2009. "Reconsidering the Theory on Adolescent-Limited and Life-Course Persistent Anti-Social Behaviour." *The British Journal of Criminology* 49 (6): 863–78.

Spencer, Dale, and Amy Fitzgerald. 2009. "Sex Offender as Homo Sacer." *Punishment & Society* 11 (2): 219–40.

———. 2015. "Criminology and Animality: Stupidity and the Anthropological Machine." *Contemporary Justice Review* 18 (4): 407–20.

Taylor, Ian, Paul Walton, and Jock Young. 1973. *The New Criminology*. London: Routledge & Kegan Paul.

Taylor, Bruce, Apollo Kowalyk, and Rachel Boba. 2007. "The Integration of Crime Analysis into Law Enforcement Agencies: An Exploratory Study into the Perceptions of Crime Analysts." *Police Quarterly* 10 (2): 154–69.

Walsh, Anthony, and John Paul Wright. 2015. "Rage Against Reason: Addressing Critical Critics of Biosocial Research." *Journal of Theoretical and Philosophical Criminology* 7 (1): 61–72.

Wolfgang, Marvin E., Robert M. Figlio, and Thorsten Sellin. 1972. *Delinquency in a Birth Cohort*. Chicago: University of Chicago Press.

Wright, John Paul. 2009. "Inconvenient Truths: Science, Race and Crime." In *Biosocial Criminology: New Directions in Theory and Research*, edited by Anthony Walsh and Kevin M. Beaver, 137–53. New York: Routledge.

Zedner, Lucia. 2009. *Security*. Key Ideas in Criminology Series. UK: Routledge.

7

DECRIMINALIZING SETTLER COLONIALISM IN CANADA

Entryways to Genocide Accusation and Erasure

ANDREW WOOLFORD

IN ITS FINAL SUMMARY REPORT, *Honouring the Truth, Reconciling the Future*, the Truth and Reconciliation Commission of Canada (TRC) refers to the history of Canadian settler colonialism as one of cultural genocide (TRC 2015, 1). These words were carefully chosen. The TRC did not simply call this history one of genocide, because Chief Commissioner Justice Murray Sinclair understands genocide to be a legal term only applicable through a court of law and the TRC did not possess adjudicatory power (Sinclair and Murray 2014). At the same time, Justice Sinclair had spent the previous five years hearing testimony from Indian Residential School Survivors, who often described themselves as victims of genocide. It is therefore clear that he wanted to acknowledge how Survivors experienced forced assimilation as a world-destroying event (see Benvenuto, Woolford, and Hinton 2014). Cultural genocide was thus a means for the TRC to invoke genocide without making a legal accusation. It gave authority to the experiential knowledge of Survivors, while sidestepping technical debates about the case for genocide in Canada. As William Schabas notes, the term "cultural genocide" has "no legal implications" and the term is not used in international law (as quoted in Schwartz 2015).

This legal reality is contrary to the intentions of the originator of the genocide concept, Raphael Lemkin, who promoted inclusion of techniques of cultural destruction in genocide law. How is it then that cultural forms of group destruction have been largely left out of legal frameworks ostensibly created to protect groups as groups? And what consequences does this omission have for practices of accusation related to group destruction?

There are two foundational sources frequently drawn upon when engaging in genocide accusation: 1) the collected works of Raphael Lemkin, the originator of the term, who sought to define and enshrine in law the crime of genocide, and 2) the United Nations *Convention on the Prevention and Punishment of the Crime of Genocide* (1948; hereafter UNGC). This chapter traces the criminalization of genocide and the development of its lore of accusation (see Pavlich 2007) through the engaged scholarship of Raphael Lemkin and the discussions at the United Nations that led to the codification of the UNGC. Through this overview, the restrictions placed on genocide accusation are noted, in particular how the drafters of the UNGC sought to defend their national sovereignty and protect themselves from accusation. Special attention is given to Canada's involvement in the lore-formation activities related to the creation of the UNGC, with emphasis on how Canada contributed to the marginalization of cultural techniques of group destruction and thereby sought historical erasure of its policies of Indigenous elimination.

As Pavlich notes, "Criminal accusation transposes ethically ordered visions of custom into law; this move is profoundly constitutive for it creates a sense of order through legally authorized renderings of rupture (disorder)" (2007, 86). Genocide law, in this manner, represents a particular vision of the global order and calls into account specific forms of disorder. This vision is constituted through a grammar of accusation that is itself the product of the assumptions, dispositions, interests, and other bases of ethical calibration that subjects participating in the formation of genocide law brought with them to identify which forms of disorder would be of concern to the international community. By looking to these entry points to genocide accusation, I draw attention to the settler-colonial order that is preserved and legitimated through genocide law, as well as the modalities of settler-colonial disorder that are excluded from consideration. This point is illustrated by reference to the case *Daishowa Inc. v. the Friends of the Lubicon*, where the term "cultural genocide" was not deemed justiciable. Based on this discussion, I gesture toward unsettling modes of genocide accusation that refuse complicity in erasing Canada's efforts to destroy Indigenous groups as groups, and open up broader understandings of what it means to destroy a group.

The notion of erasure in this chapter speaks to the other side of accusation. Past the limits of accusation rest those actions that are deemed not accusable, no matter their harmful nature. They are buried within visions of order rather than identified as sources of disorder. In this manner, the authorization of specific forms of accusation simultaneously authorizes the silencing or erasure of order-sustaining harms. Past wrongs are thereby placed beyond the remit of the lore of accusation so that they can be minimized and forgotten. With respect to the genocide concept, the narrowing of its grammar of accusation to prohibit Indigenous accusations of group destruction has served to erase the violence of Canadian settler colonialism and feed into a myth of the peaceful frontier.

Authorizing Accusation
The Criminalization of Genocide

Raphael Lemkin
Genocide lore begins with Raphael Lemkin, a Polish Jewish jurist who made it his life work to criminalize the destruction of groups. Genocide scholars celebrate Lemkin as a hero, role model, and emblem of engaged genocide scholarship (see Cooper 2008; Jacobs 2014; Power 2002). As the coiner of the term, Lemkin (1944) certainly played an important role in constituting genocide as a legal and scholarly concept. It is often assumed that the inspiration for his concept of genocide came from the Holocaust, which Lemkin survived only because of his professional networks, leaving behind many family members who were killed by the Nazis. The Holocaust

undoubtedly had an influence on his thinking about genocide, but Lemkin's work to criminalize group destruction began before the Nazi genocides were under way. In his autobiography, Lemkin traces his interest in preventing group destruction to Henrik Sienkiewicz's novel *Quo Vadis*, which offers a fictional retelling of Nero's atrocities against Christians in 64 CE (Frieze 2013). Lemkin writes, "I became so fascinated with this story that I looked up all the similar instances in history, like the destruction of Carthage, of the Huguenots, of the Catholics in Japan, of so many Europeans by Genghis Khan" (Lemkin 2013, 1). Later, as a law student, he was drawn to the story of Soghomon Tehlirian, who in 1921 assassinated Talaat Pasha, one of the architects of the Armenian genocide. Likewise, he closely followed the trial of Shalom Schwarzbard, a Jewish tailor who in 1926 shot Shymon Petliura, the Ukrainian minister of war, who had been accused of perpetrating the massacres that had killed Schwarzbard's parents. Lemkin described Schwarzbard's act as a "beautiful crime" in an article he wrote on the trial (2013, 21). These formative events, Lemkin suggests, set him on a path toward ensuring that law protects not only individuals, but also groups. For Lemkin, the group has value in and of itself, both as a source of meaning for the individual and for its contribution to global diversity.

In 1933, when offered the opportunity to present at an "international conference for the unification of penal law" in Madrid (Lemkin 2013, 22), Lemkin made his first attempt to draft a law to prevent the destruction of groups. Unfortunately, he was not permitted by the Polish minister of justice to attend the conference because the minister worried that Lemkin's quest was directed solely at saving his own race and would reflect poorly on the Polish government. Lemkin therefore was limited to submitting the text of his proposal for conjoined laws against barbarity and vandalism: "The first consisted of destroying a national or religious collectivity; the second consisted of destroying works of culture, which represented the specific genius of these national and religious groups" (Lemkin 2013, 22). It is worth noting that, for Lemkin, a "nation" referred not to an already existing sovereign entity, but to ethnic/cultural groups that possessed distinct institutions and persisted across time through the transfer of cultural knowledge to future generations (Irvin-Ericson 2013; Moses 2008; Short 2010).

The rise of the Nazis to power and their invasion of Poland put Lemkin in immediate danger. He managed to avoid capture, securing passage first to Lithuania, Latvia, and then Sweden, eventually making his way across the USSR by train. From there, he went by boat from Japan to Vancouver, before finally arriving in the United States. He initially took up residence in North Carolina and taught at Duke University, but relocated to New York where he made tireless lobbying efforts to get the United Nations to recognize the crime of genocide, a term he coined in 1943, combining in one term his previous categories of barbarism and vandalism (Lemkin, 2013). In his 1944 manuscript, *Axis Power in Occupied Europe*, Lemkin defines genocide as follows:

> *Generally speaking, genocide does not necessarily mean the immediate destruction of a nation, except when accomplished by mass killings of all members of a nation. It is intended rather to signify a coordinated plan of different actions aiming at the destruction of essential foundations of the life of national groups, with the aim of annihilating the groups themselves. The objectives of such a plan would be disintegration of the political and social institutions, of culture, language, national feelings, religion, and the economic existence of national groups, and the destruction of the personal security, liberty, health, dignity, and even the lives of the individuals belonging to such groups. Genocide is directed against the national group as an entity, and the actions involved are directed against individuals, not in their individual capacity, but as members of the national group. (79)*

In this definition, it is clear that Lemkin viewed the group to be constituted by more than the individual lives of its members, and therefore he speaks of the "different actions" that target the "political and social institutions" that are the "essential foundations" of group life. These "political and social institutions" are what hold the group together and therefore are deemed to be most relevant to its survival.

Initial recognition of this new term came when it was included in the indictment for the Nazi war criminals tried by the International Military Tribunal (IMT) at Nuremberg. However, genocide was not amongst the charges laid at the tribunal because it was not included in the statute for the IMT, which placed emphasis on crimes of military aggression, including crimes against humanity that occurred through such aggression. For Lemkin (2013), the focus on military aggression was grotesque—many crimes preceded Nazi military aggression, but only those crimes associated with military aggression were held to account at Nuremberg. Lemkin thus turned his attention toward the United Nations, hoping for a law of genocide that would recognize the threat of group destruction beyond the confines of the laws of war.

The UNGC

Working through his many contacts, Lemkin succeeded in convincing nations such as Panama, Cuba, and India to sponsor a resolution on genocide before the UN General Assembly. He wrote a draft resolution in 1945 and it was presented to the General Assembly in 1946, followed by an expanded 1947 Secretariat Draft for which Lemkin was a co-author rather than the primary author. His influence, however, was apparent in all of the early drafts, which included details of physical, biological, and cultural techniques of destruction. For Lemkin, these techniques were not understood as separate forms of genocide or as distinct types; instead, they were interconnected techniques that typically conjoined within specific processes of group destruction (Short 2010). Following Lemkin's lead, the Secretariat Draft Convention for the Prevention and Punishment of Genocide of June 6, 1947 identified the following acts of genocide that aligned with Lemkin's division between physical, biological, and cultural techniques: "Causing the death of members of a group or injuring their health or physical integrity"; "Restricting births"; and "Destroying the characteristics of the group" (Abtahi and Webb 2008, 116).

Not all parties involved in the creation of the UNGC, however, were convinced that these techniques should appear equally within the Convention. Lemkin, commenting on the importance of retaining cultural genocide in the June 26, 1947 Secretariat Draft, voiced his opposition to his co-authors, Professor Henri Donnedieu de Vabres from the Paris Faculty of Law and Professor Vespasian Pella, President of the International Association for Penal Law, who both felt the cultural element should be excised (Abtahi and Webb 2008). The three experts subsequently raised the question for the UN delegates of whether or not the international definition of genocide should include acts to destroy the hallmarks of culture. In the *travaux preparatoires*, Lemkin argues, contrary to those who felt cultural genocide represented an undue extension of the notion of genocide, that "a racial, national, or religious group cannot continue to exist unless it preserves its spirit and moral unity...If the diversity of cultures were destroyed, it would be as disastrous for civilization as the physical destruction of nations" (Abtahi and Webb 2008, 234–35). Presaging some of the opposition he would face, which will be discussed below, Lemkin assured the UN representatives that their efforts to integrate minorities into their societies would not be subject to genocide accusation, and he suggested that the assimilation of minorities was acceptable when conducted through "relatively moderate methods" (Abtahi and Webb 2008, 23).

Lemkin was more agreeable when discussion turned to leaving out political groups as potential targets of genocide, which was another sticking point amongst the various national representatives participating in the discussions on the UNGC. In the end, Lemkin disagreed with Professor Donnedieu, who worried that the exclusion of political groups could be perceived as authorization for their elimination. In contrast, Lemkin argued that political groups do not have the permanence and specific characteristics of the other groups potentially protected by the UNGC (Abtahi and Webb 2008).

The *travaux preparatoires* of the UNGC capture the intense negotiations that go into giving shape to an international crime. At times, the national representatives participating in these discussions were very direct in stating their desire to define genocide in a manner that would absolve their nations for what they perceived to be legitimate acts of nation-building and empire. This was evident in discussions of the question of whether or not the article on cultural genocide should be retained. Indeed, for some delegates, the very idea that their nations had been complicit in the destruction of cultural groups through civilization and uplift seemed ridiculous. Evolutionary standards for assessing the value of groups were still in vogue, and even Lemkin was hesitant to suggest that sovereign nations did not have some right to try to integrate subject peoples. In this vein, reflecting on the inclusion of cultural techniques of genocide in the ad hoc committee draft, Mr. Petran, the representative from Sweden, noted, "The acts which, according to article III [on cultural genocide], would constitute cultural genocide might be far less serious than those specified in article II; for instance, in the case of measures of educational policy, it might be difficult to estimate their scope in relation to the cultural position of a minority. The question could arise whether, for example, the fact that Sweden had converted the Lapps to Christianity might not lay her open to the accusation that she had committed an act of cultural genocide" (Abtahi and Webb 2008, 1506). The thought that a lore of accusation could be established to impugn colonial actors for their efforts to transform Indigenous peoples struck the delegates as outrageous, so barely worth consideration that they did not hesitate to bring up their "civilizational" efforts in condemning the article on cultural genocide. Mr. Goytisolo from South Africa, for example, brought the spectre of cannibalism into the discussion, noting that there was "danger latent in the provisions of article III where primitive or backward groups [sic] were concerned. No one could, for example, approve the inclusion in the convention of provisions for the protection of such customs as cannibalism" (Abtahi and Webb 2008, 1513).

Other representatives, though also likely worried about their own susceptibility under the terms of cultural genocide, simply declared: a) that physical and cultural genocide were too different to combine under the same law; b) cultural genocide was covered by other legal protections (such as those concerning minority rights to be included in the UN Declaration of Human Rights that was being negotiated at the same time); and c) that the article on cultural genocide was too vague to be of any legal utility. Mr. Federspiel from Denmark raised two of these objections in his remarks, where he expressed his astonishment "that the Ad Hoc Committee should have submitted so vague a text," and argued that "it would show a lack of logic and of a sense of proportion to include in the same convention both mass murders in gas chambers and the closing of libraries" (Abtahi and Webb 2008, 1508). Some nations such as Egypt and China countered these arguments, pointing to the destructiveness of forced conversions and other assaults on the cultural life of a group, but to no avail: in the Sixth Committee, twenty-six nations voted in favour of excluding cultural genocide from the UNGC versus sixteen against and four abstentions (Abtahi and Webb 2008).

Aside from the debates about cultural genocide, which are revisited below, the *travaux preparatoires* provide further insight into the modes of accusation and criminalization authorized by the UNGC. For one, these papers show how the drafters struggled with identifying the subject to be accused under the terms of the UNGC. An early draft included states as accused parties, but was soon dropped when the French representative argued that this was impossible under French law, which did not admit criminal responsibility on the part of states. Mr. Chaumont proposed instead the following language for identifying the accused: "[The General Assembly] Declares that genocide is an international crime for which the principal authors and accomplices, whether statesmen or private individuals, should be punished" (Abtahi and Webb 2008, 11). Moreover, the *individual* accused was to be a specific sort of "intending" individual, someone who had formulated the specific intent or *dolus specialis* to destroy the group in question "as such"—or, in other words, because of the animus toward the group and not for other motives. This further narrowed accusation, leaving aside various structural, exploitative, and extractive modes of violence threatening colonized peoples around the globe.

Likewise, liberal individualism also permeated the notion of the group protected by the UNGC. Early drafts of the Convention referred to "groups of human beings" (Abtahi and Webb 2008, 22) rather than simply groups, and suggested that genocide "is aimed at a group through the individual members which compose it" (Abtahi and Webb 2008, 229). By individualizing genocide, cultural genocide was further marginalized. What was to be protected by the accusatory architecture of the UNGC was not the group as something inclusive of but also more than its individual members; instead, individuals aggregated together by their group affiliations were its targets. The drafters, Lemkin included, tended to view identity as ascribed and static, rather than something constituted through fluid and complex relations of formation and reformation.

The liberal individualism of the UNGC also complemented governing efforts to protect the state, as an entity, from being held directly responsible for genocide. Social groups that promoted genocide were to be disbanded under Article XI of the UNGC, but state sovereignty was maintained by giving states priority in addressing violations of the Convention and trying those individuals (as individuals) deemed to have been participants in genocide. States, as collective actors, were of lesser concern than the individuals within the state who would be held accountable as masterminds, planners, and enablers of genocide. In this manner, the UNGC's promise to hold states accountable for genocide was hamstrung by the Convention's affirmation and preservation of state sovereignty. This would have dire consequences, as the jealous protection of state sovereignty and the prioritization of state interests would for more than forty years after the UNGC prevent action against the genocides that erupted in places such as Cambodia and Burundi.

In the end, the UNGC defined genocide as follows:

Article II: In the present Convention, genocide means any of the following acts committed with intent to destroy, in whole or in part, a national, ethnical, racial or religious group, as such:
a. Killing members of the group;

b. *Causing serious bodily or mental harm to members of the group;*

c. *Deliberately inflicting on the group conditions of life calculated to bring about its physical destruction in whole or in part;*

d. *Imposing measures intended to prevent births within the group;*

e. *Forcibly transferring children of the group to another group.*[1]

Article III on cultural genocide was removed from the UNGC. It was still present as late as the Ad Hoc Committee on Genocide's 1948 draft. In this version, Article III read:

> *In this Convention genocide also means any deliberate act committed with the intent to destroy the language, religion or culture of a national, racial or religious group on grounds of national or racial origin or religious belief such as: 1. Prohibiting the use of the language of the group in daily intercourse or in schools, or the printing and circulation of publications in the language of the group; 2. Destroying, or preventing the use of, libraries, museums, schools, historical monuments, places of worship or other cultural institutions and objects of groups.* (Morsink 1999, 1023)

Lemkin (2013) considered inclusion of Article II(e) on the transfer of children from one group to another as the preservation of one form of cultural genocide in the UNGC. Some recent authors also see in this clause a fragment of Lemkin's notion of cultural genocide (Annett 2000; Grant 1996); however, others argue that this clause was intended only to serve to address physical or biological genocide, i.e., to qualify as genocidal, children had to be removed from their homes in a manner that was permanent, thereby jeopardizing the biological and physical continuation of the group (MacDonald and Hudson 2012; McGregor 2004; van Krieken 2004). Nonetheless, in implementing the UNGC in the Canadian Criminal Code, Canada was careful to recognize only Article II(a) and Article II(b) as acts of genocide, further adjusting its domestic lore of genocide to place its own actions beyond the reach of law.

Entryway as an Escape Route
Canada's Role in Erasing Settler-Colonial Destruction

Canada's contribution to fashioning the lore of genocide accusation is particularly notable in light of recent events. These include the TRC's aforementioned use of the term "cultural genocide" (TRC 2015, 1). But they also include how, a week prior to the summary report's release, Supreme Court Chief Justice Beverley McLachlin spoke of Canada's history of attempted "cultural genocide" when she delivered the fourth annual Pluralism Lecture of the Global Centre for Pluralism, making her the highest-ranking Canadian official to use the term while in office (as quoted in Fine 2015). These public statements were in addition to more widespread use of the genocide concept (and not just "cultural genocide") by residential school Survivors, activists, journalists, and scholars (see Akhtar 2010; Bischoping and Fingerhut 1996; Chrisjohn and Young 1997; Churchill 2000, 2004; Davis and Zannis 1973; Grant 1996; MacDonald 2014; MacDonald and Hudson 2012; McKegney 2007; Neu and Therrien 2003; Palmater 2011; Powell and Peristerakis 2014; Starblanket 2015; Woolford 2009, 2015).

David MacDonald (2015) has noted the TRC had several strategic reasons for using "cultural genocide" instead of genocide, including avoiding legalistic debates with right wing detractors and others who might use the letter of the law to distract the public from the recommendations and the Survivor testimony contained within the report. But it is worth noting that Canada played a significant role in creating the lore of genocide accusation that would provide detractors with a leg to stand on in such debates. Canada was, from the beginning, involved in the discussions to create the UNGC, and was consistent in its view that the United Nations should prepare "a more limited definition of genocide" (Abtahi and Webb 2008, 624) than that found in the Secretariat Draft. Lemkin nonetheless viewed the Canadian delegation as allies in getting his law passed, despite their efforts to narrow it. During the July 1948 discussions in Geneva, Lemkin found himself unable to sleep, so worried was he that the UNGC would not receive adequate support from the UN delegates. On a late night stroll, he came across Canadian ambassador Dana Wilgress, and the two of them walked together and discussed the Convention. Lemkin writes, "When I accompanied him back to his hotel he told me it would be very good for us, and I distinctly heard the saving phrase 'for us,' to win the support of the future president of the Assembly in Paris. He was Wilgress's personal friend..." (Lemkin 2013, 142). Around the same time, however, the secretary of state for external affairs in Ottawa sent a July 27, 1948 telegram to Wilgress and the Canadian delegation at the Palais Des Nations in Geneva. It instructed, "You should support or initiate any move for the deletion of Article III on 'Cultural' Genocide. If this move is not successful, you should vote against Article III and if necessary, against the Convention. The Convention as a whole less Article III, is acceptable, although legislation will naturally be required to implement the Convention" (as quoted in Brean 2015, n.p.). Wilgress was therefore an ally, but only so long as Article III was struck from the UNGC.

The Canadian delegate expressed this view during the October 1948 discussions held at the Palais de Chailott in Paris. Here, Canada maintained the position that cultural genocide represented a "dilution of the purpose of the Convention" (Abtahi and Webb 2008, 1246). At the eighty-third meeting, Mr. Lapointe from Canada added that no revision of the article on cultural genocide would satisfy Canada—it simply had to be removed.

> Yet it was true to say that the Government and people of Canada were horrified at the idea of cultural genocide and hoped that effective action would be taken to suppress it. The people of [Canada] were deeply attached to their cultural heritage, which was made up mainly of a combination of Anglo-Saxon and French elements, and they would strongly oppose any attempt to undermine the influence of those two cultures in Canada. (Abtahi and Webb 2008, 1509–10)

What is striking here is the delegate's simultaneous act of erasure (ignoring the cultural heritage of Indigenous peoples) while claiming

Canada's adherence to the protection of culture. This allows him to support a lore of genocide accusation that is "limited to the mass physical destruction of human groups" (Abtahi and Webb 2008, 1510) without appearing in bad faith on the issues of cultural genocide and cultural preservation. Canada, he contends, supports the preservation of culture, but the lore of genocide accusation need not include cultural protection, since assaults on cultures are in his view distinct from those on the physical lives of group members.

Nevertheless, Lemkin would continue to view Canada as an ally in his efforts to criminalize genocide. A 1949 meeting with then Minister of Foreign Affairs Lester B. Pearson, during which Lemkin hoped to convince Canada to ratify the UNGC, led him to observe the following about Canadians: "One could also recognize [in Pearson] what is so appealing about all Canadians: they basically reject the theory that international feeling must necessarily be devious. 'Let us first try it straight,' they seem to imply by all their behaviour, and they remain at that point" (Lemkin 2013, 192). Lemkin thus seemed either forgiving or unaware of the machinations of the Canadian government to excise cultural genocide from the UNGC. In his memoir, he expresses his disappointment at its removal, while accepting that the majority of delegates could not be convinced of its necessary inclusion: "This very idea was very dear to me. I defended it successfully through two drafts...with a heavy heart I decided not to press for it" (Lemkin 2013, 172).

Prohibiting Genocide Accusation
The Friends of the Lubicon

The creation of the lore of genocide accusation and the carving of space therein for Canadian erasure has had a legal impact in Canada. In a 2000 article, Native American Studies professor Ward Churchill reflects on how the UNGC narrowed Lemkin's concept of genocide, as I have here (Churchill 2000; see also 2002). He argues that through these efforts at curtailing the genocide concept, Canadian courts have been able to forbid the use of the "g-word" and promote genocide denial. Though Churchill is a controversial figure in US academia, it is worth revisiting the primary examples upon which he builds his arguments: *Daishowa Inc. v. The Friends of the Lubicon Cree* [1995; 1998]. Here, one can see how the accusatory architecture of genocide facilitates settler-colonial erasure. Whereas Churchill opts for the more polemical discourse of denial to describe the court's prohibition of the use of the term "genocide" by The Friends of the Lubicon (FOL), I argue that an analysis of the lore of accusation in this context provides a means to detail the accusatory logics inherent in the genocide concept that do not simply require proper application of the concept, as is presumed by the counter-accusation of denial in that the notion of genocide denial presupposes that there exists a "reality" of the genocide concept that is being avoided or refused. Instead, following from the analysis of the contingent foundations of genocide's accusatory architecture, one can see that the genocide concept itself requires more than the reclamation of its Lemkinian roots or a mythic return to its "authentic" meaning—it demands unsettling.

The traditional territory of the Lubicon Lake Cree is located in northern and central Alberta. Though some members of the Lubicon live on reserves, the community itself does not have a reserve. Since the onset of settlement, the Lubicon have been locked in a territorial dispute with Canada. In 1899, a government party visited northern and central Alberta to negotiate Treaty 8 with Indigenous groups in this region and seek cession of their territory to Canada, but the Lubicon were not contacted. Contemporary Lubicon therefore dispute the government claim that their land was surrendered. Initially, the Lubicon sought to have this injustice resolved through the creation of a reserve and adhesion to the treaty. In 1940, lines for a Lubicon reserve were in fact drawn, but the onset of World War II resulted in delays to Canada surveying and finalizing the reserve. In subsequent conversations with the provincial and federal governments, the Lubicon came to fear administrative erasure, as they were encouraged to simply blend into existing reserve communities. Since the late 1970s, oil, gas, and timber activities have intensified within

Lubicon territory and Lubicon assertions of territorial and cultural rights have been repeatedly thwarted. In fighting against dispossession and erasure, the Lubicon have found support from international organizations such as Amnesty International and the United Nations Commission on Human Rights, the latter of which determined Canada to be in violation of Lubicon rights under Article 27 of the International Covenant on Civil and Political Rights, which states, "In those States in which ethnic, religious or linguistic minorities exist, persons belonging to such minorities shall not be denied the right, in community with the other members of their group, to enjoy their own culture, to profess and practice their own religion, or to use their own language."

The larger history of the Lubicon and their struggle is beyond the scope of this chapter (see Churchill 2000, 2002; Goddard 1991; Martin-Hill 2008). Of specific interest is the 1995 case brought before the Ontario courts by Daishowa Inc. against the FOL, a Toronto-based organization advocating on behalf of the Lubicon. In this case, Daishowa Inc. sought a legal injunction against and defamation charges for the FOL, which orchestrated a boycott against Daishowa paper products. Daishowa Inc. in 1988 announced plans to open a paper mill near Peace River, Alberta, that would be fed by forests from unceded Lubicon territory to be clear-cut by an affiliated company. The FOL were very successful in convincing the Canadian public of the genocidal impact of clear-cut logging in northern Alberta, and several companies heeded their call to stop using Daishowa paper products. In its suit, Daishowa claimed to have lost 25 percent of its business because of a boycott for which they felt wrongly targeted since they were not, in their view, directly involved in the clear-cutting operation.[2]

The lawsuit covered much ground, but of primary interest here is the discussion surrounding the right of the FOL to lodge a genocide accusation against Daishowa. The FOL, in calling on Canadians not to use Daishowa products, charged the company with contributing to the cultural geno-cide of the Lubicon. In the interim injunction hearing, which considered whether or not the FOL should halt their boycott of Daishowa while awaiting trial, Justice Frances Kiteley held that while the FOL could continue their boycott, "the defendants were prohibited from using the word genocide or similar words in its communications." She found that their use of the term "genocide" was "misleading and constituted misrepresentation."[3] For example, the FOL had distributed a pamphlet that called upon consumers to "Stop the Genocide: The Lubicon Cree see the impending destruction of their forest as the final stage of a genocidal process that began with the onset of government-backed oil and gas development in the late seventies. It is essential that the pressure be kept on Daishowa to stop any cutting on Lubicon territory."[4] The terms "genocide" and "cultural genocide" were also frequently used in letters sent by the FOL to corporate clients and customers of Daishowa. In support of the use of the genocide term by the FOL, anthropologist Joan Ryan, who had long worked with the Lubicon Cree, noted the destructive consequences of logging operations for the continuity of Lubicon culture and livelihoods. She spoke to the impact of logging on Lubicon hunting, gathering, and trapping, the spiritual and cultural consequences of these impacts, as well as how logging roads have made possible the entry of alcohol, drugs, unhealthy foods, and other substances that have harmed Lubicon communities. In making the case for genocide, Ryan referred not to the UNGC, but rather to a Webster dictionary definition of genocide as "the deliberate and systematic destruction of a racial, political, or cultural group."[5] This definition, of course, does not stray too far from the UNGC, maintaining its focus on intent, destruction, and certain types of group life (leaving aside national groups). But it also narrows the UNGC by insisting on "systematic" destruction, which is perhaps a nod to that most emblematic of genocides, the Holocaust. Nonetheless, Ryan made an expansive reading of this definition, and spoke to how Lubicon group life was under severe threat from corporate actions.

Whether Madame Justice Kiteley relied on the same definition or on the UNGC is unclear in her ruling. In her application of the law to the case, however, she wrote:

To the extent that Brewster [an affiliate of Daishowa] logged in 1990, and that logging was announced in 1991, I cannot find that that activity falls within the definition of genocide based upon the materials before me. I also cannot agree that the isolated act of signing the Forest Management Agreement is an act of genocide. Finally, I cannot agree that Daishowa's refusal to make the clear, unequivocal and public commitment is an act of genocide. I find that the plaintiff has established a prima facie case that attributions of genocide are misleading and constitute misrepresentation. I cannot find that a prima facie case of defamation has been proven. The statements made...by the defendants are most certainly within the category of "fair comment" as indicated above. Likewise, in the absence of an element of malice, I am not prepared to find that the tort of injurious falsehood has been established.[6]

In the full trial of the Daishowa case, Ontario Court Justice James MacPherson, like Justice Kiteley before him, affirmed the legality of the FOL boycott and picketing activities, but he further restricted their use of the genocide concept, finding it to be defamatory and not a case of "fair comment." He was also clearer in identifying his sources in rendering a decision on the genocide question:

In my view, the plain and ordinary meaning of the word "genocide" is the intentional killing of a group of people. "Genocide" is defined by Webster's Dictionary (Seventh Collegiate Edition) as "the deliberate and systematic destruction of a racial, political or cultural group", by the Shorter Oxford English Dictionary (Third Edition, 1991 Reprint) as "the annihilation of a race", and by the Oxford English Dictionary (Second Edition, 1989) as "the deliberate and systematic extermination of an ethnic or national group." Thus, the essence of the meaning of the word "genocide" is the physical destruction of a group identified on a racial, political, ethnic or cultural basis. The United Nations Convention on the Prevention and Punishment of the Crime of Genocide conveys a

similar meaning...Neither in intent nor in result could Daishowa's
proposed logging activities come anywhere close to these definitions.
Indeed, in a century that has borne witness over and over again to
terrible examples of genocide, it would be an enormous injustice to link
Daishowa's proposed activities with this meaning of genocide.[7]

Though he discussed the UNGC, for the purpose of assessing the
complaint about defamation, MacPherson made it clear that the plain
and ordinary meaning of the term was most important to such an assessment, since this was the meaning most likely to affect the reputation of
the defendant. While Churchill (2002) argues that in so doing MacPherson
ignored every expert on genocide, as well as what Churchill takes to be the
"real" meaning of the UNGC, the matter is not so clear. To date, genocide
case law has emphasized genocide as a crime of physical group destruction. To this extent, the dictionary definitions that guided MacPherson
were not so different than the UNGC as it is applied in the courts, as
MacPherson noted. The lore of genocide as shaped through the UNGC
in order to push aside questions of cultural destruction is very much
active in MacPherson's conviction that an accusation of genocide was not
permissible in this case. MacPherson did not so much deny genocide as lay
authoritative claim to interpreting who does and who does not have the
right to accuse, and on what basis such accusation may be levelled.

Moreover, MacPherson countered the FOL's argument that they were
using Lemkin's notion of genocide, which is more nuanced and considers
a wider range of genocidal acts, by arguing the common perception of
the term is that it refers to events like the Holocaust. He added, "in my
view the Friends cannot even bring themselves within a fair reading of
Professor Lemkin's definition. That definition speaks of 'actions aiming
at the destruction of essential foundations of the life of national groups,'
'the aim of annihilating the groups,' 'the objectives of such a plan would
be disintegration of ... culture'. It borders on the grotesque for the Friends
to try to link Daishowa's planned logging activities with such aims, objectives and plans." He thereby parses Lemkin's language and complex view

on the subject so that he can confirm his own assumptions about the lore of genocide accusation.

In this manner, whether through reference to the UNGC or the Webster dictionary rendition of this definition, the FOL were denied the right to engage in genocide accusation against Daishowa. What mattered was not how the Lubicon experienced the aggressive entry of clear-cut logging and oil exploration into their territory, or the way this economic activity was designed to marginalize the Lubicon from their territorial assertions, or certainly not the role of territory in the Lubicon's collective identity. The accusatory architecture of genocide could not open to the experiences of the Other, whereby the Lubicon sought to give language to the history of violent encounters that have endangered their persistence as a group. Instead, it was the lore of genocide accusation that determined whether or not a claim of genocidal violence was authorized and facilitated the legal erasure of Canadian wrongdoing.

The conflict between Daishowa and the FOL would eventually be resolved in April 2000 with a commitment by Daishowa not to harvest timber or use fiber from Lubicon territory until their land issue is resolved. But the efforts to open genocide law to Indigenous understandings of group destruction must continue.

Unsettling Genocide Accusation

The scourge of genocide is so abhorrent that it often discourages critical evaluation. But there is a real tension between the need to prevent the horrors of mass violence and group destruction and the work of fashioning new categories of inclusion and exclusion that are said to make possible group protection. Genocide law, while providing terms to which certain groups can attach themselves for protection, also constitutes a set of subjects deemed worthy of protection. A group hoping to preserve its collective identity must reconstitute itself under the terms of the law, namely as a racial, ethnic, religious, or national group. Thus, by enunciating legal groups and setting their boundaries, the UNGC serves to make these groups subjects of law. Genocide law therefore does not simply protect existing groups; it constitutes peculiar forms of group identity as the basic building blocks of a global plurality. Groups are protected only to the extent that they fit the UNGC ontology. As we can see with the discussions that took place in the formation of the UNGC, the criminalization of genocide also involved the creation of groups outside law, of collective forms of being that were perceived as either too primitive or unusual to be worthy of persistence (see Pavlich 2014). Here, the UNGC enacts a symbolic violence on the often complex nature of Indigenous groups that do not fit neatly into racial, national, ethnic, or religious categories (Woolford 2009), but that have nonetheless been racialized and subject to settler colonialism's logic of elimination (Wolfe 2006).

The structure of settler colonialism has sought to render Indigenous groups too uncivilized and too primitive to even make a legitimate claim as groups deserving protection. Expansionist myths of the frontier and "manifest destiny" have gone so far as to present Indigenous groups as dying races or barriers to the rightful claimants of the land. In confronting such deadly prejudice, it may seem valuable to claim status as a national, ethnic, or racial group under the terms of the UNGC to stop this onslaught. But there are costs to such efforts. Indigenous scholars describe their groups as not simply fitting one of these UNGC-prescribed categories. Indigenous groups are all of these identities, entangled together. In particular, as groups, they are "grounded ontologies," not simply aggregates of individuals, but deeply entwined with the land and life that surrounds them (Coulthard 2014). The case of the Lubicon confirms this, as advocates on behalf of the Lubicon sought to make the case that ecological assaults on Lubicon territory had serious repercussions for their group life. However, the lore of genocide accusation deterritorializes group life, so that the group cannot be too closely coupled with its places. For the Lubicon to afford themselves any protection under the UNGC, they are required to first reconceptualize themselves under its terms, delimiting their Indigenous ontologies to fit those of a European ontology, and to prioritize only certain forms of assault on their collective being, not including those directed toward their territory. In this manner, the UNGC remains trapped within a settler-colonial universe that narrows the boundaries of protection and accusation, providing Canada pathways to the very erasure it appeared to seek in its contribution to fashioning the lore of genocide accusation. The UNGC's settler-colonial foundations therefore often offset any potential benefits of counter-accusation it promises.

To protect Indigenous groups, the lore of genocide accusation requires more than a politicized process of decision that arrests the group in singular form and dilutes it into supposedly universal elements. By unearthing the ethical dimensions of genocide's accusational lore, it becomes possible to reimagine and authorize other practices of accusation. Here, we can, for example, envision modes of accusation that do not seek to reify the group when promising to protect group relations, and instead create space whereby groups can enunciate their own ontologizing practices in a manner that does not assume a group stasis, but instead articulates the group's relationality, fluidity, and hybridity. More concretely, by deconstructing the architecture of accusation that has been built around genocide, we can open ourselves and the law to each group's distinct self-understandings rather than imposing on them, in a manner that mimes genocide's destructive violence, forms of life that are not their own. With such a move, the group itself would be authorized to express its own feelings of threat and potential destruction, rather than having to fit itself within a certain mould to claim the right to a collective existence.

Moreover, a thorough critique of the lore of genocide accusation also raises questions about the subject of genocide perpetration, exposing the liberal core of our thinking about genocide as the project of an intending individual, rather than an outcome of an emergent process that draws its motive force from social, networked, and individual levels of violence. To allow genocidal accusation to address the very ways in which we live in relationship with one another as potentially genocidal opens up the possibility of critically examining the ways in which intergroup relations are structured in such a manner that they are inherently threatening to the less dominant group. Such is the case in settler colonial societies, where Indigenous groups have not just suffered from the intentions of individual actors seeking their elimination; they have rather been forced to struggle for existence in a system predicated on their erasure (Wolfe 2006). Whereas the actors who perpetrated such individual actions against Indigenous collectivities may or may not have passed on, the structures of settler colonialism, and the networks that derive from these structures, persist.

Notes

1. *United Nations Convention on the Prevention and Punishment of Genocide.* Adopted by Resolution 260 (III) A of the UN General Assembly on December 9, 1948. Entry into force: January 12, 1951.
2. Daishowa Inc. v. Friends of the Lubicon, [April 14, 1998], Ontario Court of Justice (Gen. Div.), File No. 95-CQ-59707.
3. Daishowa Inc. v. Friends of the Lubicon, [May 29, 1995], Ontario Court of Justice (Gen. Div.), File no. 95-CQ-59707; see prefatory summary, under Held.
4. Ibid.
5. Ibid., para. 184.
6. Ibid., para. 338.
7. Daishowa Inc. v. Friends of the Lubicon, [April 14, 1998], Ontario Court of Justice (Gen. Div.), File No. 95-CQ-59707.

References

Abtahi, Hirad, and Phillippa Webb. 2008. *The Genocide Convention: The Travaux Preparatoires.* 2 vols. Leiden: Brill Academic Publishing.

Akhtar, Zia. 2010. "Canadian Genocide and Official Culpability." *International Criminal Law Review* 10 (1): 111–35.

Benvenuto, Jeff, Andrew Woolford, and Alexander Laban Hinton. 2014. "Introduction." In *Colonial Genocide in Indigenous North America,* edited by Andrew Woolford, Jeff Benvenuto, and Alexander Laban Hinton, 1–27. Durham, NC: Duke.

Bischoping, Katherine, and Natalie Fingerhut. 1996. "Border Lines: Indigenous Peoples in Genocide Studies." *Canadian Review of Sociology and Anthropology* 33 (4): 481–506.

Brean, Joseph. 2015. "Canada Opposed Concept of 'Cultural Genocide' in 1948 Accord." *The Star Phoenix,* June 18.

Chrisjohn, Roland D., Sherri L. Young, and Michael Maraun. 1997. *The Circle Game: Shadows and Substance in the Indian Residential School Experience in Canada*. Penticton, BC: Theytus Books.

Churchill, Ward. 2000. "Forbidding the 'G-Word': Holocaust Denial as Judicial Doctrine in Canada." *Other Voices*, 2 (1). http://www.othervoices.org/2.1/churchill/denial.html.

_____. 2002. *Struggle for the Land: Native North American Resistance to Genocide, Ecocide, and Colonization*. San Francisco: City Lights.

_____. 2004. *Kill the Indian, Save the Man*. San Francisco: City Lights.

Cooper, John. 2008. *Raphael Lemkin and the Struggle for the Genocide Convention*. New York: Palgrave Macmillan.

Coulthard, Glen. 2014. *Red Skin, White Masks: Rejecting the Colonial Politics of Recognition*. Minneapolis: University of Minnesota Press.

Davis, Robert, and Mark Zannis. 1973. *The Genocide Machine in Canada: The Pacification of the North*. Montreal: Black Rose Books.

Fein, Helen. 1993. *Genocide: A Sociological Perspective*. London: Sage Publications.

Fine, Sean. 2015. "Chief Justice Says Canada Attempted 'Cultural Genocide' on Aboriginals." *Globe & Mail*, May 28.

Frieze, Donna-Lee. 2013. "Introduction." In *Totally Unofficial: The Autobiography of Raphael Lemkin*, edited by Donna-Lee Frieze, ix–xvii. New Haven: Yale University Press.

Grant, Agnes. 1996. *No End of Grief: Residential Schools in Canada*. Winnipeg: Pemmican Publications.

Goddard, John. 1991. *Last Stand of the Lubicon Cree*. Vancouver: Douglas & McIntyre.

Irvin-Ericson, Douglas. 2013. "Genocide, the 'Family of Mind,' and the Romantic Signature of Raphael Lemkin." *Journal of Genocide Research* 15 (3): 273–96.

Jacobs, Steven L., ed. 2014. *Lemkin on Genocide*. Lanham: Lexington Books.

Lemkin, Raphael. 1944. *Axis Rule in Occupied Europe: Laws of Occupation, Analysis of Government, Proposals for Redress*. Washington, DC: Carnegie Endowment for International Peace.

_____. 2013. *Totally Unofficial: The Autobiography of Raphael Lemkin*. Edited by Donna-Lee Frieze. New Haven: Yale University Press.

MacDonald, David B. 2014. "Genocide in the Indian Residential Schools: Canadian History through the Lens of the UN Genocide Convention." In *Colonial Genocide in Indigenous North America*, edited by Andrew Woolford, Jeff Benvenuto, and Alexander Laban Hinton, 306–24. Durham, NC: Duke University Press.

_____. 2015. "Five Reasons the TRC Chose 'Cultural Genocide.'" *Globe & Mail*, July 6.

MacDonald, David B., and Graham Hudson. 2012. "The Genocide Question and Indian Residential Schools in Canada." *Canadian Journal of Political Science* 45 (2): 427–49.

McGregor, Russell. 2004. "Governance, Not Genocide: Aboriginal Assimilation in the Postwar Era." In *Genocide and Settler Society: Frontier Violence and Stolen Indigenous Children in Australian History*, edited by A. Dirk Moses, 290–311. New York: Berghahn Books.

Martin-Hill, Dawn. 2008. *The Lubicon Lake Nation: Indigenous Knowledge and Power*. Toronto: University of Toronto Press.

McKegney, Sam. 2007. *Magic Weapons: Aboriginal Writers Remaking Community after Residential School*. Winnipeg: University of Manitoba Press.

Morsink, Johannes. 1999. "Cultural Genocide, the Universal Declaration, and Minority Rights." *Human Rights Quarterly* 21 (4): 1009–60.

Moses, A. Dirk. 2008. "Empire, Colony, Genocide: Keywords and the Philosophy of History." In *Empire, Colony, and Genocide: Conquest, Occupation and Subaltern Resistance in World History*, edited by A. Dirk Moses, 3–54. New York: Berghahn Books.

Neu, Dean, and Richard Therrien. 2003. *Accounting for Genocide: Canada's Bureaucratic Assault on Aboriginal People*. Black Point, NS: Fernwood Publishing.

Palmater, Pamela D. 2011. *Beyond Blood: Rethinking Indigenous Identity and Belonging*. Saskatoon: Purich Publishing.

Pavlich. George. 2007. "The Lore of Criminal Accusation." *Crime, Law & Philosophy* 1: 79–97.

———. 2014. "Criminal Justice and Cape Law's Persons." *Social & Legal Studies* 23 (1): 55–72.

Powell, Christopher. 2011. *Barbaric Civilization: A Critical Sociology of Genocide*. Montreal and Kingston: McGill-Queen's University Press.

Powell, Christopher, and Julia Peristerakis. 2014. "Genocide in Canada: A Relational View." In *Colonial Genocide in Indigenous North America*, edited by Andrew Woolford, Jeff Benvenuto and Alexander Laban Hinton, 70–92. Durham, NC: Duke University Press.

Power, Samantha. 2002. *"A Problem from Hell": America and the Age of Genocide*. New York: Basic Books.

Schwartz, Daniel. 2015. "Cultural Genocide Label for Residential Schools has No Legal Implications, Expert Says." *CBC News*, June 13. http://www.cbc.ca/news/aboriginal/cultural-genocide-label-for-residential-schools-has-no-legal-implications-expert-says-1.3110826.

Short, Damien. 2010. "Cultural Genocide and Indigenous Peoples: A Sociological Approach." *The International Journal of Human Rights* 14 (6): 833–48.

Sinclair, Murray, and Stuart Murray. 2014. "Canada must Confront the Truth." *Winnipeg Free Press*, November 1. http://www.winnipegfreepress.com/opinion/analysis/canada-must-confront-the-truth-281166292.html.

Starblanket, Tamara. 2015. *Suffer the Little Children: Genocide, Indigenous Nations, and the Canadian State.* Atlanta: Clarity Press.

Truth and Reconciliation Commission of Canada (TRC). 2015. *Honouring the Truth, Reconciling for the Future: Summary of the Final Report of the Truth and Reconciliation Commission of Canada.* Ottawa: Truth and Reconciliation Commission of Canada.

van Krieken, Robert. 2004. "Rethinking Cultural Genocide: Aboriginal Child Removal and Settler-Colonial State Formation." *Oceania* 75: 125–51.

Wolfe, Patrick. 2006. "Settler Colonialism and the Elimination of the Native." *Journal of Genocide Research* 8 (4): 387–409.

Woolford, Andrew. 2009. "Ontological Destruction: Genocide and Aboriginal Peoples in Canada." *Genocide Studies and Prevention: An International Journal* 4 (1): 81–97.

_____. 2015. *This Benevolent Experiment: Indigenous Boarding Schools, Genocide and Redress in North America.* Lincoln and Winnipeg: University of Nebraska Press and the University of Manitoba Press.

"HOW SHE APPEARS"

Demeanour, Cruel Optimism, and the Relationship Between Police and Victims of Domestic Violence

MARCUS A. SIBLEY, ELISE WOHLBOLD,
DAWN MOORE & RASHMEE SINGH

Introduction

While we routinely think of accused people in relation to entryways into the criminal justice system, victims and survivors, to varying degrees, are also entrants. For this population, a number of factors dictate whether or not they even attempt to open the door to criminal justice, let alone what occurs once they obtain access as complainants. While we recognize that all who come into the criminal justice system as complainants face particular issues and barriers, there are many "soft" factors that count in the prosecution of any criminal case. In this chapter, we are specifically interested in the question of demeanour in the context of prosecuting domestic violence. Axioms of justice as well as social science research tell us that the demeanour of the victim counts a great deal, especially in the crucial first encounter with police, as it is through this encounter that the initial discretionary powers of criminal justice are exercised in deciding whether or not a victim is believable and thus has a story worth pursuing through criminal investigation. In short, is she allowed to enter in?[1]

Our project goes beyond what we already know about the importance of a victim's demeanour, arguing that it can only be understood as a gateway into criminal justice in relation to the demeanour of the police when responding to and investigating the complaint. We argue, then, that a more fulsome understanding of the workings of demeanour within the criminal process must account for the dialogic relationship between police and victims. Thus, we seek to move the debate beyond "how she appears"— without understating the importance of the victim's presentation of self—to suggest that demeanour is the result of a social interaction, not an individual presentation, and that it is these interactions that ultimately decide if and how a complainant enters into the criminal justice system. The interactions we see as crucial here are those between victims and police. The importance of this interaction, while arguably extendable to other crimes, is particularly salient in the context of domestic violence, where both victims and police have certain expectations about the other's comportment as well as obligations to present themselves in particular ways. These expectations, whether met or largely unfulfilled, decide which victims are telling a story about a crime and which are simply telling a story.

What sets demeanour in domestic violence apart from other crimes, we propose, is that these expectations and obligations found at the start of a complaint of domestic violence create a scenario of what Lauren Berlant (2011) calls "cruel optimism," an experience through which both parties are led to expect much more from the other than they can ever realistically deliver. Drawing on a review of seventy criminal cases as well as twenty-five interviews with domestic violence survivors, we want to show that there is a process of setting expectations and obligations, which triggers an affective response of disappointment when these expectations are not met. We argue that this affective response directly relates to how a complainant enters into the criminal justice system. This in turn creates a sort of affective spiral as the cruelty of shattering the initial optimism often creates a sense of resentment and antagonism between these two sets of actors, if not already present. In this way, entrances cannot be thought of in the absence of consideration of their concomitant exits, especially when such exits are fraught with the relational, affective politics of domestic violence prosecutions.

Expectations, Obligations, and Cruel Optimism

Goffman (1967) breaks rules of conduct (what he later refers to as demeanour) into two categories: obligations and expectations. He writes,

> *Rules of conduct impinge upon the individual in two general ways: directly, as obligations, establishing how he [sic] is morally constrained to conduct himself [sic]; indirectly as expectations, establishing how others are morally bound to act in regard to him [sic]. (1967, 49)*

Goffman continues on to explain that both obligations and expectations are largely subconscious, automatic responses we have to the world around us. We feel compelled to conduct ourselves in certain ways, defer to authority, abide by certain social norms. We do not necessarily experience these obligations as burdensome insofar as they are just routinized parts of our day-to-day lives. At the same time, we have expectations of others that also go largely unrecognized. We anticipate deference from those whom we outrank, empathy from those from whom we seek assistance, and so on. Again, these expectations go largely unrecognized in the every day. We simply accept that these are the rules and rituals that guide our conduct, and, for the most part, we experience them as largely neutral, barely worthy of our consideration.

Goffman is clear to point out that these rules and expectations are both situation specific and tethered to a reflexive notion of self. As he argues, when we are following the rules of our obligations, we think of ourselves as the kind of person who does these things, a sense that translates into a particular version of self. We become, to use Goffman's own language, "the sort of person who would follow this obligation" (1967, 50). The same, according to Goffman, can be said of the individual of whom we have expectations. Just as the individual following rules of obligation tends toward an automatic execution of these obligations and derives a sense of self from this successful execution, so too are the individuals on whom we place expectations ascribed a particular selfhood.

Of course, not all these expectations and obligations are palatable for those on whom they are placed. In this way, obligations and expectations can be either desirable or burdensome, and, importantly, as Goffman points out, our experiences of burden and desire may shift. For our project, of particular interest is what happens when these expectations and obligations that come at the initiation of an individual's relationship with criminal justice actors are unmet. We are mainly interested in these ruptures, the points at which a person falls short of what is expected of her, and effectively exits the system in the midst of an attempt, desired or not, to enter. It is through such failures that Goffman begins his own exploration of deference and demeanour. Seeing the two as intricately bound in social relations, Goffman (1967) is careful to point out that they are not the same. As he explains,

> the analytic relation between them [deference and demeanour] is one of "complementarity" not identity. The image the individual owes to others to maintain of himself is not the same type of image these others are obliged to maintain of him. Deference images tend to point to the wider society outside the interaction, to the place the individual has achieved in the hierarchy of this society. Demeanour images tend to point to qualities which any social position gives its incumbents a chance to display during interaction, for these qualities pertain more to the way in which the individual handles his position than do the rank and place of that position relative to those possessed by others. (1967, 82)

There are two aspects of the complementarity between deference and demeanour on which we wish to draw. First, that they are mutually regulatory. A show of deference, for example, calling a police officer "officer," is meant to illicit a particular demeanour from the police—one which, from the point of view of the individual performing deference, is intended to show the officer a certain degree of respect and assignment of authority, with the expectation that more respectful and less threatening behaviour from the officer will result. The officer, recognizing this act of deference, may, in turn, treat the individual more leniently, extend additional assistance, or simply turn her attention to someone who is being less deferential.

On the flip side, an individual seeking deferential treatment must present a particular kind of demeanour. Goffman (1964) attributes much of this to acts of concealment. Returning to our example of the police officers needing to secure positions of authority, officers must conceal those aspects of themselves which, borrowing Goffman's terms, place them in undignified states: be it their expressions of fear, lack of confidence, or something more mundane, such as a stain on one's uniform or having forgotten a crucial piece of equipment like a pen or notepad.

Finally, Goffman recognizes that a failure on either part does not negate the obligations of the other to perform a certain demeanour (though this is often not the outcome). So, an individual struggling to show respect and deference to police officers for whom she does not harbour these feelings must still make an attempt to convey them. Relatedly, the police officer who does not receive or elicit the deference to which she feels entitled can still continue to conduct herself with a demeanour that commands it, even as that may escalate to threats and use of force.

Inspired by Durkheim (1954), Goffman concludes with the provocative statement that, "the rules of conduct which bind the actor and the recipient together are the bindings of society" (1964, 90). Refusing an orthodoxy to Durkheim's claims of social solidarity, Goffman asserts that instances in which the rules of conduct are articulated through deference and demeanour are rarely about social cohesion, and instead are about more micro rituals of interaction that direct the comportment of self in a given social setting. We return to this point below. For now, though we want to attempt to reinsert the social into these interactions, an experiment inspired by the work of Lauren Berlant.

Taking as her point of inquiry the ordinariness of humanness vis-à-vis the promise of optimism, Berlant argues that,

> whatever the experience *of optimism is in particular, then, the* affective *structure of an optimistic attachment involves a sustaining inclination to return to the scene of fantasy that enables you to expect that this time, nearness to this thing will help you or a world to become different in just the right way.* (2011, 2; emphasis original)

This optimistic view of the "good life" troubles Berlant, as she queries our attachments to conventional notions of happiness. Berlant relegates these attachments to the realm of fantasy, as she positions them in a liberal-capitalist structure in which their attainment is impossible, save by a select few. Berlant labels this conventional hope placed in institutions that will never deliver on the expectations we place on them "cruel optimism." She outlines her interest, which she describes as,

> gestural economies that register norms of self-management that differ according to what kinds of confidence people have enjoyed about the entitlement of their social location. The way the body slows down what's going down helps to clarify the relation of living on to ongoing crisis and loss. (2011, 5)

This ongoing crisis and loss Berlant describes as a crisis of ordinariness. Thus, the failures that result in human suffering are not aberrant; they are routine and, in fact, mundane features of the structures and interactions that direct and inform our daily lives.

We see a conversation to be had between Goffman and Berlant on this question of unfulfilled expectations and individual action. When we put the two side-by-side, important questions emerge that directly inform this collection's key theme concerning entrances into criminal justice. Thinking specifically about the actors within the prosecution of domestic violence: how do the expectations and obligations of actors (including institutions) inform their demeanour, especially at first contact? How does demeanour change when there is a failure of expectations and obligations? Do we place actors in a state of cruel optimism before the interaction even occurs by setting them (specifically victims) up to hope for an elusive sense of justice that is, as Berlant intimates, the stuff of fantasy? And finally, and perhaps implied in all of the above, there are questions about how these variables of demeanour and cruel optimism shape the ways in which victims enter into and, in most cases, exit the criminal justice system.

A sense of who the victim is, well characterized by a sense of her demeanour, is crucial to a prosecution. The perceived selfhood of the victim decides whether police lay charges, whether a judge finds her a credible witness, and, in some cases, whether or not she herself will be charged with a crime. At the same time, it is not just the demeanour of the victim that determines the course of criminal justice; how the victim experiences and interprets the demeanour of police also impacts the trajectories of domestic violence prosecutions. Here, questions of whether the police act with compassion and extend dignity and a sense of believing in the victim are all vital to what is ultimately a dialogic relationship of demeanour between the responding police and the victim.

We focus not only on the ways victims comport themselves vis-à-vis criminal justice actors, but also on the ways in which interactions between police and victims negotiate presentations of selfhood. Inspired in part by Gotell's (2008) analysis of the judicial production of good and bad victimhood, we examine demeanour as a relational process between police and victims. The demeanour of police vis-à-vis victims impacts how victims will respond to police just as much as a victim's demeanour will impact police, and ultimately prosecutors' and judges' assessment of a victim's credibility. Implicit here is not only the question of whether or not criminal justice actors trust the victim's story, but, perhaps more importantly, whether or not the victim feels that she can trust the police, and whether or not the police appear as trustworthy actors on whom the victim can rely for protection, service provision, and, in some cases, an intangible notion of justice.

Policing Victims' Entrances

Victims are explicitly invited into the criminal justice system. Websites, brochures, and leaflets on domestic violence actively all encourage victims to report domestic violence to police, providing hotlines and service supports in addition to expected outcomes and promises that somehow calling the police will stop the abuse. For example, the Ottawa Police Service (OPS) suggests that its central mandate when investigating domestic violence is grounded in services for victims of violence as well as the broader community. OPS Chief Charles Bordeleau has claimed, "Everyone deserves to be safe and we each have a role in ending violence against women and men in our community. We need to work together to report all incidents of partner assault as well as provide people the tools to prevent incidents, such as recognizing the warning signs in advance."[2] This same chief announced on December 22, 2015 that he was seeking extra resources to combat violence against women. When Bordeleau took the post in 2011, he claimed combatting violence against women was one of his top priorities.

OPS is not alone in making such promises. The London Police Service, Ontario, states its "continued dedication to providing appropriate police response to occurrences of domestic violence. To that end, we employ a collaborative approach, consulting our community and justice partners to ensure our response is effective."[3] Likewise, Toronto Police Chief Mark Saunders "believes that the Toronto Police Service must continue to work closely with their community partners to ensure that victims of domestic violence and their children get the help and support they need to leave abusive relationships and rebuild their lives."[4]

Police departments province-wide express being able to address and understand the complex dynamics of those involved in domestic violence. For example, the Ontario Provincial Police (OPP) indicate its officers receive special training in the area of domestic and family violence, creating the expectation that officers will understand the complexity and nuances of domestic violence. Furthermore, the OPP states its goal to ensure coordination with other agencies, services, ministries, and community groups, in order to develop a "consistent and seamless response to victims province-wide."[5]

Naturally, there is an invitation to optimism embedded in these claims. Practically, these promises include victim care, capturing a video statement, and connecting the victim with services to assist with the prosecution of their incident. Our interviews revealed few cases in which all—and in some cases any—of these things actually happened. In fact, in many instances, we were the first people to inform victims of their rights, tell them about victim services, and even let them know that the police should have taken them to the hospital. Almost all our participants suggested that they thought calling the police would improve their circumstances in some way and expressed their shock when this turned out to not be the case. Clearly, an expectation of the demeanour of police is a setup for victims. Again, reflecting on Berlant, our participants, for the most part, believed that contact with the police would bring positive change in their lives, or at the very least, end or mitigate the violence they experienced. Their narratives attest to the public performance of policing. The police appear to participate in a "gestural economy" (Berlant 2011) in which, at least on the surface, victims/survivors have every reason to believe that, when they call the police to report domestic violence, they will be treated respectfully, offered services, and effectively have "the law" on their side. What bears out in our research, however, is quite a different picture from this ritualistic act of accessing justice; enter cruel optimism. Though the promised demeanour of police writ large creates the expectation that their encounters with victims/survivors will be, at the very least, benevolent, this is very rarely the case. Benevolent responses are far more the exception than the norm.

Demeanour on Trial
Courtroom Testimony and Video Evidence

One place we can look in order to understand the mechanics of demeanour is the courtroom and how it affects entrances into the criminal justice system. Here, the presentation of both victims and police, especially as understood by the presiding judge and represented in written judgments, offers us a window into both "how she appears," but also the notion of cruel optimism. Though these cases have already entered the machinery of criminal justice, written judgments, transcripts, and case law often give an important perspective as to how and why a particular case went to prosecution—questions that are especially important given that the vast majority do not. An analysis of demeanour within case law offers insight into the relationality between police and victims, as well as how it is mobilized as a site of further interrogation during the prosecutorial stages of domestic violence cases.

In cases of domestic violence, we often hear multiple versions of the story. Of interest to us are the versions narrated by the police, offering their accounts of the events surrounding a violent encounter. Along with these accounts, we have the testimony of the victim, who presents herself as the temporary proprietor of her own conflict. These two court-room performances are often not complimentary. In our study of seventy judgments, we found that victims often recant their original stories in favour of ones that absolve the accused of wrongdoing, while simultane-ously sullying their own credibility. Though they've gained entrance to the system, they want out. We see this play out in many cases where women perform certain non-normative and non-credible identities in order to have their abuser's charges dismissed. Such complex and diverging sets of testimony challenge the epistemic function of the court as fact finder and trier of fact. Thus, in order to effectively evaluate the probative value of courtroom testimony, judges and juries must juxtapose "how she appears" in court with her original accounts of victimization.

In order to fully understand how demeanour actualizes in court, it is useful to understand that, from the outset, the masculinized character of the courtroom establishes a "hierarchy of credibility" (Becker 1967), historically situating the lived realities of women at the bottom (Easteal and Judd 2008).[6] Within the domestic violence trials, certain character-istics are representative of what it means to perform a good witness role. Judges will often refer to witnesses as credible when they present their stories in a logical, linear, and straightforward manner (Scheppele 1992).

Though Goffman does not make this connection himself, we treat credibility as it is presented and judged in the courtroom, as near synonymous with demeanour. This link is long established in the academic literature (e.g., Jordan 2004; Pryor and Buchanan 1984; Schuster and Propen 2010). Witnesses must also comport themselves in a way that is respectful to the majestic authority of the court, while refraining from being argumentative, contradictory, and uncooperative. These, of course, link to broader normative performances of femininity. Remaining calm, passive, and honest are characteristics of the ideal woman. Any gestures, mannerisms, or statements that challenge these tropes of femininity are often met with suspicion and routinely with allegations of deliberate attempts to mislead the court.

The uncooperative witness only gives us a partial understanding of why some witnesses are met with hostility. A witness may be uncooperative with police from the outset, refusing to comply with investigations and refusing to facilitate the investigation that would lead to the uncovering of substantive evidence that may carry strong probative value. In circumstances where repeat calls have been made to police, officers will sometimes express frustrations toward victims who do not remove themselves from abusive relationships (Russell and Light 2006). As Randall argues, "there is a perception that the women who are 'reluctant' or 'uncooperative' victims have not fulfilled their part of the bargain; in other words, they have enlisted the assistance of the state by calling upon the police for help but have then failed to follow through with the system's subsequent requirements" (2004, 138). The recanting victim, in contrast to the uncooperative witness, entrenches a cruelly optimistic interaction between police, victim, and the goals of prosecution. She, who initially appears as a cooperative witness—a good domestic violence victim— ultimately throws a wrench in the logistical flow of justice. The recanting victim, on some level, begins with the assumption, as Randall suggests, "that the 'system' can, and typically does, effectively respond to the needs of assaulted women" (2004, 138). Thus, victims are seen to be legitimately invited to enter into the criminal justice system. However, their experiences, as is indicated in court records, reveal that the system they believe they are entering is very different from the one in which they find themselves enmeshed.

The cases of *R. v. Bishop* [2011][7] and *R. v. P.G.* [2007][8] provide insight into the kinds of expectations and obligations that attach themselves to initial policing interactions and how these expectations are not always met during trial. At the same time, these cases, along with our interview data, highlight how the affective relationalities between police and victims/survivors not only shape the initial interaction between police and victim, but also how these interactions shape the future tellings of violence in the courtroom, tellings that will ultimately shape how the victim's entrance into criminal justice is received and reconciled. In *R. v. Bishop* [2011], the complainant, Ms. Moore, was assaulted by her boyfriend and extremely hesitant to cooperate with the police. Her child had already been taken from her care and sent to live with her parents, and any trouble with police would only exacerbate the existing custody-related legal troubles. Ms. Moore feared that initiating contact with the police would only lead to more violence by her abusive partner as well as eviction. This in and of itself brings us to vital questions regarding expectation, obligation, and cruel optimism. Despite repeated assurances offered by policing services that they aim to "take domestic violence seriously," victims are often jeopardized and placed in arguably worse circumstances than they were before contact with the justice system.

Still, victims of domestic violence carry the expectation that their unique circumstances will be met with compassion and understanding by police, or, at the very least, that they will be able to exercise some autonomy in their lives once they address the violence in their relationship. Ms. Moore clearly anticipated the failure of both expectation and obligation in her case, rejecting the cruel optimism that police (and ultimately courts) will seek and ultimately secure justice. She replaced this narrative instead with her own very realistic concerns that any reports to police would only have negative consequences for her. Despite this, Ms. Moore provided a video recorded statement to police shortly after the assault, indicating that Mr. Bishop had violently assaulted her after a night of drinking, drug use, and fighting. Though we cannot fully know Ms. Moore's motivations for giving a KGB statement,[9] the fact that she did, despite her misgivings expressed later at trial, suggests that she did in fact subscribe to the expectation that if she complied with police requests, they would in turn be obliged to offer her some sort of justice and, perhaps more importantly, protection. Her later recantation reveals the cruel optimism behind these beliefs. As Ms. Moore moved through the criminal process, the unavoidable juridogenic (Smart 1989) dangers of engaging with the criminal justice system became all too apparent.

Like with *R. v. Bishop*, *R. v. P.G.* [2007] embodies the cruelly optimistic encounters between police and the kinds of assurances they can actually offer victims. K.S., the complainant, was brutally assaulted by her boyfriend, P.G., resulting in a broken jaw, five broken teeth, and a laceration to her lip. Despite making a brief statement to a local hospital nurse, K.S. was extremely reluctant to provide a statement to police. Much like many of the women we interviewed, this was not K.S.'s first encounter with police. Because she was identified as a known sex worker who operated out of a local hotel, police had waited outside of her workplace to pressure her into providing an official statement. We might say that the police harassed K.S. into providing a statement, though the judge found that no police misconduct had occurred, and that her aversion to the police was "because of her chosen profession and lifestyle and not because of anything that they did."[10]

The character of K.S. was immediately drawn from preconceived notions of her criminal subjectivity. While K.S. was reluctant to provide any information to the police, she did so with the intention that it would be mutually beneficial. She would receive access to healthcare services, victims' compensation, and relief from the police harassment, and the police would obtain an official statement that would satisfy the requirements to make an arrest. During the trial, K.S. recanted her testimony, claiming it was one of her clients that had severely beaten her. The video recorded statement given to the police by K.S. ultimately played the biggest role in the outcome of the trial. While K.S. claimed to have been drunk and high on cocaine during the interview, the judge held that "her demeanour and condition, as displayed in the video tape, do not support this contention. K.S. possessed an operating mind at the time she provided her statement,"[11] and as such, the video would be entered into evidence. The fact that the police waited outside of her place of work in order to pressure K.S. into cooperating shows the very dynamics that underscore these encounters. K.S., like other victims, held the key to securing a conviction. Without her testimony, the core role of policing would have been fundamentally challenged.

There is something at work here when we think about these interactions and how the recanting victim is constituted within the legal apparatus of courtroom rules. If we return to Goffman, we might say that the recanting victim transgresses what he refers to as an "idealized performance"—one that may be required in order to secure a conviction. Goffman writes that these ideal performances "incorporate and exemplify the officially accredited values of the society, more so, in fact, than does his [sic] behaviour as a whole" (1959, 35). We expect victims to testify against their abusers because the conflict not only remains between victim and assailant, but also constitutes a much broader problem of violence against women. Because victims of domestic violence are seen as passive, confused, or unable to care for themselves in times of trauma, we place immense emphasis on their roles as key witnesses. Because the good victim is also a good witness, the obligation to testify underscores the entire interaction with police and the prosecution. Demeanour between the victim, police, and courtroom officials is constituted as a barrier to prosecution when it impedes the prospect of a conviction. The role of the victim is to openly blame her assailant, not impede the administration of justice. When this happens, the police and prosecutors must do more to secure a conviction; they must execute their own legal fact-finding skills in order to replace and impeach the testimony of the recanting victim.

How the Police Appear

Our interviews with domestic violence survivors tell a different story from the perspective of victims. In the twenty-five interviews we conducted, there was a repeated schism between the victim's expectations of police obligations and how the police actually responded. Few victims indicated they called the police because they expected or wanted an arrest. Instead, most victims wanted the abuse to simply stop, either by police providing help or reprimanding the abuser (note that these are not one and the same thing). However, victims interviewed who called the police did not have a clear indication of how the abuse should stop. Instead, they expected the police to provide some sense of guidance and help. For example, one victim stated, "I didn't know what to do, I just wanted it [the abuse] to stop and I thought the police would know how to handle it."[12] This shows that victims' expectations of the police were ritualistic and automatic responses to what they hoped the police could provide. The economy of hope comes in the belief that the police will provide some sense of protection and safety, and possibly justice. Police officers embody what they believe to be the security of the criminal justice system, creating a set of possibilities and expectations that police will be able to provide a sense of safety. Police officers thus represent a cluster of promises that victims want the police to make. Victims hope for an elusive feeling of safety and a reality that, perhaps, is impossible to attain. In this sense, as Berlant might say, the police become the institution that will never deliver.

Participants interviewed expressed feeling a general optimism when first reporting to police, relaying a sense of hope for improvement of their situation. When these set expectations were not met and the police failed to fulfill their obligations, resentment developed. Often victims whose expectations were not met showed a loss of faith in police and the justice system itself. For example, one participant stated, "I had this unrealistic belief that the police could help."[13] This loss of faith in the criminal justice system was most apparent when victims had gone through an arrest and trial. For most participants, it was not unusual for their abuser to be released within days, if not hours, of their arrest, given that their protective court orders often turned out to be ineffective remedies. This resulted in victims frequently expressing that their expectations of calling the police changed, since police involvement resulted in no significant improvement to their situation. Multiple participants stated, "what's the point of calling the police?" after an arrest had been made and their abuser had been released hours or days later.[14] Thus, not surprisingly, many victims found their efforts to call police and seek protection through the justice system disappointing and frustrating, leading them to often not call the police again. Returning to Goffman's rule of conduct, we see how the failure to meet perceived police obligations—governed at an institutional level, and by extension, by individual officers—resulted in a victim's loss of faith in the justice system. Goffman writes, "when the rule of conduct is broken, we find that two individuals run the risk of becoming discredited; one with an obligation, who should have governed himself by the rule; the other with an expectation, who should have been treated in a particular way because of this governance. Both actor and recipient are threatened" (1956, 475). Thus, for the victims interviewed in our study, police action (or inaction) communicated outcomes that were not in line with victims' expectations, resulting in expressions of hope-lessness and distrust as a result of victims' unmet expectations with seemingly standard policing practices.

Not surprisingly, few victims relayed positive interactions with police. Instead, victims often articulated a strong sense of betrayal by the police when arrests were desired, yet never made. The expectation of safety is a bare minimum; the public statements on the promise of policing for domestic violence victims referred to earlier guarantee this basic provision. Yet this contrasts with the reality of cases where charges were not laid. For example, in Terry's case, the police said, "this [wound] doesn't look like much" and told her abuser to "take a walk and come back when he sobered up."[15] Police then left her behind, without any support or advice. When her abuser returned a few hours later, she was violently reprimanded by him. After the incident, Terry was too afraid to call the police again and questioned why she bothered calling them in the first place. Terry's lack of fulfilled expectations created disappointment when the police's obligations were not met. Her initial optimism in the kind of assistance the police could provide was shattered, creating a sense of resentment and hostility toward the criminal justice system.

The majority of victims interviewed felt that police did not take them seriously. The demeanour of the police would convey their disbelief of the victim's story or the seriousness of the situation. Participants whose experiences were negative found officers either judgmental or uncooperative, often leading to degrading experiences. Some officers also seemed to discredit the victim's account by pointing out there were no visible signs of assault. For example, Emily, who was strangled, was not believed because she showed no immediate visible signs around her neck. She stated, "I felt the police didn't take it seriously because I was not bleeding."[16] As with most strangulations, her bruising was seen only days later. Such experiences with police were particularly common for Emily because her abuser would ensure there were no visible marks on her body, so that police would dismiss the incident and not press charges. Emily also asserted that on multiple occasions, police officers seemed hesitant to arrest her abuser since, she felt, the police did not think she was a credible victim. Emily's negative encounter and unfulfilled expectations of police obligations and lack of trust in the justice system finally led her to not call the police after an assault. She described that when police were called, the abuse would simply escalate after the police left.

There are times when victims lack the optimism necessary to initiate criminal justice involvement. Not all victims interviewed called the police. Reasons for not calling included: fear of future escalating abuse either by their abuser, or, at times, the abuser's affiliated gang or family members; concerns for their privacy; fear of involvement from the Children's Aid Society; or deep-rooted negative notions around "snitching." For example, some participants did not call the police after an assault, stating they "didn't want to be a rat."[17] Equally important, victims did not want their abusers to face legal repercussions, nor did they want to be permanently separated from their abusers. Female victims often expressed feeling inadequate without their abusers and therefore that they did not know what to do without them in their lives. Aaron, for instance, stated that her abuser made her feel useless without him and she would often ask herself, "how do I do this [live] without him?"[18] Some victims also voiced a general mistrust of the police in their community and felt they needed to protect their abuser from the police. As a result, when victims did not call the police themselves, the expectation was already in place that police would make the situation worse, not better. Thus, the hope and the expectation of what the police could deliver were minimal. Even when victims who did not call the police had positive encounters with officers, they saw the encounter as "one of a kind" or a matter of luck.

In the rare instances in which police fulfilled obligations by displaying certain responses, police officers were considered trustworthy. For example, victims who experienced helpful demeanour, verbal reassurances, and positive encounters with police stated the officers were dependable and helpful. Reassurances included asking about their state of mind, offering to drive them to the hospital, being patient with their emotional response, or offering other forms of assistance; these interventions left victims with the impression that their cases were under control and their complaints were being taken seriously. One victim also expressed feeling comforted when one officer stayed with her in the hospital, since this made her feel like he cared.[19] Victims often referred to police as reliable and helpful when, in addition to showing sympathy, officers provided safety information and alternative housing options. This included giving information on local shelters and community services, or continuous updates about the abuser after the arrest. Simply being given advice was often expressed as a positive encounter with police. For example, one victim stated, "one cop that was sitting at the computer said, 'get a lawyer,' so he was nice to me."[20]

Frequently, the most important aspect for participants interviewed was that police showed empathy. In particular, when victims showed physical signs of assault, they wanted the officers to take care of their wounds first, rather than take a written statement. While victims appreciated officers taking the situation seriously by taking down the facts, often they expressed feeling shaken up and needing some time to calm down before being able to convey what actually happened. At times, victims referred to police officers as being trustworthy and caring by allowing them to call someone or talking to them reassuringly. Positive interactions with police often had positive effects on the victims, suggesting that their demeanour changed according to social expectations and affirmative interactions. For example, victims expressed feeling comfortable sharing more information with officers who showed a positive demeanour toward them, giving them the feeling the officers were taking them seriously, believing their story, and taking care of their needs. Therefore, how the officer appeared and spoke established the officer as either trustworthy or careless, causing victims to adjust their response and level of cooperation.

Victims also expressed that when they experienced negative behaviour by police, conveyed through comments or body language, they experienced negative encounters with police. Victims frequently reported that their first encounter with police was positive, but that their caring demeanour deteriorated once the same victim reported further assaults. Interviewees also expressed that their perception of the police had changed after they had come in contact with them the first time. For example, one victim stated, "I wasn't expecting much at this point but they [the police] are the only option you have, [and] I wanted the beatings to stop."[21] Here, then, we see a clear trajectory of cruel optimism. For those women who felt that their expectations of police were met on the first encounter, their disappointment and clear loss of faith in the criminal justice system became all too apparent in their accounts of subsequent encounters.

In addition to a lack of sympathy, a common experience shared by victims was the officer's perceived critical judgment of their situation. Some women were asked why they kept returning to their abuser and seemed to be blamed for continuing to be abused. Victims often felt officers were ignorant of their situation and did not want to understand the position they were in; rather, officers appeared to blame them for their predicament. Emily was interviewed by four officers in her home, and stated:

[The interaction] just felt very cold; especially it being men, it is really uncomfortable. And they talk to each other and you can hear them and they talk about you when you're sitting there like, "we've been here before" and, you know, the one guy said something like, "why don't these women get it" or something along those lines.[22]

Various victims expressed that officers would talk about them in their presence, often in the third person and in a demeaning way. Victims thus felt blamed for their situation and this often led them to feel intimidated, worthless, and ashamed. Often victims expressed disappointment and disbelief at the general lack of understanding of the effects of domestic violence, particularly in relation to the police officers' demeanour or blatant expressions. For example, one woman stated being asked by the police, "why do you keep on going back [to your abuser]." As a result, she felt judged and commented that she was surprised the police did not understand that "it isn't that easy."[23] Here again, we see a sense of cruel optimism, where, as Berlant says, the object, in this case the police, represents a cluster of promises and expectations. The police's lack of understanding of the victims' predicament resulted in unfulfilled expectations, which led to disbelief, disappointment, and resentment.

Equally important, female victims felt they needed to behave in a way that fit broader societal expectations of femininity. For example, victims who described defending themselves from their abuser felt that the police's demeanour showed they were more reluctant to believe them. One victim stated that she defended herself and took the knife away from her abuser, resulting in her arrest instead of his. Another victim described feeling confused and asking, "I'm the victim here, why are you coming after me?"[24] On another occasion, one participant had felt threatened when police stated they would have to arrest both her and the abuser because she had defended herself and hurt him. Thus, participants expressed that if they did not fit a female victim stereotype, such as acting submissive, they were often faced with skepticism. Women often felt that if they displayed appropriate gender behaviour toward the police and their abuser, they would receive adequate treatment. As such, victims expressed a certain demeanour toward police, in order to be perceived as a credible victim. Thus, victims felt inclined to display traditional gendered behaviour in their encounters with police. Here, the victim's presentation of self and her demeanour toward police are directly impacted by social interactions. Furthermore, her expectation of police is higher if she feels she is acting according to appropriate social gender cues.

At the end of each interview, participants were asked what advice they would give to a friend if she was in a similar situation, and whether they would recommend calling the police. Participants who had positive experiences, where they, as victims, felt their expectations were met, were more willing to call police again. Those that advised not to call police stated it was because "it never helped," indicating that their encounters with police had resulted in unfulfilled expectations and disappointment.[25] Instead, they recommended going to the hospital for help, particularly when there were physical injuries. One victim stated she would often go to the hospital instead of the police and lie to the hospital staff about where she received her injuries. Most victims we interviewed expressed reluctance to call police if they had previously had bad experiences with law enforcement, stating they did not want to go through such a "degrading" experience again.[26]

Victims who did not trust the police because of their negative experiences felt it influenced their actions following future assaults, thereby potentially leaving them more vulnerable. For example, two participants expressed they would never call the police again, because their interaction with law enforcement was an additional dramatic experience. One victim recollected her experience stating, "I would've never called them [police] again, like he could've been killing me and I would've never called them."[27] On most occasions, victims we interviewed recommended to only call police if they were in immediate danger, while others voiced that they were simply "too scared to call the police since it didn't help the first time I called them."[28]

Conclusion

From Economies of Hope to Relations of Distrust

In *Cruel Optimism*, Berlant writes about a generalized quest for the good life that is largely unattainable. Moving beyond Bauman's (2000, 2007) cognate thesis that capitalist economies drive us to a constant state of disappointment—as the searched for status of the satiated consumer can never be fulfilled—Berlant widens the scope, locating the forever insatiable desire to be a happy person against the backdrop of a neoliberal society that constantly makes promises it cannot keep. These promises move beyond the quest for the material into the hope for love, joy, and fulfillment.

Domestic violence survivors, at least in their immediate futures, are rarely pursuing the good life as Berlant describes it. Instead, they are simply seeking a life that is free from violence, and, for many, the threat of brutal death. Still, governing institutions continue to make promises of hope, promises that invite victims into the justice system with the lure of a more subdued optimism. In Canada, after years of community rallying, a newly elected Liberal government called for an inquiry into missing and murdered Indigenous women. At the same time, the Liberal government of the Province of Ontario has enacted legislation mandating all public institutions to redraft and implement policies to directly address gender-based violence. Following this same vein, policing services across the province proclaim their commitments to taking domestic violence seriously. As feminist activists and scholars, we can only greet these measures with hope, even as our research shows us that such initiatives, presented as they are from higher levels of government, have little impact on the day-to-day realities of those experiencing interpersonal violence.

When we turn to the expectations and obligations imbedded in the relationships between police and victims/survivors, it is apparent that victims initially share this hope with us. For the most part, they believe the police will help them, will fulfill the promises made by their institutions and satisfy their obligations through the ways in which they respond to victims. Usually these hopes are quickly dashed as the demeanour of police fails to meet victims' expectations, thus changing the demeanour of victims as they move from an economy of hope to a relation of distrust. What is crucial here is that it is not, as Berlant suggests, the wider backdrop of a neoliberal society that changes the victims' demeanour, but rather their interactions with police, interactions which are typically injected with unfulfilled expectations.

Thus, in understanding the broader landscape of the policing of domestic violence and especially considering how victims gain access to justice, it is not enough to focus on the conduct of the victim as if it sits in isolation. How she appears emerges from a relationship with responding police officers, and later with lawyers and judges. It is this relationality that is vital to understanding the dialogue of distrust that is endemic to the policing and prosecution of domestic violence. Victims are led to believe that calling the police will have an ameliorative effect on their lives, only to have this optimism dashed in the face of responding officers who are dismissive, condemning, and sometimes brutal. Thus, entering the criminal justice system as a victim, though full of promise, is also potentially full of danger and unfulfilled expectations. In a system that routinely reneges on its optimistic promises, it is all too clear that victims' entrances are closely tethered to, and in some ways conterminous with, their exits. The revolving door of justice is quite trite, but here it perhaps has revived meaning. We might also think of the victim as standing at a heavily weighted portal, one which swings fiercely open and shut and is equally difficult to control.

Notes

1. We use the female pronoun here recognizing that the majority of domestic violence complainants are female identified. We do not discount, however, that male identified people also experience this form of violence. Our research, however, does not focus on male complainants, and thus we are not able to make claims about their experiences.

2. "Partner Assault," Ottawa Police Services, accessed December 19, 2015, http://www.ottawapolice.ca/en/about-us/partner-assault.asp.

3. "Domestic Violence," London Police Service, accessed December 19, 2015, https://www.londonpolice.ca/en/crime-prevention/Domestic-Violence.aspx.

4. "Domestic Violence," Toronto Police Services, accessed December 19, 2015, http://www.torontopolice.on.ca/community/domesticviolence/.

5. "Abuse Issues," Ontario Provincial Police, accessed December 19, 2015, http://www.opp.ca/ecms/index.php?id=152.

6. As a caveat, there is no doubt that the intersections of demeanour, race, and Indigeneity are also embedded in these hierarchies. We problematically limit this analysis to gender because, at the time of writing, we had no way of credibly assessing intersectionality unless race or Indigeneity were explicitly referred to.

7. R. v. Bishop, [2011], N.S.J. No. 669, NSPC 95.

8. R. v. P.G., [2007], O.J. No. 5771.

9. See R. v. B (K.G.), [1993], 1 S.C.R. 740. In R. v. B. (K.G.), the Supreme Court of Canada ruled that statements made to police, if deemed credible, could be used in lieu of, or to impeach, direct testimony. These "KGB statements" are often used in cases of domestic violence when victims recant their initial statements made to police, a frequent occurrence that otherwise makes it increasingly difficult for prosecutors to convict.

10. R. v. P.G., at para. 38.

11. R. v. P.G., at para. 39.

12. Interview with Mitch, August 13, 2015.

13. Interview with Karen, August 18, 2015.

14. Interviews on "Domestic Violence," August 13, 2015 to October 14, 2015.

15. Interview with Terry, August 20, 2015.

16. Interview with Emily, October 14, 2015.

17. Interview with Candice, September 2, 2015.

18. Interview with Aaron, August 20, 2015.

19. Interview with Emily, October 14, 2015.

20. Interview with Hope, September 23, 2015.

21. Interview with Cindy, August 20, 2015.

22. Interview with Emily, October 14, 2015.

23. Interview with Molly on "Domestic Violence," September 2, 2015.

24. Interview with Aaron on "Domestic Violence," August 20, 2015.

25. Interview with Terry on "Domestic Violence," September 2, 2015.

26. Interviews on "Domestic Violence," August 13, 2015 to October 14, 2015.

27. Interview with Emily on "Domestic Violence," October 14, 2015.

28. Interview with Terry on "Domestic Violence," September 2, 2015.

References

Bauman, Zygmunt. 2000. "Social Uses of Law and Order." In *Criminology and Social Theory*, edited by David Garland and Richard Sparks, 23–45. Oxford: Oxford University Press.

———. 2007. *Consuming Life*. Cambridge: Polity Press.

Becker, Howard. 1967. "Whose Side Are We On?" *Social Problems* 14 (3): 239–47.

Berlant, Lauren Gail. 2011. *Cruel Optimism*. Durham, NC: Duke University Press.

Durkheim, Emile. 1954. *The Elementary Forms of the Religious Life*. Translated by Joseph W. Swain. New York: Free Press.

Easteal, Patricia, and Keziah Judd. 2008. "'She Said, He Said': Credibility and Sexual Harassment Cases in Australia." *Women's Studies International Forum* 31 (5): 336–44.

Goffman, Erving. 1956. "The Nature of Deference and Demeanour." *American Anthropologist* 58 (3): 473–502.

———. 1959. *The Presentation of Self in Everyday Life*. New York: Doubleday.

———. 1964. "The Neglected Situation." *American Anthropologist* 66 (6): 133–36.

———. 1967. *Interaction Ritual: Essays in Face-to-face Behavior*. Garden City, NY: Anchor Books.

Gotell, Lise. 2008. "Rethinking Affirmative Consent in Canadian Sexual Assault Law: Neoliberal Sexual Subjects and Risky Women." *Akron Law Review* (41): 865–98.

Jordan, Jan. 2004. "Beyond Belief? Police, Rape and Women's Credibility." *Criminology and Criminal Justice* 4 (1): 29–59.

Pryor, Bert, and Raymond W. Buchanan. 1984. "The Effects of a Defendant's Demeanour on Juror Perceptions of Credibility and Guilt." *Journal of Communication* 34 (3): 92–99.

Randall, Melanie. 2004. "Domestic Violence and the Construction of 'Ideal Victims': Assaulted Women's 'Image Problems' in Law." *St. Louis University Public Law Review* 23: 107–54.

Russell, Mary, and Linda Light. 2006. "Police and Victim Perspectives on Empowerment of Domestic Violence Victims." *Police Quarterly* 9 (4): 375–96.

Scheppele, Kim. 1992. "Just the Facts, Ma'am: Sexualized Violence, Evidentiary Habits, and the Revision of Truth." *New York Law School Law Review* (37): 123–70.

Schuster, Mary Lay, and Amy Propen. 2010. "Degrees of Emotion: Judicial Responses to Victim Impact Statements." *Law, Culture and the Humanities* 6 (1): 75–104.

Smart, Carol. 1989. *Feminism and the Power of Law*. London: Routledge.

Cases

R. v. B (K.G.) [1993] 1 S.C.R. 740

R. v. P.G. [2007] O.J. No. 577

R. v. Bishop [2011] N.S.J. No. 669, NSPC 95

CONTRIBUTORS

DALE A. BALLUCCI is an Assistant Professor in the Department of Sociology at the University of Western Ontario. Her research interests broadly include the administration of the criminal justice system, criminology, policing, socio-legal studies, sociology of childhood, and theories of governance. Her current projects investigate police responses to sex crimes, prolific offenders, intimate partner violence, and how the police respond to child and youth victims of sexual assault in Canada. Her research topics are diverse, but her primary focus is on investigating the operations of legal practice, and the administration of criminal justice.

MARTIN A. FRENCH is an Assistant Professor with the Department of Sociology & Anthropology at Concordia University in Montreal, Canada. Martin's research examines the social dimensions of technology with an empirical focus on the circuits of digital information that link together the public health and criminal justice systems.

AARON HENRY is a former SSHRC Postdoctoral Fellow and is now an independent scholar. His research draws on social theory and historical sociology to critically interrogate the formation of carceral geographies and production of the criminal subject. Other interests include the history of population and production of territory in British North America.

BRYAN R. HOGEVEEN is Associate Dean in the Faculty of Graduate Studies and Research at the University of Alberta. He is co-author (along with Joanne Minaker) of *Youth, Crime and Society: Issues of Power and Justice* (Pearson). He has published on a variety of his academic interests, which include socio-legal theory, violence, martial arts in society, young offenders and the law, and justice. His SSHRC funded research project examines neoliberalism's impact on the marginalized inner-city residents of Edmonton and Winnipeg. Dr. Hogeveen has been invited to share his ideas with both national and international audiences.

DAWN MOORE is an Associate Professor of Law and Legal Studies at Carleton University. A graduate of the Centre of Criminology, University of Toronto, Moore has three published books and over twenty-five monographs and book chapters. She works on legal subjectivities, the intersection of psy practices and law, and more recently on documenting issues of prison transparency through a SSHRC Partnership Development Grant, as well as exploring the use of visual evidence in cases of domestic violence, the focus of a SSHRC standard grant with Dr. Rashmee Singh as co-investigator. Moore is also a social and union activist who also writes on feminist criminology/socio-legal studies, addictions, legal geography, law, and science, and most recently victimology.

GEORGE PAVLICH attained BA and BA (Hons) degrees from the University of the Witwatersrand, an MA from Simon Fraser University, and a PHD from the University of British Columbia. He currently occupies the Canada Research Chair in Social Theory, Culture and Law at the University of Alberta, where he is a Professor of Law and Sociology. He has published articles on social theory, socio-legal studies, restorative justice, critical criminology, and criminal accusation. His books include *Justice Fragmented: Mediating Community Disputes Under Postmodern Conditions* (Routledge), *Critique and Radical Discourses on Crime* (Ashgate), *Governing Paradoxes of Restorative Justice* (GlassHouse Press), *Law and Society Redefined* (Oxford University Press), and *Criminal Accusation: Political*

Rationales and Socio-legal Practices (Routledge). His numerous co-edited collections include *Accusation: Creating Criminals* (UBC Press).

MARCUS A. SIBLEY is a doctoral candidate in the Department of Law and Legal Studies at Carleton University. His work centres on areas related to sociolegal studies and criminology, including sex work, domestic violence, and sexual violence on university campuses. Currently, his research focuses on interrogating notions of "rape culture" as produced within legal, political, and institutional imaginaries and the ways in which these ideas histori-cally govern responses to sexual violence within the criminal justice system.

RASHMEE SINGH is an Assistant Professor in the Department of Sociology and Legal Studies at the University of Waterloo in Ontario, Canada. She graduated from the University of Toronto with a PHD in Criminology and Socio-Legal Studies in 2012. Her work examines the governance of domestic violence and the roles of grassroots organizations and quasi-legal actors in the prosecution process. Her current research project explores the use and effects of visual evidence in domestic violence trials. Her third project examines specialized prostitution courts in the United States. She has published articles in *Theoretical Criminology*, *Law and Social Inquiry*, and *Social Politics*.

AMY SWIFFEN is an Associate Professor in the Department of Sociology and Anthropology at Concordia University, Montreal, Canada. Her research expertise is in the areas of socio-legal studies and social theory, with particular emphasis on sources of legal authority as well as new and emerging areas of law.

MATTHEW P. UNGER is an Assistant Professor in Sociology and Anthropology at Concordia University in Montreal. His work encom-passes the hermeneutics of criminal accusation, colonial legal imaginaries, sound studies, and ethnography/participant observation within the extreme metal community. He examines how predominant metaphors and symbols structure aesthetic, sonic, and legal imaginaries. His continuing projects focus on accusation and governance, nature and law, and Paul Ricoeur's thought on symbols of fault. He is the author of *Sound, Symbol, Sociality: The Aesthetics of Extreme Metal Music* (Palgrave MacMillan, 2016) and co-editor of *Accusation: Creating Criminals* (UBC Press, 2016).

ELISE WOHLBOLD is a doctoral student (ABD) in Law and Legal Studies at Carleton University. Her research project explores the historical trajectory of trans rights politics in Canada, and how trans activists are using and also rejecting law as a tool to advance claims for equality. Her professional path includes collaborating and providing gender expert advice on international and grassroots projects, working with Status of Women Canada, the Conference Board of Canada, and the 2009 UNESCO World Conference on Education. She holds a MSC in Gender Studies from the London School of Economics and Political Science.

ANDREW WOOLFORD is a Professor of Sociology at the University of Manitoba. His most recent book *'This Benevolent Experiment': Indigenous Boarding Schools, Genocide and Redress in the United States and Canada* is co-published by University of Nebraska Press and University of Manitoba Press. He is author of *The Politics of Restorative Justice: A Critical Introduction* (Fernwood, 2009) and *Between Justice and Certainty: Treaty-Making in British Columbia* (University of British Columbia Press, 2005). He is also co-author of *Informal Reckonings: Conflict Resolution in Mediation, Restorative Justice and Reparations* (Routledge, with R.S. Ratner, 2007). He is co-editor of *Colonial Genocide in Indigenous North America* (Duke University Press, with Jeff Benvenuto and Alexander Hinton, 2014) and *The Idea of a Human Rights Museum* (University of Manitoba Press, with Adam Muller and Karen Busby, 2015).

INDEX

kickboxing, 112n3

Kiteley, Frances, 155–56

law
   Foucault on formation of
     subjects, 97–99, 105
   framing of social world by,
     45–46
   nature of, x
   origins of crime and law, 9–11,
     23–24, 24n8, 120

Lemke, Thomas, 86

Lemkin, Raphael, xxiv, 140,
     141–44, 145, 148, 149, 150–51,
     152

lexicons, factual, 19–20, 23

liberalism, 64, 148

Lillooet (BC), *see* Poole murder
   case

Linden, Rick, 61

Lombroso, Cesare, 50, 117, 118

London Police Service (Ontario),
     172

Loo, Tina, 42–43

lore of criminal accusation, 11, 35

Lubicon Lake Cree
   Daishowa Inc. v. The Friends of
     the Lubicon [1998], 141, 153,
     154–58
   genocide law and, 159–60
   territorial dispute with
     Canada, 153–54

Maber, Steele v. [1901], 105

Mabior, R. v. [2012], 79–80, 80–82,
     89nn21–22

MacDonald, David, 150

Macdonald, Joseph, 6–7, 12, 13, 15

Macleod, R.C., 9–10, 24n8

MacPherson, James, 156–58

Maeda, Mitsuyo, 107

Marx, Karl, 66

McLachlin, Beverley, 150

medical information, 71

Mitchell, Robert, 90n28

mixed martial arts (MMA), 108

moralization, 66

Muai Thai kickboxing, 112n3

Nanaimo (BC)
   suicide case, 6–9, 12, 13, 14, 15,
     16, 21

Nemiah (Poole murder case), 33

Ngeruka, R. v. [2015], 79–80, 83–85

Nietzsche, Friedrich, xv–xvi,
     10–11, 14, 120

North-West Mounted Police
     (NWMP), 9–10

Nuremberg
   International Military
     Tribunal, 144

obligations, 167–68

O'Connell, Thomas, 7, 8

Ontario Provincial Police (OPP),
     172

Orton, R. v. [1878], 104

Ottawa Police Service (OPS), 172

surveillance, compliance, and curfew checks, 130–33, 134

typology and characteristics of prolific offenders, 122–23

Public Health Agency of Canada (PHAC), 72–73

The Queen vs. Clarence [1888], 77–78

Quo Vadis (Sienkiewicz), 142

Race, Ken, 96

Randall, Melanie, 175

recidivism, 124–25, 132

Red River colony and famine
about, xxi–xxii, 49–51, 57–58, 65–66

colony forts and punitive measures, 63–64, 65

habit and, 62, 66–67

Heron on famine victims and subsistence, 50–51, 53, 55–57, 58–59, 62, 66

Heron's journal, 50

Heron's racial assumptions, 59–60

Hudson's Bay Company's legal order and, 59, 60–61

market policy, 54–55

post-famine, 57

relocation of "unproductive" people to, 51, 52–53

Rees, Thomas, 3–6, 12–13, 15

repression, 95

Rice, Peter Joseph, 8

risk assessment, 115, 118–19

risk-based analysis, 121

Romanowski, Barbara, 84

rules of conduct, 167–69, 178, 180

R. v. Aziga [2007], 79–80, 82–83, 89n24

R. v. B (K.G.) [1993], 188n9

R. v. Bennett [1866], 76, 88n8

R. v. Bishop [2011], 176–77

R. v. Chang [2003], 93, 108

R. v. Crangle [2010], 89n13

R. v. Cuerrier [1998], 78–79

R. v. Dee [1884], 88n7

R. v. Flattery [1877], 76

R. v. Mabior [2012], 79–80, 80–82, 89nn21–22

R. v. Ngeruka [2015], 79–80, 83–85

R. v. Orton [1878], 104

R. v. P.G. [2007], 177–78

R. v. Sinclair [1867], 76

R. v. Wildfong and Lang [1911], 102–04, 105–06

Ryan, Joan, 155

Sandstrom, Paul, 73

Saunders, Mark, 172

Schabas, William, 139

Schwarzbard, Shalom, 142

SDR Program (Canadian HIV Strain and Drug Resistance Surveillance Program), 72–74, 82, 85

United Nations *Convention on the Prevention and Punishment of the Crime of Genocide* (UNGC)

Canada's intervention in, 149, 150–52

cultural genocide issue, 145–47, 149

definition of genocide in, 148–49

draft process, 144

group identity, impacts on, 158–59

subjects of accusation issue, 147–48

See also genocide law

Valverde, Mariana, 64

victims and survivors, 165. *See also* domestic violence

Wainberg, Mark, 84–85

Walby, Kevin, 118

Waldby, Catherine, 90n28

Walsh, Anthony, 118

Wildfong and Lang, R. v. [1911], 102–04, 105–06

Wilgress, Dana, 151

Wright, John Paul, 118

Zedner, Lucia, 119

Other Titles from University of Alberta Press

Keetsahnak/Our Missing and Murdered Indigenous Sisters

KIM ANDERSON, MARIA CAMPBELL &
CHRISTI BELCOURT, *Editors*

A powerful collection of voices that speak to
antiviolence work from a cross-generational
Indigenous perspective.

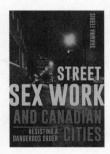

Street Sex Work and Canadian Cities

Resisting a Dangerous Order

SHAWNA FERRIS

De-stigmatization of sex work encourages efforts
toward legal changes to create safe communities for all.

Driven to Kill

Vehicles as Weapons

J. PETER ROTHE

Rothe examines the use of vehicles for assault,
abduction, rape, terrorism, suicide, and murder.

More information at uap.ualberta.ca